D1578867

NEIL YOUNG

The definitive story of his musical career

JOHNNY
ROGAN

PROTEUS BOOKS
LONDON/NEW YORK

PROTEUS BOOKS is an imprint of
The Proteus Publishing Group

United States
PROTEUS PUBLISHING CO., INC.
733 Third Avenue
New York, N.Y. 10017
distributed by:
THE SCRIBNER BOOK COMPANIES, INC.
597 Fifth Avenue
New York, N.Y. 10017

United Kingdom
PROTEUS (PUBLISHING) LIMITED
Bremar House,
Sale Place,
London, W2 1PT.

ISBN 0 86276 012 7 (p/b)
0 86276 027 5 (h/b)

First published in 1982

Design Bill Goodson
Editor Nicky Hodge
Typeset by Tradespools Ltd., Frome, Somerset.
Printed in Great Britain by
The Anchor Press Ltd., and bound by
William Brendon & Son Ltd.,
both of Tiptree, Essex.

CONTENTS

Dedicated To The Memory Of
JOHN ONO LENNON

Johnny Rogan has been actively involved in the music business since his university years. He has worked independently for a number of record companies, rock magazines and popular journals in the U.K., U.S.A. and on the Continent. Now a full time author, he has recently published two rock books: *Timeless Flight — The Definitive Biography Of The Byrds* and *Roxy Music — The First Decade.*

Introduction

The aim of this book is to show the development of Neil Young from a shy, music-loving kid to one of the world's most respected rock artists. It is less a document of his private life than a critical appraisal of Young the musician. It is this perspective that unifies the book and traces Young's musical history through a turbulent three decades.

The idea of writing a long study of Young's career seemed a logical development from my previous biography of The Byrds. I had already invested much money and exhausted all future royalties travelling across the States in search of former Byrds associates, several of whom had business and artistic connections with Young. By the time I'd visited Canada, New York and Los Angeles I figured I had enough material to make a start on this book upon my return to the U.K. Most of the book was written in the Spring of 1980 during an intensive period of total isolation in the wilds of Somerset. The work was completed in another cottage in the grounds of Lady Margaret Hall, Oxford towards the end of an extraordinary term, punctuated by the tragic news of John Lennon's assassination.

After revamping and heavily editing the text during parts of 1981, it was finally ready for commercial publication. As my main concern has been with Young's development as a rock artist, the book is strongly slanted in the direction of a critical appraisal. As I argue more fully at the end of Chapter 5, Young can tell us little about his completed songs beyond some brief and interesting remarks about his original intentions. There really is no substitute for intense critical analysis of the finished product. However, even the best criticism is incomplete if it ignores important background details and information. During my travels I was fortunate enough to be able to listen to over 140 hours of unrecorded live material from Young, including a staggering 1,400 songs performed during the past 15 years. The full contents of this research are too extensive to be included in a rock biography and would be irrelevant to all but a small coterie of Young fanatics. But the fruits of this research can be seen in the brief discussion of unreleased songs and abandoned albums. It has always been my intention to make this book attractive to both the casual rock reader and the burning fanatic. This I could only do by fusing discographical scholarship with important biographical details and establishing an easy-to-read narrative. I hope it at least succeeds as a balanced critical appraisal of a man still regarded by many as the single greatest force in rock music today.

Johnny Rogan
December 1981.

Acknowledgements

I would like to extend my thanks to all those who helped and inspired me during the writing of this book. Neil Young, his family and friends and particularly David Crosby, Nils Lofgren, Derek Taylor, Chris Hillman, Stephen Stills, Graham Nash, Roger McGuinn, Rita Coolidge, Michelle Phillips and Leah Kunkel.

Thanks also to Commander and Mrs. Quicke for allowing me to rent a cottage in the isolation of Ashbrittle and to the staff of Lady Margaret Hall, Oxford University. Additional thanks to George Kenyon, Anne Cesek, John Tobler, David Prockter, Alan Roberts and Nick Ralph for past encouragement. Further gratitude is also extended to my former tutor, Gill Chester, for her generous collaborative work in French translation during the final stages of researching foreign articles for the book. Finally, my greatest thanks is reserved for Pete Long who helped me to unravel and complete the endless lists of recording dates, unreleased songs and a discography which would have been a formidable book in itself.

ONE

The Old Folky Days

The Neil Young story begins in Canada in the mid-forties. Born 12 November 1945, the son of Scott Young, a respected sports writer for *The Toronto Sun*, Neil spent his early years in Omemee, Ontario. It was not a happy childhood, partly because Young's health was often poor. Throughout his early years, he suffered from epilesy and was subject to occasional seizures which threatened his life. At the age of six he caught polio which left him with a slight limp something which is still noticeable today, although many still assume it to be Young's awkward stage persona. According to his brother Bob, Neil was 13 when their parents split up, each having custody of one of the children. Neil had gone with his mother, nicknamed Rassy by the family, to Winnipeg, where they led a very unsettled life which resulted in his changing schools frequently. The effect of his parents' divorce, coupled with his own ill health, had a profound effect on Young's personality. He became an extremely introverted child, finding it difficult to communicate with other kids. His shyness made him easy meat for school bullies and Young became the classroom scapegoat, receiving frequent beatings from all and sundry. Although Young admits all this, he has sometimes attempted to shroud his wimpishness by relating the amusing tale of an uncharacteristic rejoinder against his "schoolfriends":

> Once I'd become a victim of a series of chump attacks by some of the bullies in my room. I looked up and three guys were staring at me, mouthing, "you low-life prick". Then the guy who sat in front of me turned round and hit my books off my desk with his elbow. He did this a few times. I guess I wore the wrong color of clothes or something. Maybe I looked too much like a mamma's boy for them.
>
> Anyway I went up to the teacher and asked if I could have the dictionary. This was the first time I'd broken the ice and put up my hand to ask for anything since I got to the fucking place. Everybody thought I didn't speak. So I got the dictionary, this big Webster's with little indentations for your thumb under every letter. I took it back to my desk, thumbed through it a little bit. then I just sort of stood up in my seat, raised it above my head as far as I could and hit the guy in front of me over the head with it. Knocked him out.

Yeah. I got expelled for a day and a half, but I let those people know just where I was at. That's the way I fight. If you're going to *fight*, you may as well fight to wipe out who or whatever it is *out*. Or don't fight at all.[1]

It's a nice tale, but the image that most clearly sticks in one's mind is of Neil feeling so threatened and insecure that even putting his hand up to ask a question is described as a major effort.

From this picture it is easy to see how Young wandered into a musical career. His frail body ensured that normal childhood sporting activities were further trials rather than enjoyable pastimes. As a result Neil was forced to search elsewhere for an interest in order to distract him from his own inadequacies. It was his father who provided him with a therapeutic crutch, when, on Christmas Day 1958, he presented his son with a plastic ukelele. The Youngs were in no way a musical family, but both Neil's father and his uncle played around on a ukelele so it seemed an appropriate instrument to give to the boy. Young remembers the old instrument with some affection:

> I learned three chords on it. Really, I went wild and learned "Blueberry Hill" and "On Top Of Old Smokey" – all those neat songs!

Within the next year, Young switched to a banjo which he eventually traded for a second-hand acoustic guitar of dubious quality. Rassy encouraged his guitar-playing mainly to stop Young from chewing his fingernails to pieces, a habit he had no doubt developed from his harrowing early schooldays. From all accounts Young's mother was an extremely dominant woman as can be gleaned from this description of her by Neil's brother, Bob:

> Rassy is a fighter, especially where Neil and I are concerned. She's largely responsible for Neil's success today. She has black flashing eyes and her voice is deep – telephone operators keep calling her "sir". She doesn't take any nonsense. She smokes too many Black Cat Plain cigarettes and she drinks quite a lot of beer. She spends her summers in Winnipeg ... and her winters playing golf and walking on the beach in Florida. At some point she became convinced that Neil's music was worth fighting for, and she's never stopped. She was Neil's first fan, his greatest supporter, and he needed her. She battled on his behalf and, too often it seemed to me, the battles were with our father.

Part of the conflict between Young's parents centerd on his mother's attitude to Neil. Scott Young, as a journalist, took an active interest in Neil's school career, and became increasingly concerned about his son's low educational attainments. Rassy, on the other hand, seemed alarmingly unconcerned about Neil's school career but took an exceptional interest in his musical ambitions. It's not too difficult to see why Rassy gambled on a show-business career for Neil since she was already involved in television as a panelist on a Canadian quiz show, *Twenty Questions*. Close to entertainers in the industry, she perceived that a singing career could prove fruitful.

2

Fortunately, Neil was already showing a strong interest in rock 'n roll and practically idolized Elvis Presley. At the age of 15, Young began spending a lot of his leisure time hanging out at local hops and school dances. One of his favorite local groups was The Reflections and their bass player, Jerry Kale, would later go on to fame and fortune as a member of The Guess Who. At that point Young himself would have settled for regional fame as a Reflection, unaware of his potential for greater things.

At the turn of the 60s with Elvis having lost much of his rock 'n roll credibility by joining the army, Young discovered a new hero in Shadows' guitarist Hank B. Marvin. Inspired by the instrumental "Apache" Young began to imitate Marvin's style. He took to writing instrumentals, gradually improving as a guitarist with each passing month. It would take Young several years, however, before he thought seriously about putting words to music. He had already made a half-hearted attempt at writing some lyrics, including "Don't Cry No Tears", but the results were not entirely satisfactory. Eventually, feeling that the time was right, Young joined a short-lived group which he now can barely recall:

> I wasn't in a group right away ... yes I was ... oh yeah ... but I can't remember ... it was the Sultans ... I think ... No ... no it was the Jades. The Jades, do you believe that? And we did a song called "The Sultan"!

In his final year at Kelvin High School Young joined what he considers to be his first real group, The Squires. Unfortunately, just as he was about to find his niche, Neil's amplifier blew up in his face. It was a desperate time for Young who promptly wrote to his father, boasting of a resurgence of interest in academic study, and asking for a loan. The plan backfired when his father received a report card which clearly revealed an abysmal decline in Neil's scholastic progress. With no chance of laying his hands on the $600 for a new amplifier, Neil and The Squires looked as though they were about to be written into history. Characteristically, Neil's mother saved the day by offering the group her savings. It was that gesture which allowed her a controlling interest in the group and she used her influence to the full.

Within months, The Squires began to become quite popular in Winnipeg, and it was no small thanks to Rassy's efforts. As booking agent and publicist for The Squires, Rassy was continually hustling disc-jockeys and local music critics in a desperate attempt to put her son's name on the map. Occasionally, however, her efforts would prove counter-productive. At this point The Squires were still at the level of playing school dances, but Rassy was way ahead of them. Using her influence she managed to persuade a disc-jockey from the local radio station to broadcast the fact that The Squires would be playing a school dance. When the principal learned that an informal dance at his school was being advertised on a rock 'n roll station he panicked. Fearing that "undesirables" from the area might disrupt the school he threatened to cancel the show. Rassy recalls how easily she dealt with this tricky situation:

> That goddam fool was afraid of undesirables from other schools. He told me all about camp followers during the Wars Of The Roses. So I told this idiot that if he wanted to cancel the dance, that was fine with

me. The contract read that The Squires got paid regardless, and I'd be right over to pick up the check. He soon backed down.

It was this kind of abrasive managerial technique that Young would once more search out in his later career as a solo artist.

The security produced by his mother's forcefulness encouraged Young to take a more active role in The Squires. By September 1964 he was coming up with his own arrangements for inclusion in the set and had also begun to experiment with songwriting. Young was so impressed by the Beatles boom of that year that he even found the confidence to attempt a couple of songs. His debut took place in the cafeteria of the Kelvin High School where he had studied two years before. Young sang, or rather screamed, "It Won't Be Long" and "Money", both of which had been included on the Beatles' current album *With The Beatles*.

As The Squires grew in popularity, Rassy became even more adept at manipulating people. By this time, the Youngs had moved from their nondescript apartment on Corydon Avenue to the comparative plush of the exclusive Winnipeg suburbs of River Heights. At first this brought more problems in the form of irate neighbors, complaining about the noise the group made during rehearsals. Rassy won the support of the landlord, however, who agreed to ignore the complaints and allowed The Squires to practice whenever they wished. Eventually, a policeman was sent round to put a stop to the proceedings, but he hadn't bargained upon meeting Rassy. At first she reasoned with him, promising to curb the noise. Following subsequent visits, however, she charmed him so completely that he ended up sitting in on drums for the group and became one of their most ardent supporters.

In spite of their regional success, it was clear that after two years on the road The Squires had not progressed much further than school dances, so they decided to go their separate ways. During their final days together they traveled to bookings at such places as Thunder Bay and Churchill, Ontario in an old 1948 hearse that Young had purchased. It was at one such gig, the Fourth Dimension club in Fort William, Ontario, that Young first met an ambitious singer-guitarist named Stephen Stills.

Stills had led a nomadic childhood moving from his birth place Houston, Texas to Louisiana, Florida, the Republic of Panama and even Costa Rica. During his wanderings he had assimilated many different musical styles and learned to play a variety of instruments from tambourine to guitar, keyboards and drums. After a musical apprenticeship that included directing a school marching band and appearing in a number of high school groups, Stills was enlisted in a Tampa, Florida combo, The Radars. Returning to Gainsville to complete his interrupted education, Stills briefly joined another band, The Continentals, before heading out to New Orleans to try and make it as a folk singer. There he teamed up with singer Chris Farns, who would later become road manager of the Buffalo Springfield. Following Farns to New York Stills became involved in the Greenwich Village folk scene and played with a host of aspiring musicians including Richie Furay.

Furay had formed a folk group in Ohio and like Stills he had decided to try his luck in New York. He was fortunate enough to be given a residency at the Four Winds. Impressed by each other, Furay and Stills formed a musical partnership and recruited eight other friends in order to found a bizarre 10-man vocal group called the Au Go Go Singers. They succeeded in releasing an album and even managed a television appearance and concert tour. It proved impossible to maintain such a large group for any length of time, so, not surprisingly, the Au Go Go Singers split after only six months together. Stephen next formed a folk group called the Bay Singers, then he changed their name to Company. Ever on the move, Stills and The Company toured Canada, eventually making that all important appearance at the Fourth Dimension club in Ontario.

During that evening Stills and Young found out that they had a mutual admiration for each other, and they were pleasantly surprised to discover that neither was particularly excited by his current group. Stills had been in-and-out of so many groups that The Company was just another stop-gap. By contrast, Young had now been gigging with The Squires for what seemed an eternity and he needed a fresh challenge. Stephen was so impressed with Neil that evening that he attempted to persuade him to form a new group immediately. Stills even seemed willing to become a member of The Squires himself if it meant a chance to play with Young. Apparently, it was Young's unusual repertoire that most impressed the visiting American:

> Neil ... was playing folk-rock before anybody else. He had his Gretch, a rock and roll band that had just recently turned from playing "Louie Louie" to playing the popular folk songs of the day with electric guitars, drums and brass. It was a funny band 'cause they could go right from "Cotton Fields" to "Farmer John".
>
> And they'd just come back from Churchill, Ontario, and Neil had written, I think, his first song "Let me tell you 'bout a thing called snow where it's 45 below", and we had a great time running round in his hearse and drinking good strong Canadian beer and being young and having a good time. Being young. At first I thought, "Well, I'm gonna quit this idiot group and go play with him right now".[2]

However, the problem could not be solved this easily. Firstly, Stills was an American citizen and it would obviously take some time before the immigration authorities would allow him a Canadian work permit. Characteristically, Stills felt that it ought to be Young who made the move from Canada to the U.S.A. though this would probably prove even more difficult to fix. Stills was confident, however, that he could get Young some employment in the States and thus make him eligible for an entry visa and work permit. It was all a bit idealistic, however, and after Stills had left, Young more or less forgot about the half-drunken promises.

Young had underestimated Stills, however, who was deadly serious about forming a group with the Canadian singer. Stephen gives his account of the immediate events following that first meeting:

> I'd toured Canada with a folk group and I'd met this cat called Neil Young who had a band and I almost left the folk group to join him – but there were hang-ups with entry visas and work permits and things like that, so I arranged to go back to New York when I'd finished this folk tour and fix up some club gigs and working papers so that he could bring his band into the States. Well, he thought that was a pretty far out idea, so when I got to California, I left the folk group, headed back east, fixed up some jobs, phoned ... only to find that he'd quit

the group, they'd split up and he'd gone back to being a folksinger and was living with this folksinger chick.[3]

Although it seemed as though Young had temporarily blown his chance of forming a very important group, this was not the entire truth. His fears that Stills would not be able to overcome the immigration regulations were not unfounded. The decision to move to Toronto was taken because Young, quite rightly, realized that legally it was virtually impossible to get work in the States, with or without Stills' aid.

The disappearance of Neil was a serious setback for Stills' master plan. Depressed, he rang Furay in an attempt to start another group in New York, but Richie refused, feeling that the time was not right. Eventually, Stills managed to get hold of Young's Toronto phone number and made him the same proposition. Unfortunately, the call was ill-timed, for Young had suddenly become enchanted with the idea of remaining a folk-singer. It was to be a brief whim, but, unaware of this, Stills concluded that his chances of forming a group with Young were no more:

> ... Neil went to Toronto, fell in with this chick, Vicky Taylor, I think her name was, who was a folksinger, who convinced Neil that he was Bob Dylan. So Neil broke up the band and decided to be Bob Dylan, and was playing rhythm guitar, you know, he would just go in and play acoustic guitar in coffee houses. So he started doing what I had been doing for three years and which I decided I didn't want to do any more. He wanted to be Bob Dylan and I wanted to be the Beatles. We were, as I said, very young. All of a sudden he decided he was gonna ... go play coffee houses and so I just threw up my hands in disgust and went to California.[2]

With no group and no commitments, the nomadic Stills remained hopeful that his luck would change on the West Coast.

Meanwhile, towards the end of 1964, Young was getting into his new career as a folksinger. In common with such contemporaries as Joni Mitchell and Gordon Lightfoot Neil played at the Penny Farthing and the various coffee houses of Toronto's Yorkville district. The folk circuit provided good experience, but Young was getting nowhere fast and he resented singing in order to keep managers alive. Disgruntled, he decided to take a vacation in New York half-hoping to meet up with the brash Texan who had promised him fame and fortune only a few months before. There was no Stills, of course, but Young did manage to meet some old musical acquaintances and he was eventually introduced to Richie Furay one day in Greenwich Village. Furay recalls his first meeting with Young:

> I was living with some friends from the old Au Go Go's when one day Neil Young came visiting. He was down to audition his tunes for someone. That was my first acquaintance with him and he seemed very sure of himself, of where he was going. I couldn't get a word in edgewise, so I just listened a lot. He taught me, "Nowadays Clancy Can't Even Sing" at the time. Back then Neil was as intense as he is now.[4]

Following a brief stay in the Big Apple, Young returned to Toronto determined to form another group in order to survive. Work in the coffee houses was not proving fruitful and Young was swiftly becoming a caricature of the starving folk singer. His luck changed one afternoon, when he was approached in the street by a musician named Bruce Palmer.

Palmer, like Young, was a Canadian who had been through a series of groups and was now faring well as bassist in a rock and blues orientated group, the Mynah Birds. According to Palmer he had noticed Young wandering around Yorkville with a guitar-case and decided to check him out. Like Stills, Palmer was immediately impressed by Young's youthful enthusiasm. Realizing his potential Palmer arranged for Young to audition for the job as Mynah Birds' guitarist. Group-leader, Ricky James Matthews, described by his friends as a black Mick Jagger, was impressed and wasted no time in enlisting Young, who was pleased to join:

> There were a few people who liked me very much and a great many people who didn't know what I was doing. I joined the Mynah Birds so I could eat. It was the first band I wasn't leader (of).

Young's first gig with the Mynah Birds was almost a repetition of his amplifier-blowing days with The Squires. When it was time for his first long solo, Young in an unparalleled fit of excitement leapt into the air and clean off the stage. In doing so, he jerked the plug of his guitar from its socket, and the rest was silence. Young quickly adjusted to the Mynah Birds, however, and found that his guitar technique was improving. The group managed to elicit some record company interest and recorded a couple of singles for Motown, which were almost immediately deleted.

Ironically, it was the minor success of the group that eventually produced its downfall. Signed to Motown, the Mynah Birds spent an increasing amount of time in Detroit and looked set for a series of future recordings. Then, on one fateful day, United States officials burst into the studio and arrested Ricky James Matthews. He was charged with being a deserter from the United States Navy, and was immediately taken back into service to serve his time. Neil, Bruce and the other members of the Mynah Birds were completely shattered. The shock was worsened by the fact that Rick had never even hinted that he was a deserter. In fact, the group had been under the misapprehension that he was a Canadian citizen like themselves. Without Ricky James Matthews, the Mynah Birds lost the spirit to continue and following their return to Canada, they went their separate ways. Years later, Matthews would get a second shot at fame as Tamla star Rick James.

Without a group, Canada proved as depressing as ever and Young soon found that his savings were dwindling away. Finally, the last link with the Mynah Birds was severed when Young was forced to sell their equipment in order to make ends meet. Meanwhile, Stills was in almost equally dire straits in Los Angeles. He had attempted to form a partnership with Van Dyke Parks, in a belated effort to emulate the success of The Byrds by electrifying folk music. However, this project failed to reach fruition. His next big chance came when he auditioned for the part of the dumb blond in The Monkees. Stills looked promising until Don Kirshner noticed his crooked teeth – and that would never do for a Monkee. As a result, the job went to Peter Tork, leaving Stills once more on the street. Moving frequently between Los Angeles and San Francisco, Stills met Barry Friedman who became a friend and musical and financial adviser for the next couple of years. Friedman suggested that Stills should look further afield in order to start another group. Stills discussed the matter with Dick Davis (later to become manager of the Buffalo Springfield) and they agreed to call Richie Furay in New York. Stills' love of exaggeration reached unprecedented lengths during that conversation in which he claimed to have a really hot group on his hands that would set California alight. Apparently, all they needed was a strong lead vocalist and Richie had been nominated as first choice. However, when Richie arrived in California he was shocked to learn that the hot combo he had flown across America to join did not even exist. After some strong words with Stills, Furay reluctantly decided to continue their partnership – at least for the moment.

It was not only Furay who was disappointed by the reunion. Stills' future manager Dick Davis had also fallen victim to Stephen's rhetoric and believed that Furay was nothing less than the hippest cat on the West Coast. When he met Furay at the airport, Davis was more than a little taken aback:

> He stepped off the plane in a Brooks Brothers' suit and a crewcut.
> Steve and I didn't look like that at all. I thought right then that
> nothing was going to happen.

Davis' first impressions were to prove incorrect. Furay, possibly because he had no choice, adapted to the situation quickly and began playing some new songs. He remembers sitting for hours in a room with Stills going through every song they had ever known.

The attempt to form a group around Stills and Furay was gradually proving disastrous. Friedman had managed to recruit Ken Kublin, the bassist in Neil's former group The Squires, and he agreed to sit in for awhile. Kublin quickly became disillusioned with the entire proceedings, however, and left the duo to their own devices. Stills and Furay came to the grim realization that unless they found additional instrumentation immediately, their careers as professional musicians would effectively be over.

Coincidentally, Young and Palmer were undergoing the same problems in Canada. Since the demise of the Mynah Birds work had become scarce, and now the situation was desperate. Predictably, they decided to team up together and head out to Los Angeles in the hope of finding a suitable gig. In spite of the problems of entering the States, Neil realized that to remain in Canada would seriously stifle the development of his career.

Although neither of them had work permits or entry visas, they hoped that fortune would smile on them. It didn't, at least not at first. Along the route Neil's hearse was involved in a serious traffic accident and Young was admitted to a hospital in Albuquerque, New Mexico suffering from shock and exhaustion.

After a few days rest, Young was free to travel again and the duo completed the trip, arriving in Los Angeles in early 1966. Young was still determined to find the elusive Texan whom he had not seen since that Ontario gig of 1964. After a seemingly pointless search, Young and Palmer decided to take in the city as tourists, and drive out to San Francisco. At that point one of the most talked about legends in the history of rock 'n roll took place when the four musicians met up under extraordinary circumstances. The long-awaited reunion was largely due to a

Los Angeles traffic-jam in which Stills and Furay were stuck. While they were patiently waiting to move, a hearse appeared on the other side of the road. Furay vividly recalls the day of the reunion:

> For about a month or so we rehearsed and looked for musicians. Just when all was looking dim, we ran into Neil driving down Sunset Boulevard on his way to San Francisco. We were driving in a white van and I saw a black hearse with Canadian license plates going the other way. I remembered that Stills had told me that Neil drove a black hearse. So we chased him down. We persuaded him to at least come and listen to our arrangement of "Clancy". He listened and liked it so he and this bass-player decided to form the group.[4]

The quartet began rehearsing at Barry Friedman's house and tentatively decided to christen themselves The Herd. Their next aim was to enlist a permanent drummer as soon as possible. In a matter of days Stills appeared with Billy Mundi and was enthusing over the drummer's technical ability and pliable personality. Mundi might have remained the original drummer throughout the group's career were it not for their astute manager, Dick Davis. In addition to The Herd, he had another group under his belt called Maston and Brewer, a competent duo who also required a drummer. Davis, realizing that it would be some weeks before The Herd were ready to perform, persuaded Mundi to join Maston and Brewer whose need was clearly more urgent.

What seemed another setback was quickly resolved when, within a few days, Neil discovered another drummer, Dewey Martin. It was an incredible stroke of luck because Martin had just been fired from The Dillards. Martin had briefly worked with another rock group, the MFO, but he felt more at ease with Young and Company. This was no doubt due to their collective musical experience, coupled with the fact that two of their members were, like Martin, Canadian. It was Young who pushed hardest to ensure that Martin was accepted in the group, no doubt sharing many experiences with the drummer about life in Ontario. The other members of the group were equally impressed with Martin's musical history, for he was clearly more experienced than any of them. Three years older than Stills and Young, Martin had achieved fame as a session-player backing such artistes as Patsy Cline, Roy Orbison, Carl Perkins and Faron Young, as well as appearing on the Grande Ol Opry. Ever restless, he moved to Seattle, Washington and formed his own group Sir Walter Raleigh and The Coupons, before finally settling in Los Angeles at the end of 1965. With his country background, it was not a particularly difficult task for Martin to secure a place in The Dillards, and when they branched out into rock Dewey's future seemed even more secure. It was their decision to revert temporarily to their more traditional folk sound which had left poor Dewey redundant.

With Stills, Young, Furay and Palmer, however, Martin would be facing a greater challenge. With their diverse musical experience, the quintet looked potentially the most eclectic unit to appear on the West Coast scene since the formation of The Byrds. One thing they wanted to do, however, was to find a more suitable and representative name for the group. Like so much of their story, their christening came about through an incredible coincidence. One day while they were hanging out at Friedman's house, they happened to notice a vehicle standing outside in the street. On the side of this steamroller or tractor, depending upon which member of the group you believe, there was printed the place of manufacture, Buffalo, Springfield. Without hesitation, the quintet decided to take that as their permanent group name.

TWO

1966 – The Struggle For Fame

What the Buffalo Springfield needed most desperately was an important gig where they would be noticed. At this point all was looking far from well and the group were so poor that they were reduced to practicing by the side of the road. Their big break came very soon, however, when they were allowed to appear at the Orange Grounds, San Bernadino in March 1966. It was a prestigious first gig and the Springfield rose to the occasion by giving one of their best performances. Furay believes this period to be the Springfield's finest:

> The very beginning was the best. The original five of us, as far as I am concerned, had the magic. The original five of us were as tight musically as we ever could've been. Our record was exciting, very exciting …
>
> The early days were great. We had such regard for each other, we were all so delighted to be making music together. No one was critical of each other, that would come later. Everyone was helpful, constructive and creative.[4]

Brian Friedman, however, was still concerned that Stills should be receiving the best possible deal. He began negotiations to sign Stills and Furay to Epic, but this was bitterly opposed by manager Dick Davis who argued that it was contrary to the interests of both artistes. Predictably, a managerial clash took place and the group sided with Davis, which resulted in Friedman being forced to abandon his grand design. Before closing his account with the Springfield, Friedman did them an enormous favor by introducing them to The Byrds.

It was Byrds' bassist, Chris Hillman, who first saw the enormous potential of the Springfield. In fact, he was so impressed that he actually considered the possibility of managing them. Hillman went as far as to approach fellow Byrd Jim McGuinn about the project, but in the end they decided that it would require too much responsibility and unwanted pressures. Instead, Hillman gave the group the benefit of his experience in the business and managed to pull a few strings. Hillman's most important contribution at this stage was securing a very important series of gigs for the Springfield at the prestigious Whisky A Go Go. Hillman introduced the group to Elmer Valentine, the manager of the Whisky, and persuaded him to give the group a six-week engagement at the club. It was a solid residency, requiring the Buffalo Springfield to play six nights a week. What was to happen during those weeks was more than anyone could possibly have imagined.

After the first few nights, word spread around Hollywood that a very unusual group were playing the Whisky. What first attracted people was not the music as much as the image and the unusual name Buffalo Springfield. Onstage, the group were visually more appealing than anything that had been seen on the Strip since the halcyon days of The Byrds at Ciro's. It seemed that each member of the Springfield had a distinctive image of his own, and on stage the audience's attention would constantly move from one member to the other. Richie held the center stage and impressed the teenyboppers with his cute balancing act. This consisted of moving across the stage on tip toes with his feet turned inwards. After several gigs, Furay perfected this to such an extent that it became almost as famous as Chuck Berry's celebrated duck-walk. Furay also adopted a clever pose to emphasize his vocal abilities. He would stand far away from the microphone during the introductory riffs and breaks, and then dramatically burst into song. In any other group Furay alone would have been the visual focus, but in the Springfield every member had some gimmick to show off. Young, for example, began to check out all the various boutiques in Hollywood, before finding the perfect stage outfit:

> There I was making a hundred and twenty a week at the Whisky as a musician. I've always liked fringe jackets ... fringe jackets are groovy. I went out and bought one right away with some pants and a turtleneck shirt ... Oh yeah I thought I was heavy. I wore 'em on some T.V. shows and whenever we worked. Then I went to this place on Santa Monica Boulevard near La Cienega. I saw this great Commanche War shirt – the best jacket I've ever seen. I had two more made.
>
> The group was Western, the name Buffalo Springfield came from off a tractor, so it all fitted. I was the Indian.[5]

The stage roles adopted by Stills and Young were a perfect reflection of their complementary roles in the group. They each took their places on separate sides of the stage and appeared almost to be competing with each other in order to gain the audience's attention. Stills saw his role in the group as that of a musical director:

> At the beginning, Neil would sort of stand off at the side and play his axe and be very cool, and everybody dug that about him. And I was on the other side of the stage calling it. I would call the show.[6]

Dewey Martin, as a drummer, could not realistically compete with all this but even he chose flamboyant shirts and neckerchiefs, typical of an era dominated by Carnaby Street fashion. Bassist Bruce Palmer might have easily been submerged by all these onstage theatrics, but in many ways he was the most visually appealing of all. Palmer, throughout his career in the Springfield, retained a mystique which made him seem a much more intriguing figure than the other members of the group. While Furay danced around the stage and Stills and Young battled it out on the side lines, Palmer remained unmoved, almost uninterested in what was going on around him often with his back turned towards the audience. He seldom talked to the press and when he did he remained evasive. He refused to disclose his age, even his musical background or family origins, and this would later intrigue the fans. Young learned a lot from his fellow Canadian and in later years he would remember how easy it was to manufacture a mystique by refusing interviews and appearing moody. Even in these early shows the Springfield were playing dangerous games. Palmer's manufactured "moodiness" and the play-acting rivalry between Stills and Young were personas which might all too easily be transformed into distinctive personality traits.

Within a couple of weeks of their residency at the Whisky, the audience grew to unforeseen proportions. Chris Hillman recounts their sudden rise to local fame:

> What happened to the Springfield at the Whisky was similar to what happened to us at Ciro's. First there were just a handful of people and then word spread and everybody wanted to be there. It became *the* place to be. Everyone was there – Barry McGuire, Sonny and Cher, the Mamas and Papas. It was a great gig.

David Crosby, who was also in The Byrds at the time, recalls those early shows at the Whisky:

> I first met Neil at the Whisky when Chris Hillman took me by to hear him. I thought he was real good. I thought he couldn't sing too well, but I thought he played real well. He and Stills were into doing this guitar duet stuff, which I thought was fantastic. "Nowadays Clancy Can't Even Sing" and stuff like that – it was great.

It was now clear that the Springfield had a lot more going for them than visual effects. The patronage that they received from other Los Angeles musicians was a strong indication that their sound was highly regarded. According to Stills the live sound that the group generated in their early days was never effectively captured on vinyl:

> ... I wish that someone had been recording those concerts live. Because by the fourth or fifth concert we were so good it was absolutely astounding and the first week at the Whisky was absolutely incredible.
>
> We were just incredible, man, that's when we peaked, just like Clapton's band, The Cream, peaked at the Fillmore the first time and after then it was downhill. We peaked at the Whisky and after then it was downhill. Our producer didn't know how to record such a thing ...[2]

Although they were beginning to draw the crowds and buy outlandish clothes, the Buffalo Springfield were a long way from being millionaires. Young was still living in a sleazy rooming house sleeping next to a guy who had contracted hepatitis. Such living conditions were hardly conducive to a body as frail in health as Young's, but the successful Whisky stint kept him together. In April 1966, just after they had secured the residency, he wrote his mother Rassy an optimistic note:

> We have formed a group in which we'll do our own material ... The group is called Buffalo Springfield for no particular reason.[7]

Superficially, it seemed that the group's first taste of fame had not changed them. According to Stills, however, there was a discernible change of attitude as early as the Whisky days. He admits that there was a period of solidarity but stresses,

> That was before the ego trips, when we were a band, when we lived together. We did everything, y'know. We'd cram ourselves into a car together and all go off to the gig. But then we started working the Whisky and all those strange chicks started me and Neil and it kind of blew the whole balance.[6]

The conflict that threatened to break up the group, however, would lie dormant for a considerable while longer.

The successful stint at the Whisky brought its own immediate rewards as well as its problems. The audience reaction had not gone unnoticed by record company a'n'r men, and the group shortly found themselves in the center of a bidding war. The presence of the Mamas and the Papas in the audience ensured that their record label, Dunhill, would be an interested party. Impressed by what they saw, Dunhill made a tentative offer of $5,000. However, they could not compete with the bigger labels who were also quick to see the group's potential. Warners literally doubled Dunhill's offer, promising an advance of $10,000.

Realizing that things were hotting up, Dick Davis became a little concerned. His managerial experience was limited and so he was unsure whether to accept Warner's offer or wait for an even higher bid. After discussing the problem with the group he decided to seek the advice of Charlie Greene, who had formerly managed the hugely successful duo Sonny and Cher. Stone and Greene agreed to give their opinion of the group and an audition was arranged. After hearing the Buffalo Springfield's repertoire Stone and Greene were suitably impressed and ensured that they would get a slice of any future action by publishing their music. They also introduced the Springfield to Atlantic Records president Ahmet Ertegun who was invited to one of the rehearsals. Ertegun also saw potential in the group and ensured that they be signed to Atlantic's subsidiary label Atco by producing a $20,000 advance.

Work soon began on a first single, "Go And Say Goodbye", a Stills composition. It seemed to have commercial potential with its fast beat and country/pop sound. Lyrically, it was far from demanding, but it showed Stills to be capable of writing in the third person and eager to moralize to teenagers. According to Stills a guy must never leave his girl on the sly but come out and say goodbye to her face. It was typical teenage fodder, but Stills knew it had hit potential.

The projected flip-side of the single, "Nowadays Clancy Can't Even Sing" was a much more ambitious piece of work. Lyrically, it was a puzzling song, almost a dramatization of paranoia. Nobody has ever bothered to analyze the song in any depth except for Greil Marcus in a piece for *S.F. Good Times*. However, Marcus' interpretation of "Nowadays Clancy Can't Even Sing" is almost totally impressionistic and little of it seems to be related to the song at all. Marcus argues:

> In one of the most touching, depressing songs ever written, "Nowadays Clancy Can't Even Sing", Young told the story of a kid he'd gone to school with up in Canada. The boy used to spend his time making up songs and singing them, or perhaps it's the other way round. I

wouldn't know. But the kids in the town banded together and teased this boy, shamed him, scared him, made him afraid of himself and his own natural impulses to express himself with the little melodies he gathered up throughout the day ... It was a rare song – a song about friendship. It shows just how scary and cruel childhood can be.

The premise of the whole piece is based upon Marcus' assumption that the song is the story of kid whom Young had attended school with in Canada. One would obviously assume this to be a fact told to Marcus by Young himself. However, Marcus cites no authorial authority and appears to be making his own assumption about the inspiration behind the title. Even if Clancy was a kid whom Young knew at school, this fact bears little relevance to the song as we have it, and even less to Marcus' subsequent "analysis". A glimpse at the lyrics is enough to see that there is pretty well no information about "Clancy" beyond the title itself. It is not even clear whether it is Clancy who is making up the songs. Within the song, there is not a shred of evidence to support the contention that "the kids banded together and teased this boy, shamed him, scared him etc." We look in vain for "the town" that Marcus insists is in the song. In fact there are no geographical references at all and not even one direct allusion to "childhood". Having begun with a premise not substantiated by the song, Greil Marcus has been forced to fill in imaginary details all along the line in order to make his interpretation sound plausible.

Following the song through logically line by line one sees that it is actually a long series of rhetorical questions. We are never actually told who is saying, "Baby that don't mean a thing 'cause nowadays Clancy can't even sing". Or are we? There is a definite perceptual movement in the song which gives us some clue as to the speaker's identity. The narrator is convinced that someone is attempting to hurt him ("Who's that stomping all over my face?") or at least prevent him from enjoying a freedom and pleasure which he believes he once had ("... putting sponge in the bells I once rung and taking my gypsy before she's begun"). The questions continue in this manner until they become less concerned with threatening external forces, and increasingly obsessed with speculations on the self ("And who's all hung up on that happiness thing? ... Who's trying to act like he's just in between?"). One suspects that the "he" is not another person at all, but the narrator chiding himself ("... don't bother looking you're too blind to see"). The paranoia implicit in the song is laid bare towards the end ("Who's seeing eyes through the crack in the floor?") before Young finally unravels the thread. The final question ("Who should be sleeping but's a-writing *this* song, wishing and a-hoping he weren't so damn wrong?") indicates that the "he" is the songwriter himself. Thus all the rhetorical questions voiced throughout the song are by implication directed towards the self: the songwriter should be sleeping but is in fact "a-writing this song" ("Nowadays Clancy Can't Even Sing"). It is the songwriter who is destroying himself ("stomping all over my face") and restricting his own former freedom ("putting sponge in the bells I once rung"). As a first piece of recorded work this is a very impressive composition with a clever twist. Unfortunately, the lead vocal work was given to Furay, as it would be on several of Young's early compositions. Although Furay provides a technically superior vocal performance, much of the anguish and intensity of Young's own interpretation, as heard in later concerts, is absent. Overall, however, a passable "b" side for a first single is what the group must have felt at the time.

While awaiting the release of the first single the Springfield managed to secure some more important gigs through their old friends in The Byrds. They were taken on a one week tour of Southern California as support, and sampled the power of Byrdmania, as Roger McGuinn remembers:

> After Chris had got the Springfield that Whisky residency they toured with us. We were very big at the time and had a strong following. I think they were impressed by the intensity of the fans who would stop at nothing!

The Springfield were a huge success, even attempting to upstage the Byrds by pulling out their plugs while they were playing. After that, however, gigs became scarce, though the Springfield managed to get a booking with The Turtles at Redondo Beach and another important support with the Rolling Stones at the Hollywood Bowl.

At the end of July, "Go And Say Goodbye" was set for release, but at the last moment it was relegated to a flipside. Atlantic had been besieged with calls from distributors who unanimously stated their preference for "Nowadays Clancy Can't Even Sing". Aesthetically it seemed a good decision, but in commercial terms is was obviously a mistake. The single was a minor U.S. Top 30 hit, but at this point the Springfield were obviously hoping for something bigger. In retrospect, it is easy to see why the single fared so badly. It was banned in many states because the lyrics included the word "damn"; some disc jockeys felt that the name Buffalo Springfield was a little long; more complained that the title "Nowadays Clancy Can't Even Sing" was too long; finally, there were objections to the length of the single which clocked in at three minutes twenty seconds. It was a difficult product to break, and although other artists had successfully overcome such petty resistance in the past, the Springfield were not so lucky.

The last minute decision to flip the single was not particularly welcomed by Stills and caused some friction within the group. Already a strong sense of rivalry was beginning to develop between individual members, particularly Stills and Young. When they finally signed their publishing contracts with Stone and Greene, the first signs of greed and resentment were very evident. June Nelson, who worked with Stone and Greene, recalls the tension during their first meeting:

> They were up in my office and they didn't know anything about contracts or publishing. So I said, "Listen, somebody's got to be the leader, because this thing has to be legal". Everybody went, "Well ... ah ..." and just sort of looked at each other. So Stills said, "Okay, I'll be leader", and Neil looked over to Stills and said, "Okay, you be leader!"
>
> Then the major conflicts began over whose material would be done. Stills knew the more songs he had on the album, the more money he would get. Then everyone realized the significance of the thing in terms of money. So Neil began to say, "Let's get some of my songs done too, Steve."

It was in this frame of mind that the group set out to record their first album.

16

The recordings began during the summer, but there would be a long delay before the final release of the album. The group found themselves not only arguing with each other but also with the executives of Atlantic. Having completed the recording, the group listened to the tapes and were far from pleased. They felt that the stereo effects were practically inaudible because of the mix and also complained about the disparity of the harmony work. The group demanded that they be allowed to re-record the album, but Atlantic initially refused. The delay caused by this wrangling seriously affected the release schedule. By the time the problems had been sorted out it was mid-winter. Atlantic, realizing that the release of a debut album just before Christmas would be suicidal, put the record back once more until the New Year.

The problems that had beset the Springfield's progress during 1966 showed no signs of abating. Shortly after the completion of the album a further disaster took place when Neil Young was arrested. While driving with a friend, Neil was stopped by the police who quickly discovered that the Canadian had no permit. At the police station, Young was confronted by an officious cop who called him an "animal" and threatened to throw him in a cage. After exchanging insults, Young was severely corrected by two other officers. At that moment Brian Stone arrived with the necessary money for bail, but he was also assaulted and imprisoned. Young was next taken to a Neuropsychiatric hospital to undergo examinations. At this point Neil was apparently still subject to the nervous attacks that had plagued his childhood, but fortunately they did not last too long.

Following the recording of their first album, the Buffalo Springfield had quickly drained their financial resources and the gigs were not forthcoming. During the winter they managed to secure a brief residency at the Fillmore (11–13 November) but they became increasingly alienated by the snobbery of the audience. Disillusioned, Young spoke of quitting and returning to Canada. Meanwhile, Stills temporarily returned to Topanga Canyon in order to work on some new material. He emerged with an exciting new composition, "For What It's Worth", which provided hope for possible success in the New Year.

THREE

The Touring And The Damage Done

The group's debut album, *Buffalo Springfield*, was finally released in February 1967 and received favorable reviews. What it showed most clearly was that Stills and Young had assumed creative control of the group. Of the twelve songs included on the album, seven were written by Stills and the remainder by Young. Furay originally had one song intended for inclusion, "My Kind Of Love", but its standard was not deemed high enough. Although Stills takes most of the writing credits, his compositions are well below the standard of Young's contributions. "Sit Down I Think I Love You", "Hot Dusty Roads" and "Paid The Price" are fairly average 1966 pop songs with very little lasting appeal. "Leave" is the token rocker on which Stills manages to let rip, and "Everybody's Wrong" shows his first recorded attempt at writing a protest song. In retrospect, this material is noticeably unexceptional, and Stills appears merely to be following the kind of music that the Beatles had brought to public attention four years before. The Beatles' influence is particularly discernible on "Baby Don't Scold Me" and, as if to punctuate this, Stills deliberately includes the riff from "Day Tripper" at the end of the song.

In contrast to Stills' work, the four Young compositions are generally excellent and stand well alongside "Nowadays Clancy Can't Even Sing". "Burned" sounds as though it might have been a slow number but it emerges as a rocker. It is probably best remembered as Young's singing debut:

> My first vocal ever done in a studio, late 1966 (Gold Star). The boys gave me some uppers to get my nerve up. Maybe you can hear that. I was living in a $12.50 per week apartment at the time and everybody on the floor liked it too. We stayed up all night listening to it.[8]

Although a reasonable debut, "Burned" was hardly worth staying up all night for, especially when we compare it with his other compositions on this album.

"Do I Have To Come Right Out And Say It?" was a predictable love song from the early period, dealing with the problem of commiting oneself to a relationship. Furay, who took lead vocal on much of Young's early material, gives a great performance. The care with which Furay handled the vocal is underlined by comparing this with an earlier alternate take, currently in circulation, in which Richie plods along without any attempt at putting meaning into the song. Whether the impetus for the re-recording came from Young's protests or Furay's good taste is an interesting question.

The remaining songs, "Flying On The Ground Is Wrong" and "Out Of My Mind", show more clearly the direction Young's writing would take during the next few years. Both songs deal with his attempt to rationalize the meaning of stardom, and to determine its effect upon his life:

> All I hear are screams from outside the limousines
> That are taking me out of my mind.

Young expresses the feeling of a tremendous and inexplicable loss, caused by the sudden changes that stardom brings: "Left behind, by myself and what I'm living for". Finally, as in "Flying On The Ground Is Wrong", there is the hint of a personal loss underlying this depression: "... if you miss me I've just gone". Young's awareness of the pressures of superstardom at this early stage of his career is very ironic when we consider his determination to succeed. According to his contemporaries, Young more than any of the other members thirsted for commercial success, and when it was denied him he became extremely depressed. In fact, in many respects, it was Young's impatience for success which would most threaten the continuance of the group.

The Springfield's hopes for commercial success were increased when "For What It's Worth" was issued during the same month as their debut album. A statement of concern about the tension between police and kids, "For What It's Worth" was perfectly timed. With student riots and anti-war marches a part of everyday American life, it could not have been more topical. It was soon shooting up the American charts and eventually reached as high as Number 7. Atlantic, observing its success, decided to include it on all future pressings of the group's current album as a replacement for "Baby Don't Scold Me". In spite of the single's success the group were still far from satisfied. Both Young and Furay felt that the disc was only a "regional" hit and claimed that it should have achieved a higher placing. At least having a Top 10 single gave the group more drawing power as well as offering the possibility of further touring. In the wake of the single's success they accepted a ten day booking at a New York Club called Ondine's and it proved to be one of their more memorable gigs. It even gave them a chance to reach a new audience by opening for the legendary Otis Redding. During the Ondine's residency the group entered Atlantic's New York studio one evening to record their next single, "Mr. Soul". Written by Young the song was a continuation of the "Out Of My Mind"/ "Flying On The Ground Is Wrong" theme of anti-stardom, but with a new twist. Young replaced the depression of those songs with a surprisingly wry, often cynical humor:

> For the thought that I caught that my head is the event of the season
> Why in crowds just a trace of my face could seem so pleasin'.

The mood of the song is very close to satire, which indicates a shift in Young's sensibility. He is now capable of achieving an ironic distance, not previously discernible in his introspective lyrics. It was almost as if Young concluded that it was not he who was "out of his mind", but the fanatical public: "She said, 'you're strange but don't change'; and I let her". In the last line of the song Young plays with the girl's phrase in order to ask the question: "Is it strange I should change I don't know why don't you ask her?" This implies a realization on Young's part that the changes in his own musical career might be more effectively answered by his audience, rather than himself. That final line of "Mr. Soul" would later sum up Young's attitude towards conducting interviews with the music press. Although another hit, "Mr. Soul" did not come any nearer to giving the group the Number One single they so coveted, but would never achieve. In a way, it was hardly surprising. Although "Mr. Soul" contained some clever lyrics it was extremely derivative musically. The stolen riff from the Rolling Stones' "Satisfaction" was blatant and did much damage to the Springfield's artistic credibility.

While plans were being formulated for a second album release, more problems occurred when bassist, Bruce Palmer was arrested for being in possession of marijuana. With commitments looming in Los Angeles, the group were forced to leave Palmer in the custody of the New York Police Department. The subsequent trial went particularly badly for Palmer who was sentenced to three months in prison and deported to Canada. Without Palmer, the group were close to disarray and it could not have happened at a worse time. With an important television appearance due in the near future they desperately needed to find a replacement. Manager Dick Davis was finally forced to appear with them on *The Hollywood Palace* television show masquerading as a bassist. The Buffalo Springfield recordings from that show were later included on the soundtrack of Young's *Journey Through The Past*. Following the television appearance, the group managed to secure a booking at Garazzi's, a club on La Cienga Boulevard, Hollywood. Love's bassist, Ken Forssi, agreed to stand in on a temporary basis until a suitable replacement could be found. Eventually, the unpredictable Ken Kublin agreed to fly down from Canada and become a full time member of the group. Although Kublin was a good friend of Young, he was not an adequate replacement for Palmer.

During the next couple of months the Springfield toured extensively. An appearance at Hollywood's Hullabaloo was followed by an evening at the Rolling Hills High School. Following these warm-up gigs the group toured the States, but they often found themselves relegated to second or third place on the bill. In fact the only performance where they actually got their name included in the concert program was with Peter, Paul and Mary and The Byrds. On one occasion the group broke their contract by refusing to continue a show. Their reasons were not entirely unjustified, for only twenty people had turned out to watch their set.

The group returned defeated and morose and attempted to complete their second album. On this occasion, they were directly produced by Atlantic president, Ahmet Ertegun. Although they were reputed to have recorded more than an album's worth of material, the sessions were abandoned and no record appeared until later in the year. At the time of these sessions it was revealed that the new record was to be titled *Stampede* and later in the year an album bearing that title was advertized in several trade papers. Whether *Stampede* was a completely different album from the work that finally appeared, *Buffalo Springfield Again*, is conjectural. The fact that both albums contained the same serial number strongly suggests that they were identical. At least, it seems unlikely that during the very brief period in which the cover art work was altered an entirely new album would be substituted for *Stampede*. The facts are extremely confusing, but my guess is that the group began to record an album early in the year with Ahmet Ertegun which was tentatively titled *Stampede*. Those sessions produced a number of songs but presumably the material was not considered of consistent enough quality to make up an entire album. The sessions were therefore abandoned and later in the year the group recorded an entirely different album. Satisfied with the results, they decided to release it at the end of the year. At that point they chose the title *Stampede* which, of course, was to have been the album released earlier in the year. Finally, Eve Babitz appeared with a more elegant cover, so the group rejected the *Stampede* art work and settled for *Buffalo Springfield Again*. This change was effected so rapidly that the serial numbers on both covers remained the same.

The confusion caused by this state of affairs has led many commentators to assume that a last minute switch took place at the end of 1967 involving two totally different albums. It is my contention, however, that by that time the situation had been resolved, an album was prepared, and only the art work was altered. Of course that still leaves us with two questions – what happened to the rejected recordings of the first session, and how many of them later appeared on record? It is possible of course that the best songs from the original "Stampede" sessions were salvaged and included on *Buffalo Springfield Again* but we do know that many others were not. "Down To The Wire", Young tells us, was originally planned for inclusion on *Stampede* but did not surface on any official recording until the *Decade* compilation in 1977. This was a great mistake because it is undoubtedly a strong composition and one of Young's more powerful moments. Its non-appearance is probably explained by the fact that the other members of the group were pushing for their own material, and Young had already moved on into new ideas involving orchestration. It is worth noting that an alternate take of the song exists with Stephen Stills on lead vocal. Although his interpretation is acceptable, it is far less impressive than Young's version. Two other tracks from the original sessions subsequently appeared on the group's postumously released third album ("Pretty Girl Why" and "Uno Mundo"). That leaves at least three very impressive acoustic numbers generally accepted to have been recorded during this period. Stills' rendition of "So You Got A Lover" surprisingly turns out to be one of his finest songs from that era. Backed only by an acoustic guitar and additional harmonies during the last verse, it takes the form of a lecture directed against an unfaithful lover. However, the emotion is controlled and the sentiments deliberately restrained, unlike the self-indulgent rantings that could be heard on Still's own later work. Young's "There Goes My Babe" is a solo acoustic love lost song, while "One More Sign" argues the necessity of expressing pent-up emotion. All three numbers are simple, charming love songs unmarred by any melodramatic use of orchestration or ostentatious production tricks. Finally, "We'll See" is also reputed to be an outtake from these sessions and is very close in feel to "Baby Don't Scold Me" from the first album, though the lead guitar work has noticeably improved. Although most of these songs range from fair to very good it is difficult to believe that they were ever considered as anything more than outtakes. The three acoustic numbers, in particular, impressive though they be, are essentially solo recordings and would not have fitted easily onto a group album without additional instrumentation. The tracks that have surfaced then, strongly indicate that there was no completed *Stampede* album as such, but a session consisting of introductory acoustic songs and sub-standard pop material similar to Still's recordings on the first album. Only "Down To The Wire" looks a really serious contender for the second album. Several other tracks such as "Neighbor Don't You Worry", "(Come On) Here" and "My Angel" sound dated enough to have come from the first album sessions, or even earlier. Young has gone on record as saying that several tapes of unreleased Buffalo Springfield recordings of superb quality are in his possession, but in naming the tracks, he has merely repeated the above titles. Whether material of a higher standard lies buried in the vaults remains to be heard.

The problems caused by the deportation of Palmer continued to hound the group throughout the first half of the year. The unpredictable Ken Kublin suddenly decided that he did not fit into the Springfield set-up and abruptly departed. He returned to Toronto and formed Three's A Crowd with Trever Veitch and David Wiffen and although they managed to release an album later in the year, it was not a commercial success. With tour commitments to fulfil, the Buffalo Springfield quickly enlisted Jim Fielder from The Mothers Of Invention as a replacement. The subsequent tour of the Mid-West, however, was another disaster as tempers began to fray between various members of the group. Stills soon realized that Fielder's style of playing was not suited to the Springfield and argued in favor of employing another bassist. The other members argued against such a sudden change, particularly in the middle of an important tour. It now seemed that everybody was at each other's throats, particularly Stills and Young. Young began to object to Stills' domination of the group and gradually insisted on making the Springfield a more democratic unit. By this time, Young was signing his own songs but he also wanted more say in arranging his own material. The resultant arguments gradually became more and more violent as neither member was willing to give way. Stills recalls how close these clashes came to destroying the group:

> My temper was starting to get in the way 'cos I would watch the shit go down ... and I sensed that Neil was resenting the fact that I was starting to play lead guitar. I was the arranger, and all of a sudden I was treading on his territory, so he started getting into mine and so forth and we just got into this ridiculous 21-year old boys in the band gig. Then we were finding fault with everything. Everything started to lose proportion and it got stupid, y'know. It was just dumb, a kid's trip.[6]

In order to escape the tension, Young spent less and less time with the group and began associating with a young producer/arranger named Jack Nitzsche. Nitzsche had previously worked with Phil Spector and impressed Young with his imaginative and innovatory ideas about recording. Young's absences throughout this period emphasized his increasing disenchantment with the Buffalo Springfield and his willingness to try something new. While on tour the group were still attempting to complete their all-important second album while the arguments continued to rage. As a result it soon became bedlam in the studio. Stills and Young would often appear three hours late for a session which not only wasted time and money but caused bad feelings between themselves and the other members of the group. By this time Furay was also becoming upset by his role in the group. With Young demanding more time, Furay's lead vocals were being cut, and his stature in the Springfield was gradually being undermined. Like Young, he reacted aggressively, and began insisting that the group record his own compositions. Stills and Young were so busy fighting amongst themselves that Furay managed to seize the opportunity to use the wasted studio time to record his own material. What made it even easier for Furay was the fact that Stills and Young were avoiding each other to such an extent that they began working on their own material individually. On stage, however, they had to face each other and it became more than Young could take.

The break-up of the group seemed imminent when dramatically Bruce Palmer returned to the fold. He had managed to pass the Canadian border without the necessary papers and he was now ready to take his place in the group once more. Fielder was immediately fired, much to Stills' relief, and for a time it seemed that the Springfield might rediscover its former stability. Young, however, was becoming increasingly disillusioned with the group and even the return of Palmer was not adequate to keep him in line:

> It seemed like every two months he'd be gone. I mean we'd go off to gigs and he wouldn't show up. In Boston, in some club there, we played a gig one night and the guy said, "Don't come back" because we weren't a whole band without Neil.[4]

It was not long before Young himself realized that his attitude was helping to destroy the group. After discussions with Nitzsche he called an extraordinary general meeting inviting his managers, producers and the other members of the group. There he officially announced that he was leaving the Buffalo Springfield:

> Well I sort of dropped out of the group. I couldn't handle it. I don't know why but something inside of me felt like I wasn't quite on track. I think it was when we booked the Johnny Carson Show. Right around the time of the Monterey Pop Festival.[9]

As Stills recalls, Young's decision came at a time when everyone was confused about the ultimate direction of the group:

> I was beginning to wake up a little and realize that the pressures of really getting big and making a lotta money which it looked like was gonna happen, would destroy the band. Which was eventually what happened. We were supposed to go back to New York to do the Johnny Carson Show for a whole bunch of money and that would have probably led to a spot on Sullivan's show, which was at the time the big thing to do ... Neil flipped out and quit and wouldn't come, and went off and hid in the San Fernando Valley at some chick's house, so we couldn't do the Johnny Carson Show.
>
> But by that time everybody was too crazy, just too crazy, and that's when Neil had to quit, exactly at the time when it meant the most. He decided that it wasn't worth it, probably he knew the same thing, that Bruce wasn't gonna be able to handle it, and he probably thought that I was just as crazy as he was.[2]

The group continued to tour without him but it was soon very obvious that the performances lacked punch, so the inevitable decision was made to find a replacement. Doug Hastings, lead guitarist of the San Franciscan group, The Daily Flash, was accepted as Young's replacement and accompanied the group on their next series of gigs. The Springfield's luck changed after Young's departure and they managed to secure themselves a couple of prestigious bookings during the summer. The most important date was the historic Monterey Pop Festival on 16 June. In order to prepare for that day they rehearsed their set by playing three nights at the San Francisco Fillmore some weeks before. The extra effort paid off, and even though several members of the group were stricken with illness they managed to put in a fine set. The favorable reaction at Monterey was due partly to the fact that David Crosby of The Byrds sang with them. After that performance rumors circulated that Crosby might be joining the Springfield as a permanent member, but nothing came of it. Crosby denies that he ever considered joining the Buffalo Springfield:

> Neil left about a week before Monterey, so I rehearsed with them for a few days and I said that I'd sit in with them to cover. I was just trying to help. I wasn't in the Springfield and I had no intention of being in the Springfield.

Following Monterey, the group received a lot of good publicity and found themselves back in demand. A lucrative supporting tour with the Monkees in Chicago ended a most successful summer. The Springfield had not only survived without Young, but seemed to be at the peak of their popularity.

When Young became aware of the publicity that his old group were receiving he began to feel that his decision to quit might have been a little hasty. In retrospect, Young maintains that his attitude throughout this period was caused by a combination of nerves and immaturity:

> I just couldn't handle it toward the end. My nerves couldn't handle the trip. It wasn't me scheming for a solo career, it wasn't anything but my nerves ... I was going crazy, you know, joining and quitting and joining again. I began to feel that I didn't have to answer or obey anyone. I just wasn't mature enough to deal with it. I was very young. We were getting the shaft from every angle and it seemed like we were trying to make it so bad and were getting nowhere.[10]

What Young fails to mention is the lengths to which he went to ensure that he would regain his place in the Springfield. He began to turn up at Dick Davis' office gradually winning his sympathy and persuading him to encourage the group to re-enlist their former lead-guitarist. Sessions had already begun for a projected future album and Young was allowed to submit a couple of songs.

Re-establishing his role in the Springfield, Young was finally re-enlisted when the group fired Doug Hastings in September 1967. After a stormy period it seemed as though the Springfield might have reconciled their differences sufficiently to continue.

FOUR

The End Of The Line

With Young back in the Buffalo Springfield, the final months of 1967 went relatively smoothly. Their second album, *Buffalo Springfield Again* was finally released and immediately sold in excess of 250,000 copies. Babitz' art-work on the sleeve was excellent, making the album one of the best designed covers of 1967.

If the sleeve was stunning the music contained within the covers was nothing less than incredible. Young had developed even further as an artiste, but probably the biggest surprise was the dramatic emergence of Stills with some of the finest songs of his career. If the Stills/Young duo had been rivals on stage, it was nothing compared to the competition that must have inspired these songs in the studio. Perhaps the most remarkable aspect of the album was its musical variety and experimentation. It showed two artistes working at white heat in an attempt to establish creative control. David Crosby maintains that neither artiste suppressed the other:

> I felt Young and Stills were about equal. It worked differently to me and McGuinn in The Byrds. Neil liked Stills' work; McGuinn resented mine. Neil did not resent Stephen, he encouraged him and he recognized his work.

The traumas of 1967 appeared to have worked very much in Stills' favor. Although under heavy fire, he had managed to maintain leadership of the group and he ended the year with the release of four new songs, three of which "Everydays", "Rock 'n Roll Woman" and "Bluebird" outstripped any of his previous recordings. The guitar interplay between Stills, Young and Furay on "Bluebird" is undoubtedly one of the highlights of the album. A worthy candidate for the best ever Buffalo Springfield cut, "Bluebird" became Stills' most famous song for the next few years of his career.

In the face of such intense competition, Young's songs did not go unnoticed. An alternate take of the "Mr. Soul" single provided the opening song on the album, which Neil dedicated "to the ladies of the Whisky A Go Go and the women of Hollywood". The song served as an effective contrast to the more ambitious songs which Young contributed while under the strong influence of Jack Nitzsche.

"Expecting To Fly" showed Young's desire to experiment with new ideas. The lyrics, relating the tale of a broken relationship and its effect upon the two participants, are beautifully complemented by the elaborate but controlled orchestration and the powerful choral ending. Young's perfectly pitched vocal gives some idea of the amount of work that went into producing this cut. Young explains precisely how the song was composed and the reason it was produced with such clarity:

> "Expecting To Fly" took a long time to write. It came from two or three songs that I molded together and changed around and fitted together. We spent three weeks recording and mixing it. Some people have said that you can't hear the lyrics too well. I like to hear the words to it. They are buried in spots, but the general mood of the song is there. That's what matters in that particular song. It's not like a modern recording, it's based on an old theory. The new style is to try to hear every instrument clearly, the old one is the Phil Spector idea of blending them all so they all sound like a wall of sound."

Young's final contribution, "Broken Arrow" is probably the strangest song he ever wrote. Although Young takes the credit for the production, it is difficult to determine precisely how much he was involved in playing on this record. He receives no credit for the guitar work which was apparently done by Stills, Furay and roadie Chris Ferns. Don Randi plays piano on the track and the clarinet is uncredited. Clocking in at over six minutes, this collage of ideas is held together by Young's observations of different types of personal and political idealism. In the first verse he examines the role of the rock star, using the "Mr. Soul" motif to give us a frame of reference. On this occasion, however, the song is almost drowned by screams which, aptly enough were taped from one of the Beatles' concerts in Los Angeles. The performer is manipulated by the audience and is not allowed to express his own art. His role is simply to remain a hollow godhead. The screams reflect the absurdity of the audience's idealism in its preference for a pleasing illusion rather than the reality that the performer attempts to convey to them. That reality is expressed in the performer's own difficulty in coming to terms with his situation:

> The lights turned on and the curtain fell down
> And when it was over it felt like a dream.

When the audience finally does confront the artiste at the stage door, their roles are reversed. Young exposes the fan's idealism as merely a repressed form of narcissism: "They stood at the stage door and begged for a scream". Rather than worshipping their hero, the fans actually beg him to worship them.

In the next section Young moves from an observation of the myth surrounding a rock star to an examination of another illusion, the American Dream. Here he portrays the breakdown of an adolescent through his realization that the norms and values he has inherited from his parents are being challenged and superseded by a new order:

> He saw that his brother had sworn on the wall
> He hung up his eye lids and ran down the hall

His mother had told him a trip was a fall
And don't mention babies at all.

Like the rock star, the adolescent comes to realize the inadequacy of myth, and the result of this awareness is emotional disorder.

In the final section, Young fuses the American Dream concept and the myth of the superhuman rock star into an allegory. The King and the Queen are representative of the archetypal fairy tale – the belief that it is possible to achieve everlasting happiness: "The streets were lined for the wedding parade/... They married for peace and were gone". In every idealistic tale or comedy there is traditionally a dance or a wedding to conclude the festivities. From *Cinderella* and *The Sleeping Beauty* to *Twelfth Night* and *As You Like It* the message has always been "and they lived happily ever after". It is the prerogative of the King, Prince or Duke to make these things happen and it is a myth shared by the people who "lined for the wedding parade". Young applies this ideal rather obliquely to contemporary America by allegorical association with the Kennedy myth. America's perennial dream of establishing its own royal family appeared to reach fruition during the Fifties with the much publicized wedding of John Fitzgerald Kennedy and Jacqueline Bouvier. Yet that myth was itself destroyed by an assassin's bullet – "the sun rays of dawn" that shattered another aspect of the American Dream.

The chorus, as Young explains, reiterates the main theme of the emotional turmoil that follows the destruction of myth:

It's an image of being very scared and mixed up. The broken arrow is the Indian sign of peace usually after losing a war. A broken arrow usually means that somebody has lost a lot."

"Broken Arrow" was Young's own observation of his time, an era in which presidents and rock stars would die and later be apotheosized not because of what they were, but rather for the myths that their deaths created. The impact of "Broken Arrow" may have substantially waned since it was originally released, but it remains a fascinating example of Young's desire to experiment with new ideas. Both "Expecting To Fly" and "Broken Arrow" showed Young's determination to move beyond standard rock songs in order to incorporate different musical elements from jazz to orchestration.

While Stills and Young dominated *Buffalo Springfield Again*, Furay's voice did not remain unheard, and he managed to get three of his compositions included on the album. "A Child's Claim To Fame" was by far the finest and remains one of Furay's most famous tracks. The ballad "Sad Memory" was an average cut made good by Young's tasteful background guitar-work. In fact, the only unquestionable dud on the album was Furay's "Good Time Boy", an inconsequential composition, made worse by allowing Dewey Martin to sing lead vocal. In spite of its minor flaws, however, *Buffalo Springfield Again* remains a classic of its period and it deserved far more attention than it received in 1967.

Young's thirst for fame remained unquenchable during this period and he continued to pin his hopes on a massive selling single. In view of his later apparent aversion to superstardom, it comes as a surprise to see how obsessed he was with achieving international fame. In one interview of the period, his thwarted ambition made him sound like a desperate man:

So whatever is right will happen ...
We know it's gonna definitely happen.
It's gotta happen. When it does happen
it's gonna be a real big one. We've got
an underground following now and we've
got a lot of people who dig us. We've
only had one big record and I didn't think
it would be a number one record. Everybody
heard it and it was a hit.[11]

In spite of their recent success, Young and the group were still suffering from uncertainty. This was not helped by the growing tensions within the group. It seemed that no sooner had one feud ended between Stills and Young, then another would brew among the other members of the group. Looking back, Stills is self-critical:

I was trying to be Boss cat and trying to keep the thing in order. You gotta dig that part of my upbringing in the South was very militaristic. I was in this military school and being taught how to be an *officer*. Wow, I was like 11, and that stuff can't help but stick way down. Anyway, a lot of the ways I relate to situations like that is to simply take command. Because someone has to, because that is the only thing that will work and of course somebody like Neil or Bruce is instantly going to rebel. So there was chaos.[2]

Having received his moment of glory on *Again*, Dewey Martin became more assertive and followed Furay's lead by demanding more time. Martin had begun songwriting himself and he felt that he had as much right as the other three to have his material included on the third album. Following Martin's outburst there were further problems with Palmer. Bruce had always been the great stabilizing force in the group and he had frequency acted as an arbitrator between Stills and Young. During his exile in Canada, the clashes between Stills and Young had reached boiling point, but his return had helped them both to settle their differences, at least temporarily. By the end of 1967, however, Palmer seemed to be tiring of his role as peacemaker and, even more alarmingly, he seemed rapidly to be losing interest in the group. Palmer had always been a little eccentric, living in a tree house and acting the role of the loner, but his musicianship was regarded as exceptional. By this time, however, he seemed to have turned away from rock music and was arguing the case for Indian ragas, much to the perplexity of the rest of the group. Stills remembers Palmer's growing disenchantment with the Buffalo Springfield:

I remember particularly one time in New York, before Bruce really began to withdraw. He just looked at me and said: "This band is jive, this band is getting jive, man!" He very seldom talked, when he did it was philosophy and stuff like that. An extremely intellectual man, really self-contained.[6]

It was at that same New York gig that Palmer and Stills had a major confrontation:

We went to New York as a band with a reputation, and we end up in this pretty small club for a rock 'n roll band to play in. We were all playing little bitty amplifiers to try to make it tolerable. Bruce was playing so loud that nobody could hear themselves and like my hearing is bad anyway and there's a certain wave-length where everything cancels out. Bruce struck it with his bass that night. I said, "Bruce, turn down, I can't hear myself, nobody can hear themselves, you're playing too loud", and he slapped me across the face. So I went completely purple with rage and put him through the drums, right in the middle of a club in New York and everyone was very shocked, but like I said this was in the middle of when we were all really, really flipped out. Neil, Bruce, me, the lot of us.[2]

It was evident that in order to ensure their continuance, the Springfield required commitment, hope and stability. All three of these were irrevocably lost in January 1968 when disaster struck once more.

Bruce Palmer's luck once again ran out when he was arrested on a drugs charge. He was taken to a detention camp near San Diego and deported to Canada once more. His second departure proved almost too much for the group who were ready to split at any moment. Almost perversely, however, they decided to carry on without him. Jim Messina, who had worked as an engineer on the second album was enlisted as a replacement, but the changes did not stop there. Dick Davis became involved in a dispute with the group and amid bitter reprisals he was fired. Joni Mitchell's manager, Elliot Roberts, replaced Davis but lasted only two weeks. Finally, the group persuaded Beach Boys' manager Nick Grillo to take them under his wing. For most observers outside the group it seemed that the end was in sight. Young, however, was still hoping against hope that somehow the group might get that Number One single that he had always longed for:

All we need is what we always tried to get ... a smash hit record. If we have just one that we think is a success then we'll know that we have actually communicated. If we can survive that without going through changes, then there's no telling what will occur.

Whatever might have occurred ended dramatically in true Bruce Palmer fashion when the entire group were arrested in Topanga Canyon on a drugs charge on March 20. The arrest took place one evening during a jamming session between members of the Springfield and Eric Clapton, then of Cream. The police were well aware of the Springfield's notorious reputation following the Palmer trials so, in many respects, another bust was inevitable. This time, however, it signalled the end of the group. After many weeks in prison, the group were freed and at that point they more or less went their separate ways. They occasionally regrouped to fulfil their few remaining commitments and played their final gig in Long Beach soon after. On May 5, the Buffalo Springfield were no more.

In retrospect Young feels that the Springfield never really had a chance to appreciate what they were dong:

It was good, but we didn't know what we were doing so we didn't know how much fun we were having until it was over. Everybody thought, "Wow, that must have been a lot of fun". We were just there.[9]

Although many have lamented the break-up of the Springfield, Young is not one of them:

> Well, it's like this guy just before was saying how he thought the break-up of the Springfield represented the end of an era or something. It was just the end of the Springfield, that's all. Yeah, I think the Springfield broke up at the right time. I don't think they were improving when they broke-up.[5]

The recording sessions for the third album that had been half-completed towards the end of the previous year were salvaged by Furay and Messina and made into an album, *Last Time Round*, that was released posthumously in August 1968. Neither Stills nor Young were actively involved in compiling the album, as Neil reveals:

> The last real album that group made was *Buffalo Springfield Again*. *Last Time Round* was pieced together by Jim Messina because neither Steve nor I gave a shit ... we just didn't want to do it, y'know. It's weird.

Although *Last Time Round* is a very patchy album and far below the quality of *Buffalo Springfield Again*, it was welcomed as a posthumous release containing a high proportion of good quality music. Indeed the worst one could say of it is that in a couple of cases more suitable tracks might have been used. The gatefold cover reveals a shattered mirror image of the group with Young looking in the opposite direction to everyone else. In many ways that summed up his attitude to the group during the previous year.

Although Furay had almost total control in selecting the material he is to be commended for not misusing his power and releasing a solo album under the banner of the Buffalo Springfield. Again, there is one stand-out track, the haunting "In The Hour Of Not Quite Rain", written by Furay and Mickeala Gallen. The lyrics, with their poetic descriptions of nature, are extremely romanticized. The description of the moon, which takes up nearly half the song, is impressive in its imagery and one suspects that Furay had little or no involvement in these lyrics. Musically, it stands up well too, however, and Furay's singing has never been better. Unfortunately, Richie's remaining contributions were fairly unimpressive.

Strangely enough, Young is allowed only two songs on this album which demonstrates his lack of involvement during the final days of the group. Young was already beginning to retain his best material for future projects so what we have here appear to be songs written earlier in his career. Although neither "On The Way Home" nor "I Am A Child" were anywhere near his best recordings they were destined to become two of his most famous songs during the early Seventies. "On The Way Home" is best remembered as being the opening number to Young's acoustic sets, but here it is a pure pop version complete with clichéd and inappropriate backing vocals by Stills and Furay. It is a pity that this saccharine version succeeds so well in distracting the listener from Young's lyrics, which are quite intriguing. In "Mr. Soul", Young told us that after the lights had gone up and the curtain fell down, the whole experience of being a rock star felt "like a dream". In this song, he goes one step further and tells us "When the dream came ... I went insane". The confusion that Young felt in his role as a would be rock 'n roll star caused him much insecurity, which perhaps more than any other factor accounts for his persistent absence from the Buffalo Springfield during 1967. In "On The Way Home" he reveals his indecision about returning to the group:

> Now I won't be back till later on
> If I do come back at all
> But you know me, and I miss you now.

The final verse appears to be a flag of truce:

> Though we rush ahead to save our time
> We are only what we feel,
> And I love you,
> Can you feel it now?

In the wake of the Springfield, Stills shared Young's positive feelings about their working relationship:

> Neil is just about my best friend in the world. If you really want to
> know what I think about Neil there is a song he wrote about me
> called "On The Way Home" on the last Springfield album. That's
> pretty much where it is.

Young's final contribution to the Springfield, "I Am A Child" was completed as the group was on its last legs:

> The group was falling apart by this time. We all cooked separately in
> the studios. The Sunset Sound receptionist's boyfriend on bass. The
> rest is me.[8]

Although the performance is slightly cloying, it is easy to underestimate what is a very clever composition. Most of the contemporaneous rock songs written about the wonders of childhood, such as Goffin and King's "Goin' Back", were a nostalgic and pathetic realization of lost innocence. Young goes one step further, however, by attempting to take the child's perspective and see the world through his eyes. Essentially, it is the "Goin'Back" theme in reverse:

> I am a child, I last awhile
> You can't conceive of the pleasure in my smile.

Instead of looking back at lost innocence, the child looks forward, realizing that his childhood will be short. In some respects, this is the one fault in the composition. Young cannot resist giving the child a double perspective – as both child and man. In attempting to create a child persona Young can do no more but put an adult's mind into a child's body. His attempted embodiment of innocence in the form of the child is ultimately permeated by experience, and the two perspectives are irreconcilable.

The scarcity of Young contributions on *Last Time Round* leaves Stills in the relatively unassailable position as the dominant force on this work. Of Stills' five contributions at least one stands out as worthy of appearing on the final Springfield album. "Four Days Gone", the story of an escaped convict or perhaps a deserter from the forces, is one of Stills' best narrative songs. With the perfectly complementary piano work, it would have easily fitted onto a Stills solo album. Stephen's other material ranging from acoustic to Cuban-style rock showed his musical versatility to the full.

Following the release of *Last Time Round*, the Springfield gradually became recognized as one of the most important rock groups of the late Sixties. The success of their post-Buffalo Springfield work resulted in several compilations, but of these only one contained any previously unreleased material, and even then it was simply the elongated version of "Bluebird". Since then there has been much talk about the hours of unreleased Springfield material locked away in the vaults of Atlantic Records, but like the group, it all seems to be history now.

FIVE

Carefree Country Days In Topanga

The dissolution of the Buffalo Springfield in May 1968 left many people wondering whether the individual members might not go on to even greater fame in their subsequent ventures. For the less talented members of the group, this would not be the case. Bruce Palmer spent most of 1968 getting himself back together following the traumatic arrests and courtroom sessions that had so seriously affected the development of his career in rock music. Dewey Martin, on the other hand, was far more active and decided that his best chance of fame would be to form a new group, using the Buffalo Springfield name, and take it in the road. This he attempted in September 1968, but he was prevented by the other members who wisely took legal action. Martin later went on to form Dewey Martin's Medicine Ball, but he ultimately failed to rediscover the fame that he had enjoyed in the Springfield. Richie Furay was, not surprisingly, a little more successful than his cohorts. Influenced by Jim Messina, he had moved closer to his country roots, so it seemed logical that they should both form a new group. With three excellent musicians, Rusty Young, George Grantham, and Tim Schmit, the duo formed Pogo, which quickly became Poco, one of America's most respected country-rock groups.

It was the other two members of the Buffalo Springfield, however, whom the critics were most anxious to observe. Neil Young was the first to take steps towards recording a solo album:

> Started working on my own album, right away. Couldn't get off Atlantic fast enough. I mean only because I wanted to be separated from the Springfield. I didn't want to be a member of the Springfield, competing with other members of the Springfield on the same label.[9]

Although Young explains that he began work on his album immediately, this is somewhat of an exaggeration. For at least part of 1968 he began playing various folk venues with only an acoustic guitar backing. It was not a particularly rewarding experience, however, since at most of the gigs he was largely ignored. He secured a brief two-week residency at The Bitter End, New York but the punters stayed away in droves, leaving Young feeling even more insecure than in his Springfield days. Disillusioned, he moved West to Hollywood, settling in the mountainous region of Topanga. There, he spent his days gradually composing the songs that would subsequently be recorded for his debut album. While frequenting Topanga's "Canyon Kitchen", Neil struck up a friendship with the proprietor, Susan Acevado. Their relationship deepened, and within a surprisingly short space of time they were married. Forgetting his recent series of unimpressive club dates, Neil decided to settle in Topagana with Susan and her 7-year old daughter, Tia. For the next few months Young put all his efforts into working on their four-storey redwood house, perched magnificently atop one of Topanga's hills in total isolation. Young explained the way in which this idyllic lifestyle gradually altered his perspective of the importance of rock 'n roll:

> I moved out there and got married and settled down and everything and I just started really digging on being home. I have another life that doesn't have anything to do with rock 'n roll, you know ... that, I think is a reason why I think I might be a little different from most of the people who live rock 'n' roll twenty four hours a day. I think I have something else outside of it. I really feel that I like to go home ... and when I sing about that you know, I really mean it. That's probably why it comes across. I just can't keep away, you know.[5]

Young employed two separate producers for the album, first his old friend Jack Nitzsche, assisted by Neil and guitarist Ry Cooder. The remainder of the album, however, was produced by David Briggs, at whose house Young lived for a while until he himself bought a splendid home in the Canyon. After a series of sessions, *Neil Young* was completed in the late autumn and released in January 1969. The critical response was fair, but relatively lukewarm. That the album was unheralded was a great injustice, however, because it remains one of Young's most interesting and consistent efforts.

In retrospect, one can see why the album did not immediately arrest the public's attention. It was generally a low-key affair and even the strings employed by Nitzsche were not used to dramatic effect, but rather to complement the mood of the piece. The opening track, "The Emperor Of Wyoming" was very much a statement of intent, an indication that it was the mood rather than the vocals or instrumentation that should interest the listener. Young's work in the Springfield had been best remembered for its lyrical and emotive quality and a boldness in experimenting with different ideas in order to produce songs such as "Expecting To Fly" or "Broken Arrow". "The Emperor Of Wyoming", however, held no great mysteries, with its pleasant country-style guitar and jaunty air. Young had opened his solo album with, of all things, an instrumental, immediately challenging the established notion that an album must open with its strongest or most accessible number. To those listeners who came to this album expecting a series of epics in the "Broken Arrow" vein, or a work filled with surrealistic lyrics, the opening track must have seemed a complete mystery. What it did demonstrate, however, was that Young was very much his own man, and the country influence revealed another example of his growing assimilation of different styles of music.

"The Loner" was probably what was more expected of Young, though it had a musical aggression not too often heard in his Springfield work. According to Neil it was the first recording made for the album, and included some fine playing by Jim

Messina on bass and George Grantham on drums. The organ and the fuzz-guitar also worked most effectively, while the vocal was mixed into the background. This mixing down of the vocal was unusual, and would later become one of the controversial features of the album. Apparently Young, in a fit of modesty and insecurity, had begun to feel uneasy about his vocal abilities, something which had troubled him since the early days of the Buffalo Springfield. As a result, he had allowed the vocal parts to be buried low in the mix so that occasionally their audibility was impaired. Young would later sorely regret this, but to what extent it was an artistic error is very contentious as, on the whole, the low-mixed vocals tend to enhance and even help to create, the low-key mood of the album. The voice often becomes almost another musical instrument, embedded between the guitar and organ, but never overwhelmed by them. Much the same must be said of Nitzsche's use of strings which are delicately introduced only at specific moments in certain songs. Even though Young's vocals are sometimes not sharp enough, this could never be blamed on the orchestration, which is generally discernible at an even lower level in the mix. How successful a fusion of voice, instruments and orchestration is achieved on "The Loner" remains debatable. It is probably the hardest, most aggressive song on the album and therefore might have benefitted from a more abrasive vocal but on the other hand one might argue that the vocal effect is all the more powerful for holding the emotions in check.

The emotional conflict evident in "The Loner" can be gleaned from a reading of the lyrics. In the first line the loner is compared to a fox, a predator, whose cunning is emphasized in the description of him as a manipulator of other people's feelings "a feeling arranger". Young presents the Loner as a potentially powerful figure and yet in the explanation of his paranoid actions on the subway, he emerges as isolated and insecure. It is only in the final verse that the mood shifts from derision to a hint of sympathy when we learn that the isolation of the loner is the result of a broken relationship:

> There was a woman he knew about a year or so ago
> She had something that he needed and he pleaded with her not to go.
> On the day that she left, he died – but it did not show.

Over the years, it has generally been assumed that the subject of this song is Stephen Stills, "the keeper of the key" to the Buffalo Springfield. When asked if he was the loner of the song, Stills replied with some sarcasm that the sentiments of the composition were more applicable to Young's situation than his own.

The next track, "If I Could Have Her Tonight", seems similar in theme to songs such as "Do I Have To Come Right Out And Say It" and "One More Sign", but a close analysis reveals that Young is dealing with a different aspect of the unrequited love theme. Here the situation is imaginary, and "If I Could Have Her Tonight" attempts to unravel the complexities of a relationship that has not yet even begun. Essentially, it is a song of wish-fulfilment in the same way as say the Beach Boys' "Wouldn't It Be Nice". Here, however, the song ends in disillusionment and despair as the narrator begins to realize that his wishes may be an impossible dream:

> Lately I've found myself losing my mind
> Knowing how badly I need her

It's something hard to find.

"I've Been Waiting For You" is virtually a thematic extension of "If I Could Have Her Tonight" with its search for the imaginary perfect woman. Musically, however, this song is much more adventurous with the drums and organ providing a solid backing followed by a very impressive lead break by Young, during which the stereo effects are used to the full. According to Young, "I've Been Waiting For You" was recorded in segments with a different instrument being added every day:

> ... when I put on the lead-guitar I was really into it that day, you know, and all the moods I was in at all the times that I put those things on ... in the beginning we put down acoustic guitar and bass and drums, that's the smallest track that I ever did, one guitar, bass and drums ... Jimmy Messina, who plays the bass on it, played the bass part over and then he made up a different bass part so we took off the first one completely and played a whole new one ... and then we dropped the acoustic guitar 'cause it didn't fit with the other things that I put on ... so then there was nothing left except for the drums. The pipe organ was put on ... part of these things were done in different cities. The vocal was done at a different studio ... it does stick together though. It's very rare.[12]

In the closing cut on side one Young personifies death as the Old Laughing Lady. Again we see a shift in perspective, this time from the notion of death as a destructive force, "When she leaves, she leaves nothing at all", to the realization that death must be accepted: "There's the Old Laughing Lady, ev'rything is all right". The sombre mood of this song more or less sums up most of the first side. It is a song that gradually builds up from a barely audible acoustic opening to a chorus of girl singers, and then down again to an acoustic fade-out. Young's vocal is mixed very low on this track, and one feels that this was probably a mistake. In concerts of the period, Young provided a fine acoustic rendition of the song which seemed a far more direct and arresting statement of the central theme. However, the positive feature of the album cut is that it does include the girl chorus, once compared by Greil Marcus to the Brides Of Dracula. There is no doubt that the wailing effects enhance the eerie mood of the piece providing a chilling reminder that this is a song about death.

The second side of the album, like the first, opens with an instrumental, "String Quartet From Whisky Boot Hill". This brief but effective use of strings by Nitzsche would appear to be from some uncompleted project that Young was working on during this period. "Whisky Boot Hill" would appear again in Young's "Country Girl", the following year, but no explanation has ever been forthcoming as to whether this was an uncompleted song, an abandoned concept album, or a projected movie score.

"Here We Are In The Years" remains one of the standout cuts on this album. Once more, Young's voice is mixed down to a whisper at times, but the song's strong composition with Nitzsche's strings coming in at just the right moment, is very impressive. Lyrically, the song is more or less self-explanatory, exposing the insensitivity of city dwellers to the countryside.

There is a certain charming naivety about Young's lyrics on this album, and this is particularly true of "What Did You Do To My Life?". In the first line, "when we were living together, I thought that I knew you would stay" Young sums up his disillusionment in realizing that even his certainties were merely suppositions. The remainder of the song, however, views the relationship with the selfishness of a child:

> I don't care if all of the mountains turn to dust in the air ... It isn't fair
> that I should wake up at dawn and not find you there.

The sentiments summed up by the phrase, "It isn't fair", show all the immaturity of a child who has just had his teddy-bear confiscated for the night.

"I've Loved Her So Long", the penultimate track on the album reintroduces the old age motif. In "The Old Laughing Lady" we can see that Young personifies death in part of the song but he also introduces a non-symbolic old laughing lady who, as we remember, is loved by the drunkard of the village. In "I've Loved Her So Long" the symbolic lady is again replaced by a flesh and blood figure whom Young presents as the last of her kind:

> She's a victim of her senses, do you know her?
> Can you see her in the distance as she stumbles by?
> Veteran of a race that should be over.

Like the other characters that appear on this album, she is at once a sympathetic and pathetic figure. Added force is given to this track through the combined voices of Merry Clayton, Brenda Holloway, Patricia Holloway, Gloria Richetta Jones, Sherlie Matthews and Gracie Nitzsche.

"The Last Trip To Tulsa" is probably the closest that Young has got to imitating the surreal lyrics of mid-period Bob Dylan. With its fast strumming acoustic guitar and seemingly unrelated verses it seems totally out of place with the other songs on the album. It is almost as if Young were attempting to recreate the old folky days with one long rambling song. But this is not the entire truth. Parts of "The Last Trip To Tulsa" are particularly intriguing because they seem to comment upon Young's own career in rock 'n roll up until this point. One of the earliest images in the song is an apocalyptic vision of a California earthquake: "The West Coast is falling I see rocks in the sky". This gives Young leave to think about salvation, and, in turn, comment upon the decline of organized religion in Western Society:

> The preacher took his Bible and laid in on the stool
> He said, "With the congregation running, why should I play the fool?"

From religion, Young turns to that other favorite pastime, sex. In an amusing verse deliberately riddled with sexual innuendoes, Young makes some vague comments about the absurdity of male and female role-playing:

> Well I used to be a woman you know, I took you for a ride
> I let you fly my airplane, it looked good for your pride ...
> She got down on her knees, and said, "Let's get on with this thing?"

In that last line what is supposed to be a reference to the wedding service is deliberately loaded with sexual connotation.

In the third verse, Young concerns himself with the plight of the unknown folksinger who becomes either the bait of unscrupulous management or is forced to play on the street "for free" to unappreciative audiences:

> Well, I used to be a folk singer, keeping managers alive,
> When you saw me on a corner and told me I was jive.

Young's reflections on the ill-fated folksinger take on an autobiographical slant by the end of the stanza when he alludes to his own identity crisis:

> Well, I woke up this morning with an arrow through my nose
> There was an Indian in the corner tryin' on my clothes.

This is an obvious allusion to the way Young himself adopted the role of the Hollywood Indian while he was with the Springfield:

> Yeah, well when I was in the Springfield for the most part I was really
> on a whole Hollywood trip and I was living in Hollywood and I was a
> Hollywood Indian, you know … I was on a trip.

Re-introducing the death-motif via the "friendly coroner", Young goes on to produce a memorable description of paranoia:

> I was driving down the freeway when my car ran out of gas
> Pulled over to the station but I was afraid to ask.

Young loves to express his insecurity by playing on a seemingly normal and everyday activity such as buying some gas, and loading it with inexplicably menacing connotations. This would later become a very distinctive feature of his work.

The image of the palm tree, that ends the song, might well be an oblique allusion to the dissolution of the Springfield:

> I was chopping down a palm tree when a friend dropped by to ask
> If I would feel less lonely if he helped me swing the axe.

However, in Young's desolate world it seems that even "friends" cannot be allowed to swing their axes together, and the final image is one of irrational destruction: "I chopped down the palm tree and it landed on his back". "The Last Trip To Tulsa" is a very unusual song, and many would agree that it does sound very dated today and has lost most of the impact that it had at the time of the album's release. Although Young originally liked the song, he too quickly became disappointed with it:

> After the album came out that's the one I really didn't like, and I still
> don't. It sounds overdone. It just sounds like it's a mistake to me, and
> luckily it's cool.

In spite of Young's words, "The Last Trip To Tulsa" remains weird enough to be interesting. Perhaps Young himself came to this conclusion when, several years later, he began to include an electric version of the song in his live performances.

Neil Young is still one of the most underrated of his albums, even by the artist himself. For years after its release Young maintained that the bad mixing had ruined the album. Eventually, he attempted to persuade his record company to allow purchasers of the original album to exchange their old copy for a brand new remixed version. This idea was, of course, totally impractical and would have involved such a loss for the record company that it was never seriously considered. Finally, Young did manage to get the remixed copy issued in the States, although for some inexplicable reason all the copies issued in the U.K. even up until today, have the original mix. Pleased with the results, Young has continually voiced the merits of the remixed copy whenever the subject of his first album has been raised. According to Young, the differences on the remixed version are so substantial that it virtually warrants consideration as a separate album. However a critical listening of the remixed album actually inclines one to say that this is little more than an unwarranted exaggeration. It is possible to detect a greater clarity on certain tracks but overall most of the songs sound relatively unchanged except for some additional guitar on "Here We Are In The Years" and "What Did You Do To My Life". Apart from those two changes, however, there is very little to add. Young's voice is not noticeably clearer or more pronounced than on the original mix, which makes the entire remixing exercise something of a disappointment.

In spite of all this, the original seems adequate enough to stand on its own as a great record and it remains without doubt a startling debut album. What it revealed was Young the lyricist gradually moving from songs of broken relationships to concerns such as death, old age, ecology and religion. Young remains very modest in summing up the album's lyrical quality:

> ... a lot of the songs weren't really very good, but they all said a thing like here they are ... in the years they get a little hung up, a little overdone, you know – but I was trying to say something without going on a pollution and conservation kick, because I really don't want to dedicate myself to any cause, because it's limiting. But I do believe in that, and I've written a few things about that which is about the only thing, specifically, that I've written about – the other things are sort of fantasies.[5]

That final comment is particularly interesting for it indicates the danger in assuming that all Young's lyrics are autobiographical. It also demonstrates that we should be wary of accepting Young's own interpretation of his lyrics in case we fall victim to the "intentional fallacy". Once a work of art has been written it no longer is the private property of the artist, but has escaped into the public domain. In creating the work, the artist necessarily divorces himself from it. He may attempt to explain his intention in writing the piece, but this tells us only the original idea behind the work of art. The conscious and unconscious processes of creation often alter the original intention beyond recognition. What we are ultimately left with is the final product, the composition, and its meaning is composed of a complex variety of linguistic correspondances that we must fit together in an attempt to make a perfect whole. In this respect, Young's interpretation of his own songs may be less valid than the schooled critic since he depends entirely upon his ability to piece together the linguistic materials in the song in a way that is logically consistent. This is not to say that Young's own comments on his compositions are not intriguing and revelatory, but they usually tell us only what he hoped to put into the work and not what is actually there. This explains why Young seldom discusses his work in any detail, for he realizes that his own interpretation of his compositions may produce more questions than answers. In fact, Young admits that most of his songs are the product of his unconscious mind at work:

> When I write the songs ... I guess I'm writing about a part of me that I don't know if I'll ever share ... I'm writing about the way I feel inside, and no matter how many people are around me, I keep talking about all the things that are going on inside me. I guess that by talking about it, it helps. But, in my case, I talk about it more than anybody else that I know, and it still keeps on coming out. I don't know where it comes from it just comes out. Everything I write ... even when I'm happy I write about being lonesome. I don't know why. The images that I write ... I really don't know where they come from. I just see the pictures in my eyes. Sometimes I can't get them to come but then if I get high or just sit there and wait, all of a sudden it comes – it just comes gushing out. I've just got to get to the right level. It's like having a mental orgasm.[13]

SIX

Three Careers Are Better Than One

1969 was to become one of the most musically eventful years of Neil Young's life. His first album had just been issued and he hoped that he was on the way to establishing a new identity as a solo artist. According to Young, the one thing that he never again wanted was to play in a group. During two years in the Buffalo Springfield, he had experienced so many problems that he had become totally disillusioned with group formats. Now, guided by an aggressive manager, Elliot Roberts, Young was determined to succeed on his own. What literally changed his mind overnight, however, was a chance meeting with a group he had once known, but long since forgotten – the Rockets.

The nucleus of the Rockets consisted of three musicians: Ralph Molina, Billy Talbot and Danny Whitten. They were not a new group, but had been involved in the music business since the early sixties. Originally as a vocal group, Danny and the Memories, they had made a couple of unsuccessful singles for the Valiant label, following which they retired to California and took up day jobs. Their musical instinct was too strong to be suppressed, however, so they reformed at the end of 1965 and began to think seriously about becoming an acoustic folk group. In true Pete Townshend fashion, Danny Whitten locked himself in a room and practiced for months until his guitar-playing was proficient. The other members of the group borrowed and bought what equipment they could, and soon they felt that they were ready. Christening themselves the Circle, they recorded some material under the auspices of Sly Stone, who was then a San Francisco disc-jockey and part-time producer. The recordings were again unsuccessful, however, but shortly after this they found new inspiration. During a visit to a San Francisco club, they saw an early performance by The Byrds which absolutely astonished them. After the gig, they all agreed that what they most needed were electric instruments. The line-up of the group at this time was Talbot (bass), Molina (drums), Whitten (guitar) and a guy called Dino on lead-guitar. When Dino left the group to get married, the trio recruited Leon and George Whitsell, and violinist Bobby Notkoff and moved to Laurel Canyon where they formed the Rockets.

Neil Young, meanwhile, was in the middle of recording the first Springfield album. At the time he had a girl-friend named Robin Lane, a show-biz kid who, like Young, was perfecting her varied musical skills singing, playing guitar and writing songs. Lane was already well-known in folk-rock circles for her songwriting and had established a close friendship with fellow musician Danny Whitten. Lane invited Young over to the Laurel Canyon house to watch the group rehearse, and Neil soon began to join in. Although Young was very unsure about his singing at the time, Whitten strongly encouraged him, feeling that Neil's voice was extremely effective. After a while, Young began to grow in confidence and he spent many nights in the Canyon singing along with Robin Lane and the Rockets in what seemed an ideal set-up. Eventually, however, his commitments with the Springfield meant that he lost contact with the group, and shortly after this his relationship with Robin Lane ended. What Young had learned from Whitten, however, was that his voice could be used to good effect and from that point on, he began to sing lead on his own compositions.

While the Springfield achieved national stardom, however, the Rockets were content to proceed at their customary slow pace. With producer, Barry Goldberg they made some recordings for Atlantic but, ironically, that champion of the Buffalo Springfield, Ahmet Ertegun, became impatient and threw them off the label. Eventually, they recorded an album on the Turtles' label, *White Whale*, but it too flopped. It was clear that the Rockets were destined to be one of those great live groups that would never fully capture their sound in the studio. They continued to appear at gigs as often as they could and after two years they established a small but loyal following.

It was on one fateful night at the Whisky in early 1969 that Neil Young dropped by to catch their set. He was so impressed by the gig that he immediately revoked his vow to remain a solo artist and took the group under his wing. He persuaded Molina, Talbot and Whitten to join him in a group that would be called Crazy Horse. The trio agreed, but only on condition that they could also continue with the Whitsell Brothers as the Rockets. This was agreed, but soon Young had forced such an extensive touring and recording schedule upon them that it was impossible for the Rockets to remain in existence.

After only a few weeks rehearsal, Neil Young and Crazy Horse entered the studio and cut some tracks including "Cinnamon Girl", "Down By The River", and "Cowgirl In The Sand". They then went on a brief warm-up tour, and upon their return completed the album with remarkable rapidity. *Everybody Knows This Is Nowhere* was released in May 1969 and met with a mixed reception from the critics. Years after its release, however, many people still argue that it is Young's finest work, which is a tribute to its longevity.

The opening cut, "Cinnamon Girl" remains one of Young's favorite live songs, and is still frequently used as an encore number. With its strong guitar work and driving beat, this powerhouse rock number was a classic opening cut. Essentially the song seems to be about an average day in the life of a rock 'n roll group. It is difficult to say whether the "Cinnamon Girl" was a groupie or not, and Neil is cryptic enough not to provide any clues:

> Wrote this for a city girl on peeling pavement coming at me thru Phil Ochs eyes playing finger cymbals. It was hard to explain to my wife.[8]

"Everybody Knows This Is Nowhere" was one of the weaker cuts, which says much for the quality of the album. As an "electric" country-tune, it provides light relief from some of the heavier material on the album. The slightly off-key backing vocals by Crazy Horse would later be recognized as one of their most distinctive trademarks.

"Round And Round" revealed Neil duetting with his old girl-friend Robin Lane, who provided some superb backing vocals. In fact, only Young, Lane and Danny Whitten appeared on this cut. Young spoke with much enthusiasm about the recording of the song:

> "Round And Round" is one of my favorites on the second album, because some of the things ... I guess you sort of have to listen to them, 'cause I didn't bring them out very much ... but the echo from the acoustic guitar on the right echoes back on the left, and the echo from the guitar on the left comes back on the right and it makes the guitars go like this ... there's a one line start goin' like da-da-dnow ... and then you can hear like one voice comes in and out, and that's 'cause Danny was rockin' back and forth ... those things are not featured, they're just in it, you know, and that's what I'm trying to get at. I think they last longer that way. Doing it live and singing and playing all at once just makes it sound more real.[12]

The closing cut on side one is the epic "Down By The River". Young's guitar work is at its most distinctive here, building up to new levels of intensity, prior to each climactic chorus. In analyzing the lyrics, Young advises us to beware of an over-literal interpretation of the line "I shot my baby":

> Naw, there's no real murder in it. It's about blowing your thing with a chick. See, now in the beginnin' it's "I'll be on your side, you be on mine." It could be anything. Then the chick thing comes in. Then at the end it's a whole other thing. It's a plea ... a desperation cry.[5]

Young need only have added that the song ends in almost total despair: "This much madness is too much sorrow/It's impossible to make it today."

"(When You're On) The Losing End" which opens side two is another electric country tune containing some of Young's most depressing lines: "Things are different round here ev'ry night my tears fall down like rain." Sung as a slow acoustic number this might have been extremely moving, though with lines as clichéd as "my tears fall down like rain" it is difficult to imagine that it would have sounded convincing. Young cleverly avoided the temptation of saving it as a future acoustic track and instead he buried the lyrics under a brash country 'n western backing.

In spite of the two epics that close both sides of *Everybody Knows This Is Nowhere*, it is "Running Dry (Requiem For The Rockets)" that is, in many respects, the most powerful track on the album. Young's words of despair are perfectly complemented by Bobby Notkoff's haunting violin. By the end of the song Notkoff's violin-playing reaches a level where it is almost screeching setting the scene for a requiem of intense proportions. However, Young saves the song from falling into excess and avoids the pathos that might have been produced by a self-pitying tone. At first, of course, one does detect a degree of self-indulgent whimpering:

Oh please help me, oh please help me, I'm livin' by myself
I need someone to comfort me, I need someone to tell.

By the second verse, however, the mood has shifted to one of humility. The song becomes self-confessional, in the true sense of the term, as the narrator admits a secret guilt, which becomes even greater when he realizes that his humility is only transitory:

I'm sorry for the things I've done
I've shamed myself with lies,
But soon these things are overcome and can't be recognized.

The confession is completed with the facts of his callousness and the despair that it has brought him to: "My cruelty has punctured me and now I'm running dry." "Running Dry" stands as one of the most impressive tracks that Young recorded before his rise to international fame.

The ten-minute plus "Cowgirl In The Sand" is the dramatic closing cut on the album, and it was this track that the critics unanimously acclaimed as Young's finest to date. According to Young, it was written under unusual circumstances:

... wrote this with 103° fever in bed in Topanga. Lying in bed sweating with scraps of paper covering the bed.[8]

What began in delirium ended as the album's *tour de force*. Structurally, "Cowgirl In The Sand" was similar to "Down By The River" with elongated guitar breaks gradually building to a chorus that would provide dramatic relief until the next section began. Apparently, Young overdubbed this song very carefully in order to achieve perfect synchronization between the vocals and guitar work during the chorus. What was most surprising about the song was how easily Young adapted it to an acoustic number in his later concerts. In fact, it is probably the only Young song, apart from "Hey Hey My My" which is equally famous as an acoustic and electric cut. On the acoustic version, the stunning guitar-work is abandoned and Young attempts to compensate for this by concentrating on the lyrics. He once said of "Cowgirl In The Sand":

This is a song I wrote about beaches in Spain. I've never been to beaches in Spain ... but here's an idea of what it was like over there.[14]

The song shows the typical thematic movement that we expect from Young, beginning with deceptively positive feelings:

When so many love you is it the same?
It's the woman in you that makes you want to play this game.

to a final image of vulnerability and rejection: 'To be a woman and to be turned down." The song was most notable for another line: "Has your band begun to rust", which, ten years later, would provide Young with the theme for both an album and a film. *Everybody Knows This Is Nowhere* was an album that was recorded very quickly and Young maintains that it captured the raw essence of his early work with Crazy Horse:

I just wanted to go ahead and do it, I just wanted to catch it ...

because there is something on those records that was recorded ... like it was when we were really feeling each other out, you know, and we didn't know each other, but we were turned on to what was happening. So I wanted to record that, because that never gets recorded. And that's what the album is, it's just the bare beginnings. And the change between that album and the next album is really gonna blow a lot of minds.[12]

With two albums under his belt in the space of a few months, and both of them revealing very different aspects of his talent, Young must have been hopeful of achieving commercial success. With such an impressive and prolific display, one would at least have expected him to have outflanked the other members of the Springfield. This, however, was not the case. While Young had been nurturing his solo career in Topanga, his old rival, Stephen Stills, had also been making great headway in his post-Springfield career. Within the first six months of his new found freedom, Stills found himself very much in demand. He played with Al Kooper and Mike Bloomfield and released *Supersession*, in August 1968, which eventually sold a million. During the same period he was invited by Blood, Sweat and Tears to be Al Kooper's replacement, an offer he eventually turned down. He arranged and played the guitar parts on Judy Collins' *Who Knows Where The Time Goes*, played additional guitar on Tim Leary's *You Can Be Anyone This Time Around* and even managed to find time to do some bass-work on Joni Mitchell's debut album. On top of all this, Stills continued to follow his idol, Jimi Hendrix, around the country in an attempt to learn new guitar techniques.

It was during this flurry of activity that Stills strengthened his friendship with ex-Byrd David Crosby:

At that point, I began to hang around with David quite a bit, and one day The Hollies came to town and we spent a bit of time with Willie (Graham Nash). We were all up at John Sebastian's house one day, messing around with the two songs that David and I did together, "Helplessly Hoping" and "You Won't Have To Cry", and Willie joined in on the vocals. Well, Crosby and me just looked at each other – it was one of those moments, you know?

Nash left his old group, The Hollies, shortly afterwards and following a label transfer-deal involving Poco he found himself on Ahmet Ertegun's Atlantic rostrum.

Following some rehearsals in London, the trio, plus Dallas Taylor, returned to Los Angeles and recorded their debut album, *Crosby, Stills & Nash*. Released in June 1969, the album won immediate worldwide critical acclaim, sold a million copies, and established the trio as the most important new musical partnership to emerge in recent years. Within the space of a few short months, Stills appeared to have become the most successful former member of the Buffalo Springfield. After two albums, Young's career was progressing steadily but slowly while Stills looked well on his way to becoming a millionaire as well as receiving the full critical acclaim that had been denied him during the days of the Buffalo Springfield.

In the wake of the success of *Crosby, Stills & Nash,* promoters were falling over themselves to encourage the trio to embark on a nationwide tour. After considering various proposals, Crosby and company began to discuss the problem of capturing their studio sound live:

> That album was fun and it was easy and we just did it ... but we had to go out on the road. David and Graham were in favor of us going out as a sort of augmented Simon & Garfunkel, but I didn't want that – I wanted a band, and so we worked it out that the first half should be acoustic and then we'd bring out the electric stuff in the second half.[3]

It was this need for additional instrumentation that would eventually lead Stills back to his old rival, Neil Young:

> Well I went over to New York looking for an organ player, but I just couldn't find anybody, so I went to see Ahmet who suggested Neil Young being brought in on guitar which would allow me to play keyboards. So I flew back to California, went over to Neil's house and asked him what he thought. He'd been to one of our rehearsals and really dug the vocal sound ... so he came along with us, and we became Crosby, Stills, Nash & Young, which I thought contained just enough of the family element but still retained the individual names so we could all go off in our own directions if and when it folded.[3]

While Stills implies that that C.S.N.&Y. partnership was formed almost immediately, this was not the case. Young reveals that his decision to join the trio was far from sudden:

> Well, I'd heard their music and it was just wonderful. But the story of how I joined might make you laugh. They needed people to go on the road with, and Stephen asked me to join. At first, you know, I wanted to do it right away. But it took awhile before, ah, well, we had to settle whether my name would be included in the billing, and what size it would be.
>
> I already had a good solo career going, and before I would join I wanted to make sure that the "and Young" bit was right in there. That was the trip, and it took about a month to decide. You know? The music was so good, I just wanted to join in – I wasn't into thinking I could improve it or anything.

The apparent reluctance of Crosby, Stills & Nash to allow Young equal billing was not unreasonable. After all, he had not contributed to their debut album, and it was that which had launched them to immediate stardom. By contrast, Young was a struggling performer and the chance to join Crosby, Stills & Nash as an uncredited sideman might have been reward enough for many an artist in his position. Whatever insecurities may have ruled his life, Young was definitely not lacking in self-confidence. His willingness to delay the acceptance of Stills' offer in favor of a more prestigious billing showed managerial astuteness worthy of Elliot Roberts. Young knew that to join Crosby, Stills & Nash as a sideman would further his career, but he also realized that even greater foruntes would be forthcoming if he were given equal credit. As the fourth member of Crosby, Stills, Nash & Young, Neil would at last be able to reach those people who had never heard his first two solo albums. It was a calculated gamble, but Young always suspected that they needed him almost as much as he needed them.

Although Young has frequently stated that Crosby, Stills & Nash originally did not intend to give him full billing, David Crosby does not agree:

> No. Never. It was never even considered. That's the truth. We went over to his house on the understanding that we were thinking of him being in the band as an equal. There was never any thought about billing him any less than us. I don't care what was said – it's not true. We thought of him as an equal and intended to bill him as an equal from the very first afternoon we went to his house. And that's the truth. I respected him very much and I never thought of it any other way, and I don't think that the other guys ever thought of doing it any other way either. I remember Stills saying, "C'mon let's have my buddy in the band." We already knew how good he was. All three of us thought of him as a songwriter of equal value to us. We all knew that we were tremendously successful and he hadn't been yet, but we also knew what he was. And we all thought of him as an equal. He'd already established himself as an equal with Stills in the Springfield, and thereby as an equal with us. He was our contemporary and a friend. And we never, any of us, thought of giving him any less billing.

Young's desire to maintain a separate identity outside the C.S.N.&Y. set-up was evident in his refusal to disband Crazy Horse, and his insistence that he would continue working for Reprise as a solo artist. Fortunately, this would be made possible because both companies were part of Warner Brothers–Seven Arts. Crosby, Stills and Nash allowed Young to continue his solo career and always maintained that they were four individuals rather than a group.

Following the recruitment of Young, work began almost immediately on a new album. A surprise announcement was made that former Springfield bassist Bruce Palmer had been added to the group. According to Young at the time, the sextet, including Palmer, had recorded four songs, three of which would probably appear on the next album, *Deja Vu*. Palmer recalls his brief working period with Crosby, Stills, Nash & Young:

> I hadn't played bass in over a year so I was pretty rusty. I had problems with Crosby and Nash; once we were rehearsing and I missed a chord and Nash stormed out of the room. No matter what Stephen or Neil said, I wasn't wanted. I don't mind, I wasn't enjoying myself. There was not a lot of joy in the way they made music; it was aloof and distant. They were cold, calculated and sometimes abusive.

Crosby was surprisingly reticent about Palmer's involvement with C.S.N.&Y.:

> Bruce never managed to make it into the band. Stephen liked the way he played and wanted to help him out. Stephen's a very generous man and he likes to make that sort of gesture to people. He got us into trouble a lot of times that way. Palmer was unstable.

Almost immediately, Palmer was replaced by a nineteen-year old bassist named Greg Reeves who had previously worked as a session-man with Tamla Motown. With this line-up, the group set about completing their album, and began rehearsing for their final series of gigs. From that point on life would never be the same for any of them.

SEVEN

The Woodstock Myth

The first gig by Crosby, Stills, Nash & Young took place at New York's Fillmore East on 25 July 1969. There they established a format of using no support group and playing two sets, one acoustic and one electric, separated only by a short intermission. Their adaptability at being able to play equally impressive acoustic and electric sets, plus the fact that they provided a whole evening's worth of entertainment would soon make them one of the biggest acts in America. Their rise to fame was inevitable, but the whole process was precipitated by probably their most well-known appearance at the Woodstock festival. Of all the major rock groups that played at Woodstock, Crosby, Stills, Nash & Young were the unknown entity. It was only their second gig, and the audience was still in the process of assimilating the *Crosby, Stills & Nash* album, which had only recently been released. Their performance was not made any easier by the sheer weight of musical talent that they had to play alongside. The second day of the festival introduced electric music and the line-up was as follows: Joe Cocker; Country Joe and The Fish; Ten Years After; The Band; Johnny Winter; Blood, Sweat and Tears; Crosby, Stills, Nash & Young; The Buttersfield Blues Band; Sha Na Na and Jimi Hendrix. Their placing in the line-up meant that they were sandwiched between The Buttersfield Blues Band and Blood, Sweat and Tears. Paul Butterfield was still revered as one of rock's unsung heroes, while Blood, Sweat and Tears were, at that point, one of the most commercially successful groups in America. Whatever way you looked at it, Neil Young and his friends had been thrown in at the deep end.

If the wealth of musical talent was making them nervous, then one look at the crowd must have brought on cardiac arrests. The organizers had spoken optimistically about the possibility of attracting as many as 200,000 people but no one could have foreseen the events that would turn the Woodstock festival into modern-day folk lore. Days before the festival, crowds began to arrive, and they kept on coming. By the day of the festival there were a reputed one million people on the road to the gig. It would be an understatement to call the event the most momentous gathering of people in the history of rock music. The number of people that were forced to turn back in itself was greater than any single recorded concert or festival attendance. And for their brief glimpse of heaven, the other half million were forced to endure three days of hell. The heat was stifling, the toilets overflowing and food and water were in short supply. Yet the audience remained, some like refugees from a prisoner-of-war camp, others more efficient and better equipped to deal with the appalling conditions.

The formidable task of playing before an audience of this size at such an early stage in their development was in many ways a daunting prospect. Although Crosby and Stills had each played at Monterey in 1967, that festival was like a club date in comparison to Woodstock. They began their acoustic set as a trio, with Young joining in later. One of the numbers performed that they later included on the *Woodstock* album was "Sea Of Madness", a Neil Young song unavailable on any other legitimate release. However, the song did appear on a bootleg, *Wooden Nickel*, and Neil heard it by accident one afternoon:

> When I first heard that record it was on the radio. I'd never heard it before. I don't know how they got it ... I was listening to the radio and there it was, and I'd never heard the record before. And I'm used to making my own records! *Wooden Nickel* – ever hear of it? That's a capitalist rip-off.[15]

"Sea Of Madness" was an average song with lots of swirling organ and a shaky, nervous vocal from Young.

In general, the performance of Crosby, Stills, Nash & Young at Woodstock did seem very nervous and they were probably under-rehearsed. However, they played well enough to make themselves the real stars of the festival in most people's eyes. In fact, their name was to become synonymous with Woodstock and all that it was presumed to stand for in the eyes of American youth. One person who was less than pleased with the Woodstock performance was Neil Young:

> I had a really negative attitude about all of those things, about the pop festivals and Woodstock. I thought it was going to be a joke and I went there but I wasn't really into it. It was so big and everything – I didn't know what we were dong, and I saw all these people ... It wasn't like it seems now. It was great for the people and for a lot of the musicians, I guess, but, for me, I didn't even know what I was doing there. I still don't know. I know that I couldn't hardly hear myself when we were playing, and I didn't know if the people could hear us. I saw the movie and I wasn't in it, so maybe I wasn't too good there. I don't know ...[9]

Young's non-appearance in the film was an initial blow to his status, denying him the mass recognition that the other three members would instantly achieve. On the other hand, it also helped to develop his mystique and allowed him to maintain the image of being a separate entity from the other three members. In Britain, however, Young remained extremely underrated, and the press apperared to regard him of no more importance than Greg Reeves or Dallas Taylor in their initial articles on the group. That situation might have altered if Crosby, Stills, Nash & Young had played their projected open air concert at Hyde Park in September 1969, but it was abruptly cancelled. It was not until 6 January 1970 at the Royal Albert Hall when Young performed "Down By The River" that the British press began to note his contribution. In the States, however, Young was soon receiving the recognition that he deserved and with it came the loss of his individual identity. Television appearances coupled with the other big gigs that the quartet played in 1969, soon established Neil in everyone's mind as one quarter of Crosby, Stills, Nash & Young. And in spite of a 12-year solo career, he is still best remembered by the general public in that role.

One of the main reasons for the long-standing association of the name Young with Crosby, Stills & Nash is the one studio album that they recorded together, *Deja Vu*. Released in March 1970, it was one of the biggest selling albums of the year with pre-release orders totalling over two million dollars. It was undoubtedly one of the finest albums of the early seventies, and very much a consistent four-man effort. The reviews of the period were virtually unanimous in their praise, many maintaining that it was one of the finest albums ever released.

Young's first contribution to the quartet, "Helpless", became one of his more popular songs of the period. Its longevity is surprising because it is not a particularly substantial piece of work. The nostalgia that prompted the song seems to have prevented Young from coming to grips with the composition. The descriptive images are some of the most banal that he has ever produced. The song works reasonably well in the Crosby, Stills, Nash & Young set up though, mainly because the harmonies are extremely well executed. Crosby, in particular, was very complimentary in his appraisal of the song, though a little critical of Young's attitude:

> "Helpless" is real emotional. I liked the harmonies and the overall power of the thing. However, I thought it was unfortunate that he did his songs so much by himself. He wouldn't let us have much to do with them. He would cut the tracks by himself then we would arrange them vocally and sing them.

"Country Girl" the longest track on the album remains one of the most neglected songs in the Young canon. Admittedly, the lyrics do seem to be rather a hotch potch of songs, very loosely connected in order to make one track. Crosby feels that the separation of the song into (a) Down Down Down (b) Whisky Boot Hill and (c) Country Girl was simply Young's devious way of improving his publishing royalties. In spite of its segmented construction Young's vocal is very strong, the harmony work is outstanding and the overall effect is nothing short of stunning. The gargantuan production job, complete with an almost overpowering church organ backing was, in many respects, a final farewell to the inspiration of Jack Nitzsche, whose influence on Young since the Buffalo Springfield days had been enormous.

The final track on the album, "Everybody I Love You" gives Young a co-writing credit. Again, this was two separate songs that were worked on individually and later connected. Stills' "Know You Got To Run", which later appeared in complete form on *Stephen Stills II* was edited and combined with a riff that Young had recently been working on, in order to complete the song. As Stills will admit, the song is far from spectacular, but the vocals are very well performed.

In discussing *Deja Vu*, Young maintained that only three cuts ("Almost Cut My Hair", "Helpless" and "Woodstock") could justifiably be termed group efforts. Generally, Neil felt that the members spent too much time working on their own material, though Crosby quite rightly observes that Young was the most guilty party in this respect. Young's complaint, of course, is mainly directed at the group's continual obsession to strive for the perfect take and ignore such factors as spontaneity and rawness. This does not in itself produce a lack of unity, nor even does the fact that some tracks were dominated by one member of the group. Aural unity on such a record, stems from the ability of each member of the group to complement the work of the other. It is my belief that this was achieved on *Deja Vu* since the majority of tracks are distinguishable from later solo recordings. Tracks such as "Country Girl" and "Everybody I Love You", for example, have a distinctive C.S.N.&Y. sound texture which could not have easily been duplicated on a solo record. On what solo album would Neil Young's "Country Girl" have fitted in unobtrusively? The solo recordings on *Deja Vu* are minimal enough not to be overt, and generally fit well into the group context. The critics of the period were not troubled by any sense of disunity and they unanimously acclaimed the "brilliant self portraits" of Crosby, Stills, Nash & Young. The group's spirit of camaraderie would later be exposed as a myth, and as a result the so-called unity of the group would be brought into question. Yet, in rock 'n roll, reality has always been subservient to myth. Elvis was the archetypal teenage rebel to many people, even though he was actually a home-loving kid. The Beatles were loved for their zany but clean humor, though, in reality, their sordid exploits in Hamburg were reprehensible. And the Stones were apparently crude and degenerate, even though Jagger had attended the London School of Economics and was probably one of the most articulate men in rock. So it was that C.S.N.&Y. maintained a spirit of camaraderie in the Woodstock tradition of love, peace and good vibes, even though they were often at each others' throats. Whatever differences they might have had, their shared characteristics made their group recordings distinctive. Four individual singer-songwriters they may have been but when Young traded licks with Stills, or Crosby, Stills and Nash sang together they became something greater than the sum of their parts. The talent, coupled with the myth were the factors which made *Deja Vu* one of the most important albums of its day and set their later solo careers in motion. From that point on Crosby, Stills, Nash & Young were the undisputed U.S. superstars of the early seventies.

Looking back, one realizes that the mass-popularity of the quartet was the result of a complex series of factors. One of them was undoubtedly the product of America's love for the Beatles' phenomenon. When the Fab Four burst onto the American scene in the mid-sixties, they virtually wiped out every other group in sight, as did the other English groups who followed in their wake. Even the ever popular Beach Boys found that their empire had been overrun with invaders. Ever since that period, America has attempted to create its own version of The Beatles, but the nearest it reached was with The Byrds and The Monkees. Unfortunately, The Byrds were not stable or consistent enough to last the course and the manufactured Monkees, in spite of their brief flicker of fame, lacked both the depth and the talent of The Beatles. This failure of America to match The Beatles haunted the national conscience during the late sixties, and even the flowering of the San Franciscan movement failed to produce a single group who could match the Fabs for musical quality, humor and personality. By 1969, it was clear that the task was an almost impossible one for not only did America require a group whose image would be appealing enough to capture the interest of the nation but one whose music was sufficiently sophisticated to warrant high critical praise. A talented multi-million selling pop group would have been the answer in 1964 but this was 1969 and rock music had developed to such an extent that a recreation of the Beatles' primivitism would not have been adequate. Moreover, the kind of fanatical devotion that characterized the Beatles' following had not been restricted to a love of the group's music. It was the Beatles' image that captured the nation's heart – the new hairstyles, the accents, the clothes and the youthful independence brought about by post-war affluence. Suddenly there were more young kids than there had ever seemed before, and they were establishing their own music and their own philosophy which dictated "never trust anyone over 30".

By 1969 The Beatles were no longer the rallying point for youth, but they were a musical institution. They were in the unique position of being able to forge ahead musically while retaining mass acceptance. If The Beatles dropped acid and recorded "Strawberry Fields Forever" or *Sgt. Peppers Lonely Hearts Club Band* all the world listened, and commercial radio played the records. Even a single of the length of "Hey Jude" or as idiosyncratic as "The Ballad of John and Yoko" would receive national airplay. This was the position that The Beatles held in rock, and it seemed impossible for anyone else to aspire to it. If you were a pop group in 1969 you lacked class, and if you were musically sophisticated you generally lacked international mass-appeal.

What Crosby, Stills, Nash & Young achieved at the end of the decade was the closest America reached to creating an older, second generation Beatles. Many American groups of musical quality were selling albums in 1969, of course, but they were generally nameless faces. Who, excepting their fans, could name the individual members of Creedence Clearwater Revival or Blood, Sweat and Tears, or any of the other big U.S. acts? Crosby, Stills, Nash & Young by abandoning the idea of a group name were already half way towards establishing themselves as individual personalities. The press would do the rest. The quartet were also fortunate because, like the 1969 Beatles, they were still remembered as teenage idols. Crosby had been a sex-symbol four years ealier, with a fab green-suede cape and a crooked smile, which drove the girls crazy. Stills and Young had also received their share of teenage adulation during the Buffalo Springfield days. Finally, Nash provided the all-important British connection. As a former member of one of England's longest lasting pop groups, The Hollies, he had a loyal following throughout Europe. Wherever Crosby, Stills, Nash & Young played then, part of the audience's psychological response contained elements of that old fanaticism that is peculiar to teenage heroes. A musically excellent group such as The Band, for example, would always be well-received, but they would never get the same fanatical response reserved for Crosby, Stills, Nash & Young simply because they lacked that magical "star" ingredient peculiar to rock heroes.

While Crosby, Stills, Nash & Young might go some way towards duplicating the "star" quality of the Fab Four, surely they could not alter fashion, or influence young people's thinking in the way that The Beatles had done. Yet, in a strange way, Crosby, Stills, Nash & Young achieved this also. The press immediately took to fashioning individual and often stereotyped characteristics for this neo-Fab Four. Crosby, generally thought of as a loudmouth by the 1967 Byrds, was now the "spokesman" of the group and was deemed to have "poetic eloquence". Nash was the quaint Englishman – the diplomat of the group. Neil was the dark, mysterious character, nervous and moody. And to show how stereotyped these images were, Stills, for well over a year, was characterized by the music press as a shy, modest and retiring person. It was only later that the media decided that this did not fit, so he quickly metamorphozed into the brash, blonde musical general. These manufactured images may have been projected by the group to a degree, but it was the press that magnified them out of all proportion. Crosby, Stills, Nash & Young, like The Beatles and like many Hollywood film stars, achieved the kind of public image that had not been seen in the music press since the days of *Teen Set*. Crosby became famous for his fringed jackets and cowboy look; Nash's waistcoats were continually noted; Young's patched jeans had become an institution and Stills opened up new avenues for the football jersey industry. Even their marital status was good copy, making them worthwhile condidates for the popular press as well as the music weeklies. Did Nash really write "Lady of The Island" for Joni Mitchell? Was Joni's "Circle Game" a reply to Neil's "Sugar Mountain"? Was Stills in love with Judy Collins when he wrote "Suite: Judy Blue Eyes"? Was the line "Come On Sweet Rita" in "Sugar Babe" directed at Rita Coolidge? Would Crosby ever marry after the tragic death of his girlfriend? Almost every article written about the group contained an element of this kind of journalism. The simple fact was that Crosby, Stills, Nash & Young were big "stars" and as such their personal lives were inextricably bound with their music.

It was the star-making machinery that placed Crosby, Stills, Nash & Young in a position where their influence on youth became surprisingly strong. Essentially, the quartet had a ready-made set of philosophies and "new" values to bestow on to their audience. These values were, in reality, a modified form of the type that Elvis and The Beatles had unconsciously propagated in the late fifties and early sixties. The idea of enjoying your youth and rebelling against your elders was a rock 'n roll cliché which Crosby, Stills, Nash & Young revamped and placed in a late sixties context. They did this by re-enforcing the hippie ideals which had been wilting somewhat since the halcyon days of 1967. The "peace and love" movement symbolized in flower power had been nipped in the bud by the commercial enterprises before it had a chance to bloom. In Britain, it was generally seen as a passing fashion, and Carnaby Street and the boutiques of King's Road, Chelsea helped to make it one. The musical and political ideologies of the movement were generally considered too simplistic to be taken seriously. Although musically talented units such as the Jefferson Airplane and the Grateful Dead emerged from San Francisco and expounded some of its ideologies, they would never reach the scale of international popularity that was reserved for mega-stars such as Crosby, Stills, Nash & Young. Thus, although the Dead and the Airplane may have influenced the life-style of a small proportion of Americans, they lacked the popularity to broadcast the message internationally. What Crosby, Stills, Nash & Young did, was to take the old cliché "love, peace and music" and actually attempt to put some personal meaning into it. It was no small wonder that they were so closely associated with those three days of love, peace and music at Woodstock. While other groups exploited the hippie ideal, Crosby, Stills, Nash & Young had the nerve to stand up and take the whole thing seriously. At every concert and on every record the messages were the same – love, peace and music.

Nobody doubted the musical talents or commitment of Crosby, Stills, Nash & Young, least of all themselves. They always maintained that it was their love of music that brought them together. Crosby even wrote a song titled "Music Is Love" as a statement of his commitment. The quartet went on record as saying music was the most important thing in their lives, and everyone believed it. Usually, they made a single qualification in this respect such as "music – and a good woman", which introduced their philosophy of love. Now the idea of love propounded by the hippie movement in 1967 was greeted with scepticism by Mr. Normal. Surely, it was absurdly idealistic to think that we could all love each other. But what Crosby, Stills, Nash & Young did was to take that notion and put it in a personal context, exchanging idealism for a form of neo-Romanticism. All four of them sung about love, sometimes involving more than one person as in "Triad" or "Love The One You're With", but generally they directed their sentiments at an idealized individual. They made it sound credible too, because most of the songs were autobiographical. Crosby was an unmarried "widower"; Stills had lost Judy Collins and Nash's relationship with Joni Mitchell had ended.

The final requisite of peace was also frequently alluded to in their political songs and in their interviews. Crosby spent entire interviews explaining that American was about to become a bloodbath, while Stills spoke of increased fighting on the streets. They appeared to believe that the U.S. was on the verge of civil war between the young revolutionaries and the old war-mongers. Crosby, Stills, Nash & Young genuinely appeared to believe that their music and lifestyle were about to herald the beginning of a new age. The line between fantasy and conviction in Crosby's "Wooden Ships" was a very thin one. When it came to politics, they were aggressive and their political songs comprised much of their electric set. Part of their popular appeal came from this ability to sound so tender in love but so aggressive in battle. The opponents were usually those anti-pacifist politicians who promoted the Vietnam War or prompted street violence. Crosby wrote "Long Time Gone" and "Almost Cut My Hair" the night Bobby Kennedy died, a fact which was often noted in the press. Stills used the concert platform as a subject for tirades against Nixon, Agnew and Daly and suffixed his old Buffalo Springfield hit "For What It's Worth" with a political "poem" entitled "America's Children". Finally, Nash voiced his indignity with "Chicago" and advised us all to teach our children a new political philosophy.

At first, Young seemed far removed from this love and peace philosophy. While the other three were bachelors in emotional anguish, he was happily married. Similarly, Young was apolitical and did not share the radical views of his three compatriots. But Young fell victim to the C.S.N.&Y. myth, perhaps because the public could not see it any other way. If Young was happily married, who could have guessed it after listening to his repertoire, which consisted of a series of songs about lost loves and broken relationships. Even the apolitical stance could not be maintained long and soon Young was writing "Southern Man", "Ohio" and "Alabama". In short, he was now at one with Crosby, Stills & Nash and finally assimilated into the public's mind as part of this embodiment of the Woodstock ideal.

While Crosby, Stills, Nash & Young reigned, they were the darlings of the music press, and their music was the finest of its day. Implicit in the qualities that brought them to critical and public acclaim, however, were the factors which would eventually cause their downfall. Where do you draw the line between self-awareness and self-indulgence, between romanticism and narcissism, and between political idealism and the failure to confront everyday realities? And musically, where does technical perfection end and clinicism begin? These were the questions that Crosby, Stills, Nash & Young should have been asking themselves as the seventies progressed, but they never did. They remained faithful to their ideals, even as the world around them gradually turned away. It was a clear case of historical inevitability – one set of values and beliefs replacing another. Crosby and Nash continued to expound the hippie dream and were blasted from every single angle. Stills became ambitious with Manassas, but then found a formula that enabled him to release the same album over and over again, and eventually he lost himself in every decreasing circles. Young alone would survive the seventies intact due to one remarkable trait – perversity.

EIGHT

The Return And Fall of Crazy Horse And C.S.N.&Y.

While Crosby, Stills & Nash ensured that their records always sounded as perfect as could humanly be expected, Neil Young was not always of the same mind. He had a perverse element in his character that actually took pride in the odd mistake or occasional technical imperfection. It was this willingness to tolerate imperfection in the pursuit of artistic expression which would save Young's career during the seventies. As the decade progressed, he would release records which smacked of unprofessionalism by showing a total disregard for such requisites as overdubs and clarity of production. Young's aim became increasingly to show the listener his true self, blemishes and all. The records he would release in the mid-seventies would shock Crosby, Stills & Nash and be abhorred by music critics, but they would give Young a new standing in rock music.

Young's attraction to a form of music quite different from the type that he played with Crosby, Stills & Nash was evident in his continued love for the sound of Crazy Horse. When Crosby, Stills & Nash ended their long series of gigs in January 1970, they all took a well-earned rest, but Young hardly stopped for breath before he was off on the road with Crazy Horse a couple of weeks later. With the addition of Jack Nitzsche to the Crazy Horse line-up, Young went on a brief Stateside tour playing a repertoire which would have been ill-suited to the sound of C.S.N.&Y. For Young, playing in two groups seemed the perfect solution to the problems created by his determination to make technically perfect records while being free to rock 'n roll. He was fully aware that these contradictory notions might split his audience into two factions:

> They're so different – Crazy Horse is very funky. A lot of people who come to see C.S.N.&Y. because of that association might be disappointed. They might be disappointed because it's not the same kind of thing. With us (Crazy Horse), if the music doesn't get off, it doesn't make it. It's just the music. Whereas with C.S.N.&Y. even if we don't get off musically, just the fact that all those guys are there and everything – there's still enough excitement. It's really a whole different trip. Crazy Horse is more funky, more roots, you know?[5]

In searching for a better analogy Young came up with a remarkable comparison which, in many ways, summed up his paradoxical musical vision:

> Well, I'll tell you ... the ideal way to explain it ... I'm oversimplifying, but like you could compare C.S.N.&Y. to the Beatles, and Crazy Horse to the Stones. That's the only way I can put it – only they're American. That makes a difference ... Another thing I'll tell. The Rolling Stones are my favorite group.

There may be much significance in the fact that Young sets up a comparison between C.S.N.&Y. and the Beatles and Crazy Horse and Rolling Stones, and adds cryptically that the Stones are his favorite group. Are we to suppose, by implication, that he prefers Crazy Horse to C.S.N.&Y.? Young would obviously not say at this point in his career, though he came very close to admitting his preference:

> The C.S.N.&Y. thing supports Crazy Horse. Without the other trip, Crazy Horse wouldn't be doing this. I wouldn't be doing this. That's why I joined.

It is easy to assume from this that Young was just using Crosby, Stills & Nash in order to provide himself with enough fame and money to take his own group to the top. However, it should be borne in mind that these statements were made while Young was in the middle of an enjoyable tour with Crazy Horse. Moreover, in spite of his optimism and exuberance, Young would shortly discover that even fronting a group such as Crazy Horse could bring its own headaches.

At the beginning of the tour, Crazy Horse were in full flight and their performances showed great promise for a future album. Their concerts were structurally very similar to those of C.S.N.&Y. First, there would be an acoustic set with Neil playing solo, and then Crazy Horse would appear for the electric set. One of the reasons that Young could begin the tour so quickly was that a quarter of his "new" set consisted of songs he had recently been playing with Crosby, Stills & Nash. These songs included the familiar "On The Way Home", "Helpless" and the lengthy version of "Down By The River". To these Young added a selection of songs from his first two solo albums, plus a couple of old Springfield numbers, including a remarkably effective revamping of "Broken Arrow". However, it was the other songs in the set that proved the most surprising. They were rough, unpolished and totally uncharacteristic of Young's familiar recorded work. At this point Young was thinking in terms of recording a new album, and these were the tracks that he intended to use. As the tour progressed, Young and Crazy Horse found the time to begin work on this new album. According to Young, the aim of the album was to capture a quality of spontaneity and freshness that we usually associate with songs of the late fifties and early sixties. Although Young realized that this album might not sell a million copies, he was still committed to it:

> I'm trying to make records with them (Crazy Horse) that are not necessarily hits or anything like that – I don't care about that – I just want to make records that people will dig to listen to for a long time.

At first the sessions for the new album appeared to be progressing favorably.

Young discovered that working with Crazy Horse encouraged him to develop a new style of playing:

> Yeah ... it's fun ... it's groovy. It's good for me – it keeps my chops up, it really does. But it's a different style playing with this band – like when we started rehearsing it took me two weeks to calm down enough so that I could play with this band because I was rushing all the time with my guitar, you know, playing too many notes.

However, as the sessions progressed, Young became increasingly impatient with the irresponsibility of Danny Whitten whose drug habits were getting out of hand. Before the recordings were completed, Young fired Crazy Horse and the projected album was shelved. There is no doubt that the work Young had intended to release was substantially different from the next solo album that he would record. It is pointless to spend too much time speculating which tracks were due for inclusion, though it is generally accepted that "Oh Lonesome Me", "I Need Her Love To Get By", "Wondering", "Big Waves", "Winterlong", "It Might Have Been" and "Everybody's Alone" were all strong contenders. Apparently, Young's idea was to make an album of old-fashioned, down-home country 'n western music. "Oh Lonesome Me" was one song which he did re-record for his next album and it gives some clue as to how this unrealized work might have sounded. "It Might Have Been", like "Oh Lonesome Me", was another song not penned by Neil Young. In fact, Young was unsure where the song originated:

> That was a tune I learned at a church dance. I used to go there and this used to be my favorite song. It's kind of hokey. I don't know who wrote it. I don't really know any more about it than that.[16]

"Wondering", another song with a strong country tinge, would have fitted well alongside "Oh Lonesome Me" and "It Might Have Been". To go beyond these is to enter the realms of pure speculation for whatever might have occurred ended the moment Crazy Horse left the studio. Young's decision to shelve the project permanently and forget most of the songs would be the first *volte face* in a long series stretching right up to the present.

In retrospect, it is easy to be sentimental about many of the songs discarded by Young. When a song that appears in bootleg form is not released, it always seems to achieve a spurious quality simply because of its rarity. This is particularly true of these unreleased cuts by Young and Crazy Horse. If they had appeared in album form, they would probably have disappointed most of Young's audience as several of the songs that he recorded at this point had little of the commercial appeal that would characterize the tunes on his next album. Young has never been a good interpreter of other people's material and songs such as "It Might Have Been", had they been released, would have been nothing short of disappointing. Even "Wondering" and "Dance Dance Dance" lack substance, and they are the kind of songs that you imagine Young could knock off every morning before breakfast. All in all, the abandoning of the Crazy Horse album was probably the best thing that could have happened at this stage in Young's career. It encouraged Neil to search for new musicians and to think in terms of writing more suitable material for his next recording venture. Young made the obvious decision that if he could not use

Crazy Horse, then he would try and persuade some of his other friends to help him record the album. Stephen Stills and Greg Reeves agreed to interrupt their vacations in order to assist Neil, who still felt that he needed another guitarist. Eventually, he chose an unknown – Nils Lofgren.

Lofgren was an energetic young guitarist who before he met Young had attempted to enter the music business in fairy-tale fashion. He had run away from his Maryland home when he was 17 in the belief that he could find fame and fortune in Greenwich Village. After knocking on the doors of a few record companies, Lofgren realized that he needed a lot more than faith and hope. He hung around the Village until the bitter New York winter forced him to return to Maryland suffering from a severe case of pneumonia. He then formed a group which he called Grin, but though he gained experience, he remained as idealistic as ever. He spent most of his time trying to get backstage at various gigs in the hope of making himself known to important musicians. Then, one fateful evening in mid-1969, Lofgren hit the jackpot. His big break came from a chance meeting with Neil Young at a Washington club called the Cellar Door. Nils explains how he became the protege of Neil Young:

> I was in Grin and we were feal frustrated in Washington. We were thinking of going to L.A. to get something happening. At this time, Neil and Crazy Horse happened to be playing in this little club called the Cellar Door. Basically, I didn't know much about Neil, apart from the fact that he was once in the Buffalo Springfield. I was just a young musician from Washington asking, "where do I go? What do I do?" But I thought I had some good songs so I played him some tunes and he liked them. I'd never really heard his songs, but our writing was very similar in many ways. At least we both had a good sense of melody and we were telling some interesting stories. He really turned me on. I was really young and he was really nice to me – bought me cokes and hamburgers! It was neat. I spent a few days talking to him after that – a really beautiful guy.[17]

When Nils and Grin eventually recorded their debut album Young and Crazy Horse came along to help out with some vocals and lead-guitar work. It was shortly after the completion of that album that Neil temporarily ended his working relationship with Crazy Horse, so Lofgren was still in his mind as a potential guitarist for a future project.

After rehearsing with Nils in Topanga, Neil decided to re-enlist Crazy Horse drummer, Ralph Molina. The musicians began working at a studio in Los Angeles, but the results were not pleasing. Young felt that the atmosphere in the studio was not relaxed enough for the music that he wanted to play. The problem was solved when the studio allowed Neil to rent a mixing board, which was transported to Topanga. Having the convenience of a home studio meant that the musicians could play at any hour of the day. The sessions were now relaxed and profitable, but Young still felt that something was missing. Although Stills and Lofgren were providing backing vocals, Young felt that their voices were not compatible with the music he was making. Finally, Young decided to allow the other members of Crazy Horse to attend the sessions and they contributed additional vocals as well as playing on a couple of tracks. Neil's former producer, Jack Nitzsche, arrived with the other members of Crazy Horse, but he played on only one cut, "When You Dance I Can Really Love". Although he was no longer in the producer's chair, Nitzsche was not above making some critical comments on Young's work, as Nils recalls:

> I don't know what it is with Jack. I guess he feels that he is a solo artist in his own right. When we recorded *Goldrush* he came by a lot and Neil really wanted him to play piano on this particular track. Jack would get drunk and talk a lot. One second he'd be sitting there drivelling away about how much he loved Neil's music then next thing you know he'd be yelling and screaming at him, calling him names and refusing to play.

In spite of Nitzsche's sometimes scathing comments, the sessions were proving to be more fruitful than anyone could have hoped. What the musicians who attended the sessions found most remarkable was the extraordinary speed with which Young was able to write and record new songs. Nils recalls a typical Neil Young recording schedule:

> We would play through a song about four times to learn it, with Neil doing all live vocals in the same room. In four days he had written six new songs. In fact the whole thing was on tape in under a week, allowing another week or two for mixing. Neil really liked it when it was finished. He liked the concept behind the songs but it had been done so quick that he was not sure how the public would take to it. He was not sure if there was enough in it.

Young's worst fears about the album were understandable. Parts of *Everybody Knows This Is Nowhere* had been overdubbed although prior to that recording, all Young's work had taken weeks, sometimes months to complete. Yet, here was a new work taken virtually from conception to completion in the space of a couple of weeks.

In spite of Crazy Horse's attendance at the sessions, Young chose not to include the "hokey" country tunes that they had previously recorded. Instead, he had a new idea, inspired by an actor/filmmaker named Dean Stockwell. At the time, Stockwell was in Topanga attempting to film a screenplay titled *After The Goldrush*. Essentially, it was a movie dealing with the after-effects of a natural disaster in which Topanga was engulfed by a giant tidal wave. The plot was fairly predictable, using the disaster as a central theme and concentrating upon its effect on the lives of three people. One of the characters happened to be a moody folksinger, and it was this part of the plot that first intrigued Young. With the movie's theme loosely in mind, Young set about writing an album's worth of new compositions and it was these songs that constituted most of the material that was recorded at the house in Topanga.

With an album and a Crazy Horse tour completed, Young found himself in demand once more when Crosby, Stills & Nash decided to embark upon another tour. By this time *Deja Vu* was number one in the album charts and C.S.N.&Y. were being acclaimed as America's most important group. Their following had increased nearly two-fold in the wake of the phenomenal success of *Deja Vu* so the importance of this tour in commercial terms was incalculable. Young could hardly refuse the offer, even though he seemed to be moving from project to project without a suitable break.

The tour commenced in May, but after only a few dates there was trouble in the air. Greg Reeves and Dallas Taylor began to adopt more assertive roles by demanding that they be allowed to include some of their material in the set. Both had been writing songs, and the chance to get them aired before a sizeable audience proved irresistible. Not surprisingly, C.S.N.&Y. would not agree to their demands. Although the tour ended as a success, with a live album in the can and a series of glowing reviews, it would not be repeated soon. While most people considered Crosby, Stills, Nash & Young to be inseparable, they were already beginning to grow away from each other in order to indulge in their own pursuits. Young wanted even more time to develop his solo career, and the others were of the same mind. Although potentially millions of dollars were to be made through future concert performances, Crosby, Stills, Nash & Young would not appear together on the same stage for another four years.

NINE

The Soloist Rises To Fame

The Crosby, Stills, Nash & Young spring tour led many to hope that another studio album might be recorded but no attempt was made except for a rush-released single, "Ohio". This was the first political song that Young ever wrote, and it came as a surprise to the other members of the group as, up until that time, Neil had remained relatively uncommitted to the C.S.N.&Y. ideal. Crosby explains Young's political stance during his time in C.S.N.&Y.:

> Neil had the stance I have now, which I think is the right one. I don't think musicians should go and seek stands out. I don't think that it's right. I think that music is for fun. But when something slaps you in the face personally, you have to respond to it. And Kent State was too damn much. They'd gone too far. Even Neil couldn't stand it. He had to respond to it. It was as genuine and honest a thing as you could ask for. It wasn't us going out and seeking stands to take that made us look good. He was just honestly reacting to what hit him in the face. It blew his mind. He couldn't believe they'd shot those kids. It was too much.

In some ways this song brought the four of them closer together during the tour, as before Young suggested it they seemed on the verge of splitting up. Crosby remembers becoming extremely excited when Young presented him with the song and his first reaction was to rush straight to Stills and Nash and relate the good news. They were so impressed with the idea that they cancelled all arrangements and recorded it that very night. According to Nash the recording was completed within 15 minutes. The track was then mixed, cut, pressed and in the shops within eight days. Crosby confirms this extraordinary fact:

> It was done in one day. Neil and I were sitting in Butano Canyon up North. I handed him the magazine with a report of the Kent State killings. He read the article, picked up the guitar, and started writing the song. I watched him write it. He and I then got on a plane, went to Los Angeles, went into the studio with Stills & Nash, made the record and put "Find The Cost Of Freedom" on the back of it. We gave it to Ahmet Ertegun that evening; he took it to Atlantic on the plane that night, and it was out a week later.

Following so closely the student killings at Kent State University and pointing the finger directly at President Nixon, "Ohio" was both topical and controversial. It sold extremely well in spite of a nationwide U.S. radio ban. Young maintained that "Ohio" was his finest C.S.N.&Y. number. It remains one of his most powerful statements on record. That power comes from the overall performance by Crosby, Stills, Nash & Young at what is definitely one of their greatest moments. As their final studio recording, "Ohio" is a tribute to all that they might have done had they stayed together.

The seventies had opened spectacularly for Young. Since the beginning of the year he had not been out of the public eye and he seemed to be ubiquitous, appearing with Crazy Horse one month and C.S.&N. the next. *Deja Vu* had brought him some acclaim, while the second C.S.N.&Y. tour and the release of "Ohio" made him suddenly appear as a major force in rock music. All these achievements were dwarfed, however, when *After The Goldrush* was released in August. This was the work that finally gave Young a solid commercial standing outside the ranks of the C.S.N.&Y. set-up. It is probably true to say that without the C.S.N.&Y. connection this album, like its predecessors, might have passed relatively unnoticed but on the other hand all the plugging in the world could not have accounted for its enormous success. Young appears to agree with this point of view:

> For sure C.S.N.&Y. put my name out there. They gave me a lot of publicity. But, in all modesty, *After The Goldrush* was the spirit of Topanga Canyon. It seemed like I realized that I'd gotten some-where.[10]

In recent years it has become a critical commonplace to look back at the album and deem it somewhat overrated. Certainly some critics of the period termed it a landmark in the history of rock music which was perhaps a little strong, but while it is easy to determine faults in *After The Goldrush* it should be remembered that most of Young's albums are usually blemished in one way or another. What makes *After The Goldrush* an important album in the Young canon is the fact that it bore no relation to either of its predecessors. Where Young might easily have rehashed old ideas, he chose to try something new. What he probably did, along with Crosby, Stills & Nash, was to unleash a new generation of singer songwriters, some of whom were talented, while the great majority were fashion-following pretenders. Young achieved this because for the first time in his carrer he had discovered the ability to write exceptionally melodic material. In the past he had occasionally hit upon an instantly recognizable melody as in "I Am A Child", for example, but here was an album where each track seemed tailor-made for every aspiring strumming songwriter in the land.

"Tell Me Why", the opening track, showed the growing influence of Crosby, Stills & Nash on Young's work. Unlike Young's previous recordings, the vocals are precise and confident, with Neil and Nils Lofgren harmonizing and strumming in unison. One of the reasons for Young's sudden popularity was his use of what many referred to as "poetic imagery". On *After The Goldrush* however, many of Young's images were imprecise and colorful, without being particularly meaning-ful. The use of such non-descriptive metaphors as "heart-ships" impressed an audience searching for a singer songwriter whose lyrics sounded "meaningful", but whose songs were pleasantly hummable. Young clearly fitted the bill perfectly. The opening verse of "Tell Me Why" contained some of his most desolate images, with visions of "broken harbors" and a lonely, frightened figure searching aimlessly in the darkness of the night. Read in isolation, the lyrics were dark and depressing, but one would never have guessed that from listening to Young's breezy, singalong interpretation of the song. The sugar-coated bitterness of "Tell Me Why" captured the mood of the entire album. The song also revealed that, lyrically, Young was beginning to repeat some of the old lines. The chorus "When you're old enough to repay/But young enough to sell" was a thinly disguised re-working of the chorus of "Country Girl" – "Too late to keep the change/Too late to pay". Young's tendency to repeat and restate old themes and ideas would prove the most serious threat to the development of his career during the next couple of years.

"After The Goldrush" with its prominent piano and high pitched vocal was one of two songs on the album performed by Young alone. It was one of Young's most imaginative compositions up until that point in his career; it was also the most sustained and consistent piece of writing that he had attempted since the Buffalo Springfield days. The song is undoubtedly one of Young's most idealistic visions and uses the dream framework to present its imaginative theme. The dream opens with a romantic portrayal of medieval times with knights in armor and singing peasants. Young's idealistic portrayal transforms the imaginary landscape into a fairy world complete with dream-like imagery:

> There was a fanfare blowing to the sun
> That was floating on the breeze

By the end of the verse, however, the resplendent medieval world dissolves as the narrator's mind shifts to a contemporary ecological speculation:

> Look at Mother Nature on the run
> In the nineteen seventies.

Young's understanding of dream psychology is effectively demonstrated through his creation of an imaginary landscape. As in a dream, temporal and spatial distance do not exist and are replaced by the illogical workings of the unconscious. The idealized medieval setting is appropriate enough, reflecting the traditional conception of those times as a golden age. Only in a dream could such a romantic and unrealistic vision of medieval society be entertained. Young uses another feature of dream psychology by maintaining the ever present transmuting consciousness of the sleeper-narrator. Just as events and images in dreams terminate without warning when the unconscious moves on to new speculations, so Young's medieval world is left behind as the narrator ponders upon the ecological problems of the 1970s.

The second verse is, in fact, a negation of the first and, appropriately, the action is switched from medieval to modern times. The image of the "burned-out basement" contrasts strongly with the earlier medieval setting. The blowing fanfare of the first verse is now transformed into the sound of a band that the narrator hears playing inside his head. Even the sun that was pleasantly floating in the breeze in the medieval landscape is momentarily replaced by a full moon, and when it returns it no longer floats, but is described as "bursting" through the sky. As Young's vision moves to modern times, the imagery becomes more and more bleak.

The problems are resolved in the final stanza with further idealistic speculations. Here Young extends the timescale even further, and he has now moved from a medieval setting of knights in armor to the futuristic vision of silver spaceships. The idea of taking selected children of the earth to form a new, perfect civilization on another planet is an extension of the ideal presented in Crosby's "Wooden Ships". Young is actually re-stating the Crosby, Stills & Nash dream of forming a perfect society. Following Crosby's "Wooden Ships", in which the survivors of a holocaust founded a new society, Nash wrote his plea to save the future in "Teach Your Children" and Stills concluded (in "We Are Not Helpless") that it would be the children who would have "the wisdom to be free". Young fuses the ideas implicit in all these songs in the final image of the spaceship carrying the seeds of the hippie generation to "a new home in the sun".

"Only Love Can Break Your Heart" was another of the more popular songs on this album and it received extensive radio plugging when it was released as a single. Young's gift for writing strong melodies would shortly reward him with a modicum of success in the singles charts. Like "The Loner" it has been suggested by some commentators that "Only Love Can Break Your Heart" was written about Stephen Stills. Onstage in 1977, however, Young finally admitted that the song was written for his other associate Graham Nash.

"Southern Man" was the key cut on the album and judging by the number of times it has been requested at live shows, it is probably his most popular number. Part of its popularity is undoubtedly the result of Young's aggressive performance in which he damns the slave drivers of the South for their treatment of negroes. The first two verses consist of the narrator's observations of life in the South, but a climax is reached in the final stanza in which Young adopts the persona of a Southern man and screams:

> I've seen your black man coming 'round
> Swear by God I'm gonna cut him down.

That last line was to prove somewhat ironic in later years when Neil stopped playing the song because a member of his audience actually was cut down before his eyes. Young explains the incident that prompted him to cease performing his most famous of songs:

> I was at the Oakland Coliseum playing away. It was a pretty mediocre time actually. It wasn't that hot – show number 58. We were all tired and the band wasn't right in the first place. It was one of those things. By the time we'd got there everybody, every night, would yell "Southern Man", "Southern Man" – and I could dig it. It was nice. But I went to sing it, and by then I'd sung it with Crosby, Stills & Nash, I'd sung it by myself and I was singing it with these others guys. So by then I was starting to feel like a Wurlitzer, even though I really believed in the song and where I was at when I wrote it. Anyway, I was singing away: "Southern Man better keep your head, don't forget

what the good book said", and this guy in the front row jumped up and went "Right on!! Right on! I love it!" And he felt really good – I could tell. Then all of a sudden this black cop just walked up and *crunched* him. I just took my guitar off and put it on the ground and got in the car and went home. A lot of those people couldn't understand it because they couldn't see from the other end. They thought I'd flipped out or something. But there was something about it, and ever since then, I've never sung the song. I don't know why. I sang it a lot ... I sang it every night for a long time.[18]

"Southern Man" eventually re-appeared in Young's sets during the 1976 tour with Crazy Horse.

Following the stupendous "Southern Man", Young chose to end the first side on an anti-climactic note with the fairly inconsequential and fragmentary "Till The Morning Comes". Although the song lacked any real substance it did provide a nice blast of brass and some enjoyable closing harmonies.

Young's interpretation of Don Gibson's "Oh Lonesome Me" showed how unimpressive Neil could be when he chose to sing other people's material. This was a song originally done for the lost "hokey" album, and it is a pity that Young decided to revive it. His whining vocals and badly played harmonica do little justice to the number which, for some inexplicable reason, was recorded in mono. Young still likes "Oh Lonesome Me" although he realizes that it is one of his least popular songs:

"Oh Lonesome Me" is pretty good. I like it because everybody else seems to hate it so much. Well, "Oh Lonesome Me" is a real old song, so old that there wasn't any stereo when it was written!

"Don't Let It Bring You Down" is another of Young's death-songs with a suitably sparse accompaniment of piano, acoustic guitar and drums. Young uses fairly standard images of light and darkness to express the isolation of life in the city. Apparently, Young was inspired to present this bleak vision of city life following a trip to London. On the stage of the Royal Festival Hall he told his audience:

I wrote this song about London. I've been here to England three times and I've never gotten out of the city yet. People tell me that's too bad – I think it is too bad.[14]

Judging from the lyrical content of the song one would have to agree with him.

Of the remaining songs on *After The Goldrush* little need be said. "Birds" and "I Believe In You" were typically plaintive Young love songs of the period, while "When You Dance I Can Really Love" was the token rocker. As with the first side, Young chose to end the album on a light rather than a dramatic note with the amusingly irrelevent "Cripple Creek Ferry". In spite of Young's idiosyncrasies the album became one of the biggest hits of the year and finally established Neil as a solo artist in his own right.

By the time of the album's release Young had moved out of his Topanga home, which had been overrun with star-seeking fans and well-wishers. In spite of the success of *After The Goldrush* Young was not a happy man. His marriage had ended in divorce and according to his brother, he was deeply affected by the separation. Determined to re-think his future, Young returned to his childhood home of Omemee during the summer and resisted the temptation to set out on a national tour. For the remainder of 1970, he was relatively inactive. The main reason for Young's lack of personal appearances was not only his broken marriage but also his health which had worsened during this period. Throughout the latter part of 1970, Young was undergoing treatment for his back. A serious back ailment was causing him much pain and preventing him from doing any strenuous exercises. Eventually, Young was committed to the Cedars of Lebanon Hospital in Los Angeles for an operation, following a slipped disc. According to Young, the pain was so bad that, following his operation, he found it increasingly difficult even to hold his guitar up for any length of time. He was determined to tour, but in order to perform comfortably it would be necessary for him to remain seated throughout his performance. One solution to his problem would be to do a solo acoustic tour without a backing group. So, towards the end of the year, Young embarked on a series of performances, accompanied by only his acoustic guitar and piano.

The performances at Carnegie Hall in December (4th–5th) were regarded by Young as some of the most important of his career. Young even stated that he would have gladly played for free, just for the pleasure of performing at that prestigious venue. The seriousness with which Young took those performances was evident in some of his adverse comments to the audiences. He demanded silence between songs and when one punter shouted for a song Young gave him this stern reply:

> Listen, let me tell you one thing. As a performer, when you play Carnegie Hall you look forward to it for a number of years. I don't take playing here lightly at all and I think that you should have enough faith in me to know that I would plan ahead and include all of the songs that I thought you'd want to hear. That's O.K. at the Maple Leaf Gardens ... but I'm not Grand Funk Railroad.[19]

If Young was stern at Carnegie, he was downright aggressive at the Boston Gardens a few weeks later. Before even reaching the end of the opening song he shouted at a member of the audience:

> Shut up! I can't do it! Hold it, hold it, hold it! I just want to tell everybody right now that I'm just not together enough tonight to put up with any shit and I won't play if there's a lot of noise, I'll just split.[20]

In spite of these critical comments, Young gave an intimate performance at all his shows. He held audiences captive, even though a large proportion of his set consisted of new material.

The intimacy that Young achieved during these solo gigs was mainly due to the fact that all his songs were presented in their bare acoustic form. While the electric "Down By The River" had ended the sets with Crazy Horse during the early part of the year, it was suddenly transformed into the opening acoustic number of his Carnegie set. There were other surprises too, most notably the acoustic versions of

"Cinnamon Girl", "The Loner", "Cowgirl In The Sand", "Ohio" and "Southern Man" all of which were previously well known electric cuts. Young appeared effortlessly to transform them into an acoustic framework, without losing any of the power or emotion that characterized the original electric versions. Carnegie Hall was a personal triumph and fully demonstrated Young's ability to take his own show on the road without the necessity of a backing group.

During that Carnegie concert Young introduced a couple of new numbers, including "Old Man" and "Bad Fog Of Loneliness". The latter was destined never to appear on any album, even though it was equally as good, and debatably better than much of the material that would appear on his next album. It was a standard Young love song with one hook line which provided a strong melody: "Bad fog of loneliness/Put a cloud on my single-mindedness". On stage at Carnegie, Young explained that he had recently performed the song on a yet to be broadcast Johnny Cash Show backed by Carl Perkins and the Tennessee Three. That particular revelation is significant for we know from later accounts that it was after the taping of that show that Young recruited co-stars James Taylor and Linda Ronstadt and immediately recorded two new songs "Heart Of Gold" and "Old Man". While in Nashville, Young put together a new group known as the Stray Gators comprising Ben Keith (steel-guitar); Tim Drummond (bass); Jack Nitzsche (piano and slide guitar); and Kenny Buttrey (drums). Together they recorded several tracks at the Quadrofonic Sound Studios in Nashville which would eventually appear on Young's next album. However, it would be over fourteen months before that album would appear. At this point, Young was capable only of recording acoustic material, and the songs requiring electric guitar would not be attempted until the New Year.

TEN

A Long And Bitter Harvest

Young continued working on his next studio album in January 1971, and it was predicted in the press that it would be released shortly after the completion of his tour. Due to his recent back operation it was certain that the majority of the tracks on the album would be acoustic as Young confirmed that it was virtually impossible for him to play an acoustic guitar. Meanwhile, his successful tour of America was winding to a close. Having fulfilled a personal ambition by playing at Carnegie Hall, in December, Young was set for another prestigious date in early February with a concert at the Dorothy Chandler Pavilion, the largest venue in the three-theater Los Angeles Music Center. This was the final concert of the tour, and it was of particular importance because, apart from Laura Nyro, no rock artist had ever been allowed to play there before. The Pavilion was famous for its presentation of operas, ballets and symphonies, and the staff of the Forum were quite astonished when hordes of Young fans turned up to queue for tickets. Such was the demand that the concert sold out within half an hour of the opening of the box-office. Young's appearance there on 1 February was as well received as the Carnegie concert and the critics applauded the unreleased songs, several of which were heard there for the first time. Aided by a traction machine and a brace securely fastened round his waist, Young performed a very strong set and successfully overcame his physical disability. Following the concert there was a party laid on for him upstairs at the Pavilion and the press noted that he had a new female companion, Carrie Snodgrass, star of the film, *Diary Of A Mad Housewife*. Carrie was, by this time, living with Young on a ranch that he had recently purchased in La Honda, California. The idyllic setting served as an inspiration to Young whose songwriting was becoming more prolific than ever.

Following the completion of the U.S. tour, Young managed to slot in a couple of performances in Britain. These took place in late February and included an in-concert performance for B.B.C. television and a show at the Royal Festival Hall. Young's promotional visit was greeted with warm accolades in the rock press and many critics were beginning to hail him as a more important figure than his other three contemporaries, Crosby, Stills & Nash. The sudden interest in Young as a solo performer was mainly due to the enormous success of *After The Goldrush*, which, in turn, had re-opened the Reprise catalog of Young's previous two albums.

Neil Young and *Everybody Knows This Is Nowhere* had suddenly become strong, steady sellers, and it seemed that Young could do no wrong.

The performance at the Royal Festival Hall sold out almost as quickly as Young's last U.S. concert at the Pavilion. It was clear that since the beginning of the tour Young's confidence in his performances had continued to grow. While most performers visiting a European country usually choose to play safe by churning out the old favorites, Young was determined to introduce the English audiences to his new material. The B.B.C. concert performance included nine songs, eight of which were previously unrecorded. While many might have expected Young to promote *After The Goldrush* heavily, he chose to include only three numbers from that album at his Royal Festival Hall concert. During that 80 minute performance Young played 21 songs, 11 of which were yet to appear on album. Incredibly, five of those still remained unreleased 2¾ years later, and only students of ancient history would recall that such songs as "Journey Through The Past", "The Bridge", "Love In Mind" and "See The Sky About To Rain" had been performed in England during February 1971. The success of Young's British concert ensured that anticipation of the next album was high. Apparently, the public would not have long to wait as Young had already mentioned his latest work onstage at the Royal Festival Hall:

> I've got this new song that I just wrote last night. I can't remember all the words and I forgot to bring out my piece of paper with them on it. It's going to be the title song on my next album – it's called "Harvest".[14]

Young did not return to the States immediately after his performance at the Royal Festival Hall but spent three days at Barking Town Hall, recording a couple of songs with the London Symphony Orchestra, which would eventually appear on *Harvest*. Apparently, Young's back trouble was still bothering him during these sessions and a special bed had to be brought in to accommodate his slipped disc. After completing these sessions, Young intended to stay in London for a while longer but his stay was abruptly terminated when he was ejected from his London flat for consistently causing excessive noise during the early hours of the morning. Indignant at the hospitability of the British, Young decided to take the next plane back to the States and left amid false rumors that he would be returning for an extensive tour during the late Spring.

Prior to Young's departure it was "officially" announced that his next album would be released immediately following his return to the States. The new work was not to be the expected *Harvest*, however, but an anthology consisting of live recordings from three dates – New York's Carnegie Hall; Washington D.C. "Cellar Door" and New York's Fillmore East. The songs had been carefully selected and consisted of tracks from every stage of Neil's career. The full track listing was as follows: "I Am A Child"; "Expecting To Fly"; "Flying On The Ground Is Wrong"; "Cowgirl In The Sand"; "Old Man"; "Dance Dance Dance"; "Ohio"; "See The Sky About To Rain"; "The Needle And The Damage Done"; "Nowadays Clancy Can't Even Sing"; "Sugar Mountain"; "Bad Fog Of Loneliness"; "Down By The River"; "Everybody Knows This Is Nowhere" and "Wondering". Those last three tracks had been recorded at the Fillmore East back in April 1969 with Crazy Horse. The remainder, however, were all culled from the recent tour and featured Neil solo with either an acoustic guitar or piano accompaniment. It seemed a promising release and the unusual nature of the album would ensure favorable reviews, while the success of the recent concert tour appeared to guarantee its commercial success. Upon returning to the States, Young had only to complete the mixing on a few tracks, which had been delayed because of his slipped disc and the British appearance.

Although the track listings appeared in every music paper and anticipation was high, the album, for some inexplicable reason, failed to appear. This was the first example of Young's eccentricity and his later tendency to delete or alter albums at the eleventh hour. No official explanation was ever given as to why the album did not appear. The public waited for a few months and then abandoned hope of ever seeing it. Almost immediately following the announcement of the projected "live" double album, it was rumored that the release of *Harvest* was imminent. It was to remain "imminent" for a considerable period.

One of the main reasons for the long delay in the release of *Harvest* was Young's continuing back trouble. The doctors had gone as far as discussing the possibility of confining Young to a wheelchair, so he decided to undergo an operation to have the discs removed. It was a depressing period, and Young recalls being reduced to an invalid and virtually unable to walk. The doctors allowed him to remain on his feet for only four hours a day and the remainder of the time he was confined to bed. Slowly recuperating, Young managed to complete the three electric tracks for the album, and it was ready to ship. Young, however, was not prepared for its release and certainly would not be able to promote it. He had, it seemed, temporarily lost interest in the glamor of the music business just at the point when his career was about to reach a creative peak. He delayed the release of the album by objecting to the cover design on several occasions. Apparently, the Warners-Reprise art department had selected a suitable photo of Young for inclusion on the album cover, but Neil took exception to it. In fact, he took exception to having any photo of himself placed on the cover. Young had always been a little peculiar in his choice of album sleeves, which had always included dark or out of focus shots of the artist. Even on his first album, he had allowed only a depiction of himself to be included. By the time of *Harvest*, however, his self-effacing nature had become an eccentricity. The record company concurred with his demands, although it meant holding up the album for a couple more months.

Young, in the meantime, spent some of 1972 working on his first film and for the remainder of this period he remained on his ranch. Young had become a virtual recluse, and he was anxious to shut out the world in order to live a more normal existence on his ranch with his lady, away from the distractions of life as a performer. Had he been a lesser artiste, it might have cost him his career, but Young's extended vacation gave him an additional mystique in much the same way as the disappearance of Bob Dylan did following his motor-cycle accident in 1966. Vanishing from the public eye at a point when both performers were most in demand obviously captured the public's imagination and, paradoxically, made them more popular than ever. Although Young released no solo records in 1971, his career was helped by the release of the C.S.N.&Y. live double-album, *Four Way Street*, in April.

The album was very well received in the rock press, but the British music papers were already beginning to reveal their bias. One review claimed, "Neil Young dominates what is more a one-way street". The implication of that phrase was that Young was streets ahead of his three companions, but the evidence of the live double hardly supported that partisan statement. One criticism of Young's contributions must be that he failed to come up with any new material, and as a result *Four Way Street* did little to help his status as the most prolific writer in the group. Even more surprisingly, the new material came from David Crosby and Graham Nash. Admittedly, Nash had yet to record his solo album and therefore had material in reserve, but the same could not be said of Crosby who had only recently released *If I Could Only Remember My Name*. It was a credit to the duo that they chose not to repeat songs such as "Triad", "The Lee Shore" and "Right Between The Eyes" on future projects. Young, on the other hand, hardly bothered to play his current repertoire, but plundered some of his earlier work. The acoustic renditions of "Cowgirl In The Sand" and the old Buffalo Springfield number, "On The Way Home" fitted nicely into his current set. Young had discarded the dated, pop version of "On The Way Home" and slowed the tempo to change the song into what sounded like a contemporary singer-songwriter composition. Similarly, "Cowgirl In The Sand", although defused of its electric power, still sounded impressive and arresting with just the lyrics and a simple acoustic backing. Both songs showed how effectively Young's material could be restructured. "Don't Let It Bring You Down", on the other hand, did not differ substantially from the version on *After The Goldrush* in spite of less instrumentation, and though the performance was very good, the choice of material was hardly adventurous enough.

The songs on the electric side are generally staunch without being spectacular. The only two problems from a critical point of view are the elongated versions of "Southern Man" and "Carry On"; the extended jams taking the form of a guitar battle between Stills & Young, reminiscent of the early Springfield days. It would probably be justifiable to say that these songs are allowed to go on for too long and neither matches the economy of the originals. However, these long jams were very fashionable during this period and Stills and Young do manage to trade some exciting riffs in places.

Overall, *Four Way Street* was reasonably successful as a double album, but it was hardly dominated by Neil Young as some critics of the period wanted to believe. With Crosby and Nash emerging with their dignities unimpaired and producing the only new songs in the set, a balance was achieved which made this double album confirm the premise of its title.

By late 1971, Young's popularity was so high that everything seemed to be working for him even though he was contributing nothing to the rock scene. Despite his semi-retirement on his ranch and the non-appearance of new material on *Four Way Street*, the public became more and more intrigued by the man and increasingly anxious to purchase his next album. The delay in releasing *Harvest* was, probably unconsciously, a brilliant example of record company marketing. Young's new audience, hungry for his songs, began to discover not only his first two albums, but also the old Buffalo Springfield efforts. By this time, Young's back catalog was booming and shifting far more vinyl than when it had first been released. It was anticipated that Reprise would issue *Harvest* just before Christmas and milk the market dry. Even that plan failed to materialize, however, and the album did not finally appear until February 1972.

Harvest became the biggest selling album of the year with sales in excess of two million. It was not a disappointment to the public, who were hoping for an album of love-lost songs from the forlorn folksinger. Young gave them everything that they wanted, and such was the album's success that it even spawned a couple of hit singles with "Heart Of Gold" and "Old Man". Young was apparently very pleased with the work from an aesthetic point of view and deemed it his favorite album. Later in his career, Young would frequently change his mind about what constituted his favorite or best album, but there is no doubt that he placed *Harvest* very high on the list. In spite of its commercial success, *Harvest* did not please everybody; the more perceptive critics of his work and his more discerning fans quite rightly felt uneasy about the new work. The content of the new album was probably the least adventurous material that Young had ever attempted, and several of the cuts were positively weak. What was most alarming, however, was that after such a long wait Young could offer only this work as the culmination of his efforts during the last 1½ years. The album suggested most strongly that Young was running short of ideas and in common with contemporaries such as James Taylor, he was beginning to repeat himself and seemed destined to continue doing so until his career ended. Admittedly, Young had altered his sound since *After The Goldrush* by teaming up the with The Stray Gators, and producing a country-tinged album in the heart of Nashville. However, the banjo and steel guitars were not sufficient to distract the more perceptive critics from the realization that Young was simply re-writing most of the songs on his last album.

In Britain, Young's credibility was not called into question, as it had been in certain critical quarters in the States. The possibility that Young had sold-out and was merely indulging in a lazy self-imitation was a speculation that no member of the British press appeared to entertain. Generally, the reviews were as exceptional as those afforded *After The Goldrush* and adjectives such as "brilliant" were bandied about very freely. In reality, of course, there was little of anything that could be termed brilliant about *Harvest*. It was melodic, pretty and listenable, but generally unarresting, and noticeably lackadaisical. The reason for the album's mellowness was partly due to Young's health and inability to play more than a few electric cuts, though nobody seemed too bothered by this at the time. Generally, the rock audience were more interested in his acoustic material than his electric rock songs. A reevaluation of the album reveals the extent of its shortcomings.

The laid back world weariness of "Out On The Weekend" sets the mood for much of the album. It is a very average song, pleasant, but unassuming. Neil plays some harmonies and Ben Keith adds some passable steel guitar to a track which is of minimal importance in the Young canon. The most positive thing that one could say about the track is that the playing is comparable to the mood of the song although it does not necessarily follow that music must be boringly repetitive and unadventurous in order to express a state of listlessness and resignation. Yet, this is precisely what "Out On The Weekend" attempts to do. The song betrays Young's escapist nature and disillusionment as early as the opening lines:

Think I'll pack it in
And buy a pick-up
Take it down to L.A.

Yet, the mood of the song reflects a sense of resignation rather than depression or melancholia. Young sees himself as "the lonely boy out on the weekend trying to make it pay". There is a certain ambiguity here in the sense that although the boy is "lonely" and appears to be going through the motions by venturing "out on the weekend", he still retains some hope of starting a "brand new day" by finding a suitable "place to call his own". The same analogy can be observed on the title track in which an optimistic chorus ("dream up dream up") is qualified by strongly pessimistic lines ("with your mother in so much pain"). Young explained that these songs were meant to express happiness, but he realized that the mood of these pieces could pretty well be summed up by the line, "I'm so down today":

> It's just my outlook. I guess my outlook is just bleak or desolate or something. I don't know. But even when I'm happy it sounds like I'm not. And when I try to say I'm happy I disguise it. Like I really say I'm really happy in the second part of that verse. I say I'm completely happy by saying, "can't relate to joy ... tries to speak and can't begin to say". That just means that I'm so happy that I can't get it all out. But it doesn't sound happy. The way I wrote it sounds sad, like I tried to hide it or something.[13]

For almost every reviewer the key cut on the album was "A Man Needs A Maid", which had been one of the most impressive new songs on his solo tour. It had a distinctive melody, some excellent piano-work and a moving vocal performance by Young. Like many of Young's songs, "A Man Needs A Maid" was the result of a sudden inspiration:

> This is a song I wrote under weird circumstances. I don't usually write too many songs too fast, but all of a sudden I found myself not being able to move around too much, in a bed a lot, and my mind started wandering and when I got home I kept hearing this song over and over in my head. I didn't know what it meant when I first started hearing it. I'm starting to see what it means now.[15]

For some people, it was clear the song meant what its title suggested – a man's need for a female housekeeper. This opened Young to some half-serious attacks from critics who quickly seized upon its chauvinistic lines. However, the real point of the song was to document Young's insecurity about starting another relationship. The second line "I don't know who to trust anymore" indicated Young's uncertainty, and the idea of employing a maid, reflected the desire to maintain an uncompli-cated, purely platonic relationship. The last line of the song, "when will I see you again" hints at an emotional involvement but this seems to be directed not at the maid, as some critics have suggested, but rather the woman for whom the maid is seen as a suitable replacement.

While the song remains one of the album's strongest cuts, it clearly falls short of the standard it might have achieved had Young taken more care with the arrangement. When he played the song in concert it was one of his most haunting numbers and included a memorable piano accompaniment. On the album, however, much of his work is drowned by the strings of the L.S.O., and the vocal mix is nothing less than atrocious. The sentiments of "A Man Needs A Maid" reveal Young at his most selfconscious, but while the feelings appear to be simple and genuine they tread a very delicate line between self-awareness and self-indulgence. With the introduction of the booming L.S.O. Young clearly overstepped that line and made "A Man Needs A Maid" a monument to his own narcissism. The simple comment about a need for a maid is blasted out and made to appear ludicrously grandiloquent by the full scale orchestral accompaniment. This tendency is even more evident on "There's A World" in which the strings, flutes, harps and violins build the song up to ludicrous proportions and ultimately highlight its inadequacies as a composition.

"Heart Of Gold" by virtue of its success as a single is probably one of Young's most well known tracks. It is also one of the better cuts on the album with some very reasonable additional vocals by Linda Ronstadt and James Taylor. One of the reasons for the mass of advanced orders for *Harvest* was that prior to its release this track was played almost simultaneously on every radio-station across the breadth of America. Young recalls the success of the single with some amusement:

> This song put me in the middle of the road. Traveling there soon became a bore, so I headed for the ditch. A rougher ride, but I saw some interesting people there.[8]

One of the tracks to be recorded for the album was "Are You Ready For The Country" which Young recorded in 1972, following the operation on his back. In spite of the appearance of Crosby and Nash, the track is little more than average, and one suspects that Young had several other tracks which might have proved far more suitable.

"Old Man", which opens side 2, is one of the few tracks from Young's solo tour which sounds as though it has been improved by the addition of the Stray Gators. The banjo and steel-guitar work effectively together and Young puts in a fine vocal performance. Young recalls how he wrote the song:

> This is a song I wrote about my ranch. I moved up North to the country. When I bought the place there was this old man who was working there for the people I bought it from. He was about 70 years old. He was a cattleman, and that's like something that's never going to happen again. The cattle business isn't like it was 40 years ago. It's like something that's still alive, but it's dead. So I wrote a song about it.[15]

"Alabama" is another of the album's saving graces, with some distinctive harmonies by Crosby and Nash, and probably the only good guitar break on the entire album. Even here, however, it is possible to accuse Young of attempting to re-write "Southern Man" in order to get more fuel out of an old audience favorite. This is a little unfair, however, since "Alabama" is substantially different in tone. The anger that characterized "Southern Man" is largely replaced by a reasoning voice that questions why the state of Alabama is out of step with the rest of America:

You got the rest of the Union to help you along
What's going wrong?

"The Needle And The Damage Done", Young's statement about heroin addiction, seems direct, simple and sincere, yet one cannot escape the feeling that something is wrong with it. Listening to the song, it becomes clear that Young's attitude to heroin addiction is annoyingly ambivalent. His feelings can be gleaned from this statement that he made to an audience while introducing the number:

> This is a serious song I'd like to do about some people that you know, some people that I know, and some people that neither one of us knows. It's about heroin addiction. Somewhere in the universe there's probably a place where all the great art is that didn't get out. A museum of incredible art that didn't get out because of heroin. It's probably somewhere.[15]

Although Young seems aware of the problems of heroin addiction he appears to be unable or unwilling to accept the full implications of his subject. He claims he has written a "serious" song about heroin addiction, but the second part of his statement is nothing less than romanticized drivel. Young's conception of an incredible museum of lost art shows his unwillingness to face the facts of drug addiction, and the failure to come to grips with his subject is as noticeable in the song as it was in that onstage preamble.

The song appears to be an account of Danny Whitten's fall into drug addiction with references to the Cellar Door club, and the revelation of how Young lost his band, Crazy Horse, due to his guitarist's heroin problem. Given the autobiographical setting, one can accept Young's expressions of sympathy and even the exonerating line, "a little part of it in everyone" is almost acceptable in its context. What is far from acceptable or convincing, however, is Young's final simile – "But every junkie's like a setting sun". This is undoubtedly the most inappropriate image ever used by Young. A "setting sun" is one of nature's most beautiful and aesthetically pleasing images but there is nothing moving or aesthetically pleasing about a dying junkie. Ultimately, "The Needle And The Damage Done" is as sugar-coated as many of the other songs on this album. The effect of that final line is to glorify heroin addiction, something which Young surely had not consciously wished to do.

Young's closing statement "Words" is lyrically, melodically and instrumentally unimpressive. Neil's solo prior to the final verse seems intended as the highlight of the song, but his playing is merely pedestrian. Even the unusual combination of Young, Stills and Nash does nothing to salvage the song from mediocrity. A disappointing conclusion to an unimpressive album.

ELEVEN

A Journey Into Darkness

In spite of its aesthetic limitations and artistic shortcomings, *Harvest* was sufficient to maintain Young's superstar status during the early months of the seventies. Many saw the album as a natural extension of the work he had been doing with Crosby, Stills & Nash. In fact, public interest in the foursome continued, even though Young now seemed established as a star in his own right. It was reported in the press that Crosby, Stills, Nash & Young were scheduled to tour sometime in 1972 and such a supposition did not seem unreasonable. In fact, at the end of 1971 there had been a reunion of sorts at a Crosby and Nash gig. As he had done at a previous Boston date, Stephen Stills wandered on stage at Carnegie Hall, New York, and played alongside his friends for 30 minutes. He was replaced on stage by Neil Young, who also played a few songs from the then unreleased *Harvest*. That was the closest they got to recording a new abum or appearing together as a quartet. As the months passed, it became clear that the projected reunion had not materialized, and in spite of the press reports, it had never really been considered.

Rumors next began to circulate that Young was planning to commence touring early in 1972, but the dates kept getting put back further and further as the year progressed. Young did make one appearance in late March, when he again guested with Crosby and Nash during their performance at Winterland. Neil sang "Harvest"; "Only Love Can Break Your Heart"; "Heart Of Gold"; and "The Needle And The Damage Done" but in spite of the appreciative response he continued to resist the temptation to embark on another solo tour.

The success of *Harvest* was beginning to affect Young in different ways. Its most immediate effect was to provide him with enough wealth and security to feel safe on his ranch. Young was particularly optimistic during his early days on the ranch:

> I feel more free now than I've ever felt before. Last night, I sat down at the piano and played three songs for Carrie. I've never been able to do that before. I still can't play "A Man Needs A Maid", but I can play all the other ones.[13]

Contented by success, Young simultaneously felt restless, perhaps realizing the need to explore new ideas rather than merely repeat the old themes. His self-imposed isolation on his ranch was broken in order to complete the film that he had been promising to make for some time. Young's determination to become a success as a filmmaker continued, and for virtually the whole of 1972 he thought of little else. While his audience waited patiently for the next *Harvest*, Young had already moved on to thoughts of celluloid rock and other strange notions. What the rest of the world regarded as a permanent distinctive style on *Harvest* was, for Young, only one extension of his personality:

> Everybody said that *Harvest* was a trip. To me, I'd happened to be in the right place at the right time to do a really mellow record that was really open, 'cause that's where my life was at the time. But that was me only for a couple of months. If I'd stayed there, I don't know where I'd be right now – if I'd just stayed real mellow. I'm just not that way anymore. I think *Harvest* was probably the finest record that I've made, but that's really a restricting adjective for me. It's really *fine* ... but that's all.[21]

Young obviously hoped that his entry into the film-world would prove as successful as his recent selling album. At first, the project seemed promising. Young's record company, Warner Brothers, agreed to finance *Journey Through The Past* on condition that Neil would provide them with the soundtrack album of the movie. Such a clause did not seem unreasonable, although it was uncertain precisely how much music there would be in the film. Soon, it became apparent that Young would be including a substantial amount of his musical past in the movie and it was suspected that the completed soundtrack would be a musical documentary of his career. This seemed even more likely when it was learned that Neil was to use some footage of Crosby, Stills, Nash & Young in concert. A couple of years earlier, the foursome had been planning to make their own film based on the "Wooden Ships" theme. Following this abortive project, they had financed David Myers and L.A. Johnson to make a movie of Crosby, Stills, Nash & Young in concert and on the road. Although a lot of film was taken, the project was again shelved, which was very fortunate for Young who was allowed to freely plunder the footage and select what he required for his own movie.

Young next went to the major television networks in New York and emerged with some very rare film of the Buffalo Springfield shot in 1967. Young also borrowed some footage from A.B.C. television's coverage of the Billy Graham youth rally at which Richard Nixon had guested, and the whole ensemble had joined together to sing a chorus of "God Bless America". From these various sources Young intended to put together a film which would be presented in the form of a fantasy. It seemed an interesting project, and the extent of Young's commitment suggested that it had a strong chance of being both commercially successful and aesthetically rewarding.

With the continuing success of *Harvest* and a first film in production Young looked set for even greater fame. The birth of Neil and Carrie's son Zeke in the late autumn concluded a rewarding period in Young's life. From that point onwards, everything seemed to go wrong. In late 1972, rehearsals began for Neil's first tour in over 1½ years; it was to be the biggest of his career and would include dates at most major U.S. cities over a three month period. Neil decided to take the Stray Gators as his backing group, but he also invited his old friend Danny Whitten in order to assist with the lead-guitar work. Whitten was apparently attempting to overcome his drug addiction which had worsened since the days of Crazy Horse. Whitten had begun by injecting amphetamines and had almost immediately turned to heroin. By the time he reached Young, Whitten was taking large compensatory doses of various drugs and alcohol in order to satisfy his insatiable appetite for heroin. Early in the rehearsals, it became clear that Whitten would be an impossible burden on the road and there was no way that Young could work with him. The group drove him to the airport and put him on a plane to Los Angeles, allowing him fifty dollars spending money. That last generous gesture was used by Whitten to finance his own self-destruction. He scored some pure heroin, injected it that night and was found dead the following morning.

Young recalls the circumstances leading up to Whitten's death:

> We were rehearsing with him and he just couldn't cut it. He couldn't remember anything. He was too out of it. Too far gone. I had to tell him to go back to L.A. "It's not happening, man. You're not together enough." He just said, "I've got nowhere else to go, man. How am I gonna tell my friends?". He split. That *night* the coroner called me from L.A. and told me he'd ODed. That blew my mind ... I loved Danny.[10]

Whitten's death had a profound effect on Young, particularly since their last parting had not been a happy one. Neil has even suggested feeling a sense of guilt because his necessary rejection of Whitten was a factor leading to the guitarist's death. Such self-reproach seems unreasonable, however, since there is no evidence to suggest that Whitten's death was anything other than an accidental overdose. For the remainder of 1972, things continued to worsen for Neil Young. Warners decided not to release the film *Journey Through The Past* until the following year, and Young realized from their attitude that they were clearly not in favor of the album. Eventually, they withdrew their services completely, forcing Young to look for another distributor. In November, however, Warners-Reprise did issue the movie soundtrack, which was a disastrous decision. The double album was heavily criticized in almost every music paper as a flagrant piece of opportunism on the part of Young and his record company. The critics universally agreed that the material on *Journey Through The Past* was so dire that it amounted to mere exploitation. In the absence of new material Young was cashing in on the success of *Harvest* by issuing a totally irrelevant and ill-conceived two album set. Even the most partisan of Young's admirers in the British music press were forced to admit that *Journey Through The Past* was a gross mistake, and added sheepishly that perhaps the film might make some sense of the album. But the U.S. critics quite rightly argued that no film could excuse such a shambling apology of an album.

Reviewing the work, one is inclined to wholeheartedly support the American point of view. The opening cuts of the Buffalo Springfield, taken from "The Hollywood Palace" seem of little more than archivist interest. The snatch of "For What It's Worth" and the confident "Mr. Soul" sound vaguely interesting, but the recording quality is too primitive to make them anything other than of passing interest. We are told by a television announcer that the Buffalo Springfield are responsible for creating "the western sound" and in an attempt to prove it the group burst into a version of "Rock 'n Roll Woman" which sounds of even poorer quality than the preceding material. The abrupt switch to Crosby, Stills, Nash & Young provides an interesting contrast with a sensitive and harmonic version of "Find The Cost Of Freedom", traditionally the closing number of their set. On this occasion, however, it merges into a powerful electric version of "Ohio", with Neil playing his heart out towards the end and Crosby giving everything his lungs have to offer. Although this version of "Ohio" is one of the better cuts on the album, and superior in almost every department to the live version that appeared on *Four Way Street*, with two other very similar versions already in circulation on single and album one is still led to question whether it should have been included.

While side one of the album is disappointing, the second side is even worse. A demand for "Talahassie Lassie" (which might at least have been amusing!) precedes an average plodding version of "Southern Man". Again, it is the third version of the song to have appeared since *After The Goldrush* just over two years before. The song meanders on for almost 13 minutes, and one realizes that Young has now spent literally a whole album's worth of vinyl in various recordings of this one song. Irrelevent snippets of "Are You Ready For The Country" and a chorus of "Let Me Call You Sweetheart" along with the sound of chirping crickets precede the start of another familiar song, "Alabama", which admittedly does seem a good version. Unfortunately, it is cut off before it has even begun in order to revert to an earlier rehearsal in which we hear how the song was created. Although this gives us some insight into how carefully Young and his cohorts work out their harmonies, it is hardly rivetting listening.

One begins to suspect that the concept of the album may have been to start off with the worst material ever recorded by Young with the aim of defying the listener's belief by making each successive side even more horrendous. Certainly, Young achieves this on the third side by taking a sub-standard song, "Words" and showing us that the version on *Harvest* could conceivably have been worse. This "new" elongated version of the song meanders along for just under 16 minutes and ultimately gets nowhere. For this whole exercise to be placed on a record seems an unparalleled example of self-indulgence.

By the final side, one cannot believe that Young can sink any further, though he does make a fair attempt. The only thing that can be more annoying than bad Neil Young on a Neil Young album is, of course, no Neil Young at all. So, on side four, Young attempts only one cut and leaves the remainder of the side to the Tabernacle Choir and the Beach Boys. A pseudo-theological "debate" between Young and a Jesus freak is followed by a quick blast of Handel's Messiah. The "King of King's Theme" is a little more appropriate and actually does sound like reasonable soundtrack material. This is followed by more of Young's religious scepticism in the form of "Soldier" in which he states an atheistic point of view:

Jesus I saw you
Walkin' on the river
I don't believe you.
You can't deliver right away
I wonder why.

If on this side of the album Young was trying to make some kind of religious statement then the results were embarrassingly feeble. However, in the light of the "political" material on the previous side, the inanity is not particularly surprising. As a song, "Soldier" is not noticeably memorable, although it is certainly no worse than some of the *Harvest* cuts. The final track, the Beach Boys' "Lets Go Away For Awhile" (from *Pet Sounds*) appears to be included for no other reason that that it is pleasant soundtrack music.

Journey Through The Past stands as the most bizarre recording in the Young canon. It is also a very strong contender for the title of "worst album ever made in the history of rock music". One question that still remains is why the soundtrack album was ever released. Young feels that he was placed under pressure to do the soundtrack album and agreed to the idea because he wanted to appear in his own film. Although he seems to place most of the blame on the coercive tactics of Reprise he does at least admit that he sacrificed himself as a musician in order to do the project. While Young's motives seem clear, and it must be said that they appear very selfish, one wonders why he did not call a halt to the release of the soundtrack after Warners had pulled out of the project. Presumably, it was by then too late and contractual problems bound him to the project. However, this does not explain Reprise's decision to release the album. From a marketing point of view their decision was ludicrously myopic. They obviously realized the commercial impact of *Harvest* and knew that any Neil Young product would shift a lot of units. However, following *After The Goldrush*, Young had taken 1½ years to release *Harvest* and it seemed likely that it might be even longer before he released his next album. *Journey Through The Past* was, in essence, an attempt at striking while the iron was hot. No matter how dire the product, an album from Neil Young was worth its weight in gold. By the time his next album appeared his critical fortunes might have, in any case, declined, so why wait? This was, of course, illogical reasoning on behalf of the company. The long gap between *After The Goldrush* and *Harvest* had not hindered the progress of Young's career but appeared to have aided it handsomely. The release of *Journey Through The Past*, on the other hand, seriously threatened to kill the chicken that was laying the golden discs. Its release would produce a sales rush but that would soon subside in the wake of universal criticism, leaving Young's long term career in danger of premature extinction. It would take all of Young's talent to salvage his tarnished reputation during the succeeding years. Both Young and Reprise would later separate the soundtrack from the main body of Neil Young's releases, yet, at the time, the album was promoted as though it were an official new work from the artiste. Even the title, *Journey Through The Past* was deceptive, making the album seem a retrospective anthology of Young's work. One also wonders how many people must have bought the album in anticipation of hearing the unreleased track "Journey Through The Past" which, ironically, was not even included on the soundtrack. Whichever way you view the album, it remains the greatest artistic blunder in Young's career.

The failure of the soundtrack album did not bode well for the film, though Young remained confident. He managed to find a new distributor and it seemed as though the film might be in the cinemas by the beginning of 1973. However, Young had not realized the number of legal problems that would result from his decision to include certain episodes in the movie. The confrontation with the Jesus freak on the street apparently could not be shown without clearance, and neither could the broadcast of "God Bless America" without the permission of composer, Irving Berlin. As if these problems were not enough, Young's hopes for international recognition were shattered when the film was banned in Britain. Young maintains that the excessive swearing and derogatory references to Christ were the factors which upset the British censor, but this seems very unlikely. England is not one of the most conservative countries in the Christian community, and blasphemy would hardly have been an adequate reason for banning the film. It seems likely that the graphic display of a junkie injecting heroin into his arm was the real controversial element in the film and prompted the British Board of Censors to refuse it a certificate.

The film was eventually premiered at the U.S. Film Festival in Dallas on 8 April 1973. An excited audience applauded as the film began, but seemed rather less enthusiastic by the time the final credits had appeared on the screen. Their reaction was hardly surprising. In effect, the film was as disjointed as the soundtrack album had seemed. There was no plot as such but rather a series of incidents involving a central character known as the Graduate who gets beaten up and left in the middle of a desert. From there he begins to wander and he is threatened by both the Church and the Military as the film unfolds. Interspersed with this main action are some of the sequences from the soundtrack involving the Jesus freak, the Nixon rally, the concert and television footage, plus the controversial junkie scene and a recurring nightmare involving a dozen black hooded Ku Klux Klan figures. Bob Porter of *The Dallas-Times Herald* was the only critic sent to review the premier and his comments were surprisingly sympathetic:

> *Journey Through The Past* comes off as sort of a cinematic contempla-
> tion of the navel. The film will probably disappoint those fans seeking
> the music of Young and be of value primarily to those searching souls
> looking for a view of the outside world from inside the hectic,
> confused, and confusing world of rock music ...[22]

Even Porter, however, could see no real point in the film and felt that the philosophy was too simplistic to be convincing. He even briefly considered the possibility that the film might be a spoof on "arty", meaningless posturings before reaching the conclusion that the work was probably an example of artistic juvenilia: Young was not too depressed by the bad reviews which followed the film's national screening later in the year:

> The film community doesn't want to see me in there. What do they
> want with *Journey Through The Past*? It's got no plot. No point. No
> stars. They don't want to see that. But the next time, man, we'll get
> them. The next time. I've got all the equipment, all the ideas and
> motivation to make another picture.[10]

In retrospect, Young felt satisfied with his work:

> I just made a feeling. It's hard to say what the movie means. I think it's
> a good film for a first film. I think it's a really good film. I don't think I
> was trying to say that life is pointless. It does lay a lot of shit on people
> though. It wasn't made for entertainment. I'll admit, I made it for

myself. Whatever it is, that's the way I felt. I made it for me. I never even had a script.[10]

Young was so concerned about the reception the film might receive that he showed up at the premier and watched the movie from the projectionist's booth. In spite of the less than stupendous applause, Young was excited enough to appear in front of the screen and invite a question and answer session. Young's friends and even his management seemed guarded in their opinions of the film; generally, they were polite and reticent in their comments but there was a definite lack of enthusiasm. They seemed more concerned about the next film which they claimed would be a big improvement. From the public reaction in America, however, one could not escape the feeling that without Neil Young's name on the credits, the film would have been laughed off the screen. Young's final comments on the situation were that he would never make another film that had anything to do with himself or his music. That statement would later prove the most bitter irony of all.

While awaiting the premier of *Journey Through The Past* Young underwent three months of solid touring with the Stray Gators, from January to March. It was not one of Young's favorite periods. The performances were erratic which was hardly surprising when we consider that Young played something like 60 shows in three short months. Some reviews of the period stated that the shows were far too short, but most of them were the same length, if not longer than the performances during the 1971 tour. There was no question, however, that the group did play a few bad dates. One of the reasons for this was the tense relationship between Young, the group and the road crew. Apparently, the Stray Gators became dissatisfied with their wages and began to demand a percentage of the gate as compensation. Young rightly felt indignant as agreements had already been made about profit-sharing. The attitude of the group upset Young, and according to manager Elliot Roberts, it made him more cynical and gave him an even greater awareness of the problems produced by stardom. As the tour progressed, there were more problems. Drummer Kenny Buttrey was finding the performances too grueling and he was soon replaced by Johnny Barbata, whom Young had played with during the last C.S.N.&Y. tour. David Crosby recalls some of the other problems Young encountered during the tour:

> Neil had built himself a juggernaut. One of the problems he'd saddled himself with was Jack Nitzsche. He's a very bad person ... The guy isn't a nice cat. When he gets whacko, he does bad stuff. Lots of bad stuff. He tries to pick fights with people. He tried to pick one with me. I told him to stay out of my way or I'd take his head off his shoulders, and I meant it.

The pressures resulting from the tour encouraged Young to think in terms of getting some additional vocal support. Eventually, he phoned Crosby & Nash and persuaded them to join the tour:

> Neil didn't really need our help but he did call us and asked us to come, very specifically. He called me and asked me to come. He said it wasn't going very well, and that he needed our help. There was another reason why I was out there. At the time, my mother was in

84

hospital dying of cancer. I needed the music. It's my major magic. It's the one thing to hang on to when things get crazy. It was the only thing to hang on to when Christine (his girlfriend) died and it was the only thing to hang on to when my mother died. That's why I wanted to be there.

Following the recruitment of Crosby & Nash the shows generally improved and by the time Young played the L.A. Forum at the end of March the set had extended to over 100 minutes. Even at this gig, however, Young was far from satisfied. While playing the acoustic set, he chided the audience for making too much noise between and during the songs. Yet, throughout the electric set, he was clearly worried by the lack of audience response:

> Music is like everything else, it goes up and down. We played some really good nights and a couple of bad ones. But a couple of times we played pretty hot at some places, and they freaked out. We've played one or a couple of tunes better tonight, to my ears, than we did there. And I can't here you! So make some noise! It'll make you feel good when you go home or something. If you don't want to do that, then grab the person beside you – whatever it is. These places are so big, it's not intimate like a 2,000 seat place. But there's nothing like 18,000 people all boogieing at once. I don't want to force it on you, but we're gonna try to get you there.[23]

Young's devil-may-care attitude was reflected in the playing which was very loose at times. The trio did at least appear to be enjoying themselves, however, and there was much joking about the audience's need to hear old songs. As if to comment upon this, the group burst into an impromptu "Mr. Tambourine Man" and a few bars later Young sang a couple of lines from the Seeds' "Pushing Too Hard".

In spite of the onstage camaraderie, Young's comment about the lack of intimacy in playing to 18,000 people was valid. By the end of the tour, Young was tired and a little bitter about the events of the last few months. The feelings he voiced onstage at the L.A. Forum were not forgotten, but repeated very strongly when Young condemned those gigs as "circuses". Looking back at the tour, Young began to feel that he was losing contact with his audience:

> That wasn't what we were chasing from the start, was it? I've been right through that trip of massive audiences and my ego has been satisfied. I guess I had to do it and I guess all these bands that are doing it have to do it, but once you've done it, then what? You realize that's not what communicating is all about.[24]

Young vowed that he would forgo the stadiums, and return to playing small halls:

> I want to be able to see the people I'm playing for and I want the people I play to to feel that the music is being made just for them – you bounce off people that way. Get up, jump around, have a good time, get drunk – at least let's see each other. That's what I go to a concert for.[24]

Apart from the problems with his backing group one of the key factors in influencing Young's reaction against large venues was the notorious assault during the performance of "Southern Man" at the Oakland Coliseum, San Francisco. The "crunching" of the fan by an over-zealous cop not only stopped Young performing "Southern Man" but made him think about the consequences of playing at enormous stadiums:

> It was a terrible affair. It was like I was watching myself on T.V. and someone had pulled out the plug I was playing on, but I couldn't believe what I'd just seen. I was disconnected. Then I got out of that place and I said to myself: "Who *needs* it?"
>
> Who needs to be a dot in the distance for 20,000 people and give the cops another excuse to get uptight and stop kids being happy? The circus might be all right for some acts but it's not for me anymore. I'm tired of signing to a cop, that's all.

The disillusionment felt by Young during this dark period was to remain with him for a considerable time.

TWELVE

Neil Young Fades Away

The recent appearances of Crosby & Nash onstage with Young led to the familiar speculation that a C.S.N.&Y. reunion was in the offing. It seemed an even stronger likelihood when the four artists got together at Lahaina on the island of Maui in Hawaii to discuss a possible reformation. This latest attempt at making an album was a very serious project and every member thought carefully about such questions as what material to use, and whether a few warm-up gigs would be desirable. The quartet rehearsed some new songs and, according to Tim Drummond, recorded Nash's "And So It Goes", "The Prison Song" (both of which later appeared on *Wild Tales*), Young's "Human Highway" and three others. Crosby remembers the album that was never completed:

> It would have been the best album we ever made. It was going to be called *Human Highway*. "Time After Time" was saved for it, as was "Homeward Through The Haze" and "Wind On The Water". The cover of the album was to be an Hawaiian sunset. It was the last picture on a roll of film. A stunner. Nash took it; he set the timer. It was the best picture anyone ever took of us. It would have been the best C.S.N.&Y. album.

Crosby's contention is provocative, but possibly correct. The quartet certainly seemed to have enough material available to produce an exceptional work. Apart from the tracks already mentioned, several more were intended for possible use including Crosby's "Carry Me"; Nash's "Another Sleep Song" and "You'll Never Be The Same"; Stills' "My Angel" and "As I Come Of Age" and Young's "Hawaiian Sunrise"; "Sailboat Song", "New Mama" and "Mellow My Mind". With this much material they could even have made an impressive double album. According to Nash, one of the reasons that so much material was available was because at their inception, the quartet had made an unwritten agreement to hold back their best songs for possible C.S.N.&Y. projects. In Crosby & Nash's case this had even resulted in a dearth of recorded output as they continually postponed solo ventures in anticipation of another group recording. But, for all their patience, the album remained uncompleted. They moved to Young's ranch for further inspiration, but by the late summer they abandoned the project and returned to their respective ventures.

A Crosby, Stills, Nash & Young reunion would have no doubt provided Neil with critical and commercial acclaim at a time when his career seemed on the skids, but fortunately, at this stage in his development, Young suddenly seemed unconcerned about achieving mass acclaim. The fame and money that he had received since *Harvest* was gratifying, but during the past few months Young had seen the negative side of commercial success. The resentment of his backing group to the wages situation; the alienation felt from playing enormous venues; the exploitation from people he had hoped were trusted friends – all these were unforeseen results of Young's sudden rise to superstardom. It was scarcely any wonder then, that he had not pushed hard for a reunion with his superstar colleagues. The idea of scoring more hit singles, as he had done in 1977 with "Old Man" and "Heart Of Gold", also suddenly seemed unimportant:

> I've dropped "Heart Of Gold" from my concerts now, anyway, so you can see how heavily I'm into perpetuating my singles! That track was not made as a single – we went into the studio to cut the album and I guess we were hot that night and it was a good cut but it's gone now.
>
> I've seen a few artists who've got hung up on the singles market when they're really albums people. The tell-tale sign is when you try to get off a wagon that comes naturally to you. It's easy to do, but if you're wise, you stay with being what you really are. I want to be able to live with myself ... I just hope there is not a single off my next album.[24]

Young's almost intentional avoidance of commercial success seemed an extraordinary move. He realized that, for many people, his attitude would seem wrong and his decision to maintain a low profile would appear a big mistake:

> Well, I guess I can understand that view but I'm at the point where I feel the strain of having had a certain amount of success. I'm still passing through, feeling my way. I haven't come out at the other end yet, and I'm not dead. I've got to go on living, being myself, really.

The strain that Young was undergoing and the need to continue living was reinforced by what was happening all around him. Having returned from the abortive Hawaii sessions, Young learned the tragic news that C.S.N.&Y. roadie, Bruce Berry, had also died of a heroin overdose. The deaths of Whitten and Berry followed each other in such quick succession that they shocked Young into action. His depression appears to have been replaced by the need to make some sort of musical statement. Young quickly re-assembled Crazy Horse, brought in Nils Lofgren and Ben Keith to fill the musical gap left by Whitten's death, and together they began playing in a small rehearsal room at Ken Barry's Studio Instrument Rentals. In August they played a warm-up gig at the Corral in Topanga Canyon. It was a charity gig in aid of the Community Center and joining Young on the bill were both Joni Mitchell and the Eagles. Here, Young introduced a few new songs that he had been rehearsing with Crazy Horse, but the reviewers failed to perceive that anything new was happening. All that anyone noted was that Neil looked very scruffy and seemed less a musician than a farm hand. Young enjoyed the gig, however, and playing alongside Crazy Horse in his former Topanga home inspired him to develop these loose rehearsals into something more substantial.

What had began as an informal get together was suddenly transformed into an idea for a new album, totally unlike anything Young had previously recorded. Young recalls the bizarre sessions:

> What we were doing was playing those guys on their way. We all got that high – not *that* high, but we got as close as we could. I mean, I'm not a junkie and I won't ever try it out to check out what it's like. But we'd get really high – drink a lot of tequila, get right out on the edge, where we knew we were so screwed up that we could easily just fall on our faces, and not be able to handle it as musicians. But we were wide open also at that time – just wide open. So we'd just wait until the middle of the night until the vibe hit us and just do it. We did four or five songs on the first side all in a row one night, without any break. We did "Tonight's The Night", "World On A String", "Mellow My Mind", "Speakin' Out" and "Tired Eyes", without any break between 'em.[21]

Although Danny Whitten could not be there, Young believes that the music they made at those sessions captured the true spirit of Crazy Horse.

These sessions effectively demonstrated Young's new attitude to recording as there was no attempt to overdub any vocals after the event or to alter the performance in any way. Unlike Young's earlier work, this new album would not attempt to disguise his limitations as a vocalist. Even for Young, the playback of the songs that they had performed provided something of a shock:

> It blew my mind when I saw what was happening. We knew it was different when we were doing it – everything live, everybody playing and singing at the same time. There was no overdubbing on those nine songs that were done at S.I.R. That's the way the old blues people used to do it. It was really real. And we did the mixes right away.

Mixing the album also proved a formidable task since it was virtually the same as working on a live recording.

In September, having cut several tracks, Neil took this new version of Crazy Horse on the road. Almost immediately they were chosen to top the bill at the opening of Hollywood's Roxy-Theater on 20 September. With Graham Nash as support, Neil headlined two shows an evening for four nights. The gigs were not well reviewed mainly because Young was in the full throes of confounding his dedicated audience. He played nine new songs consecutively with "Cowgirl In The Sand" as an *encore*, and that was it. The audience was shouting for "Cinnamon Girl" and other well-known numbers, but Young appeared to be oblivious to their demands, and spent much time mumbling about Miami Beach and other strange things. The Roxy stage decor was also a little unusual that night. The lighting was very dim, and set in the middle of the stage was a palm tree, a wooden Indian and a grand piano from which dangled several old boots. Many of the punters assumed the whole thing to be a sleazy joke on Young's part designed to provide the Roxy with a memorable opening night. Young clearly enjoyed his rapport with the audience and probably felt a new freedom in allowing himself to drink as much as he wished, knowing that the more loose he became, the more it would complement his music. In a fit of generosity, he even offered to buy the Roxy audience a free round of drinks. According to Lofgren, Young's managers were more than a little upset about this innocent altruistic act:

> One night Neil ordered a round of drinks for the audience, on the house. Remember he was playing three nights, six sets for free, as a favor to Lou Adler and David Geffen and the other people who owned the place. Between sets his managers came up and were yelling and screaming in his face. I couldn't believe it. They said, "What are you doing ordering a free round of drinks ... do you know that's a potential $1,200 worth of profit?" I mean 400 drinks is about $50 worth of booze. David Briggs (Young's producer) just jumped up and stared in their faces – he couldn't believe it either ... What it actually came down to was his own managers were telling him and David that they wouldn't buy a round of drinks for any reason and they (David and Neil) must be really stupid ... In the end they were hassling Neil so bad that David said, "screw you guys, leave him alone, I'll pay for the drinks." Neil and David agreed to split it and his managers said, "Well OK dummy if you're stupid enough to do it we'll let you pay for it."[17]

Whether there was any real pressure upon Young from his management to curb some of the excesses of his new act remains unclear. But if the audience at the Roxy felt that this was to be merely a one-off gig, the next couple of months would prove them very wrong.

In October, Young's past caught up with him when selections from his last tour were issued in the form of *Time Fades Away*. The concept of releasing a live album consisting of all new material was an original one, and Young might have expected some critical commendation. The content of the album, however, ensured that he would receive a stormy reception. A large proportion of the public and the critics had been angered by *Journey Through The Past*, but it was still hoped that Young would come bouncing back with an album of carefully constructed love songs. *Time Fades Away* was anything but carefully constructed. It revealed a new Young, rough at the edges, imprecise, and uncompromising. For many writers it was clearly the last straw. Even the faithful English critics realized that they had lost the Young of *Harvest* fame, and one review summed up their feelings with the heading "Neil Young Fades Away".

In spite of the less than favorable reviews Neil had no regrets about releasing the album:

> ... I imagine I could have come up with the perfect follow-up album. A real winner. But it would have been something that everybody was expecting. And when it got there they would have thought that they understood what I was all about and that would have been it for me. I would have painted myself in a corner. The fact is I'm not that lone, laid-back figure with a guitar. I'm just not that way anymore. I don't want to feel like people expect me to be a certain way. Nobody

Courtesy Warner/Reprise

Neil Young in Buffalo Springfield days.

London Features International

Courtesy Warner/Reprise

Young at a
C.S.N.&Y. gig
in 1970.

London Features International/Neal Preston

Young in 1975.

Young and Stills
exchanging riffs
in 1980.

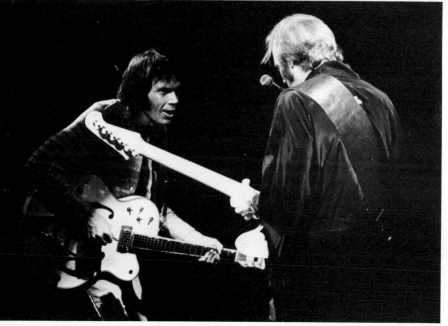

A still from
Young's film
'Rust Never
Sleeps'.

Ann Hillary O'Brien, Dennis Belfield and Neil Young.

'Rust Never Sleeps'.

Andre Csillag

Andre Csillag

Neil Young
shortly after
Woodstock in
1969.

Crosby, Stills, Nash and Young.

A portrait of
Young taken in
1973 by Alanna
Nash.

Young's former
girlfriend,
Robin Lane.

expected *Time Fades Away* and I'm not sorry I put it out. I didn't need the fame. You gotta keep changing. Shirts, old ladies, whatever. I'd rather keep changing and lose a lot of people along the way. If that's the price, I'll pay it. I don't give a shit if my audience is a hundred or a hundred million. It doesn't make any difference to me. I'm convinced that what sells and what I do are two completely different things. If they meet, it's coincidence.[10]

If *Time Fades Away* was erratic in quality and appeared to lack consistency, it was still an interesting album with some fine moments. It showed clearly that Young had taken a new step in his musical development which was more aggressive, assertive and courageous than anything he had yet attempted.

The title track, "Time Fades Away" showed Young's continued fascination with the plight of the junkie. Unlike "The Needle And The Damage Done", however, this was not sympathetic but irreverent in tone. The vocals are rough and the honky-tonk piano provides the song with a mood of abandonment as Young rocks up what might otherwise have been considered somber subject-matter. In the final verse, Young sardonically applies the parental warnings to the wayward junkie to his own adolescent days. Just as "time fades away" for the junkies on "pain street", so back in Canada Young had apparently been suffering an equally pointless existence riding subways through a haze. Young bridges the gap between the junkie and the straight, and exposes both lifestyles as equally pointless. It is one of Young's bleakest songs and the depressing theme and absurd images reveal a world-view similar to that of Samuel Beckett. "Time Fades Away" is Young's *Waiting For Godot*.

The belated appearance of "Journey Through The Past" on vinyl was hardly of great consequence. This rough and ready version is generally less impressive than his 1971 performance of the same song; its inclusion here was presumably intended as a rejoinder to some of Young's comments on Canada in the previous song. The abrupt switch to a solo work after the rip-roaring "Time Fades Away" provides a strange contrast which breaks up the continuity of this live album.

"Yonder Stands The Sinner" was another departure for Young and remains the roughest song on the album. Young described the song as "bible-rock" and warned his audiences that it was "a bit experimental". Young appeared to be almost parodying his own vocal inadequacies by deliberately straining for notes that he could not possibly reach and intentionally creating a song that sounded amusingly off-key. Young also played around with the lyrics of the song in order to create an ambivalent effect.

Even more ironic, however, is the succeeding song, "L.A.":

This is a song I wrote in 1968. Out on the West Coast people were beside palm trees, living by the ocean, worrying about earthquakes.[25]

In the song, Young vividly pictures the destruction of Los Angeles:

But when the suppers are planned
And the freeways are crammed
And the mountains erupt
And the valley is sucked

91

Into cracks in the earth
Will it finally be heard by you L.A.

Although Young appears to be deadly serious he quickly reverts to a note of sarcasm in the repeated chorus – "Don't you wish that you could be here too?" In dealing with a subject such as the obliteration of a city, one might have expected Young to use the kind of epic production that he employed on such songs as "There's A World" and "A Man Needs A Maid". However, the song is given added force by the fact that Young restricts himself to a piano accompaniment with a minimum of additional instrumentation. Although singing about junkies and earthquakes Young seems flippant, almost as if he is casually accepting the inevitable natural order of events, it was this form of stoicism that would predominate on his next studio album release.

In the closing cut on side one, Young reverted to a love song. Neil recalls the inspiration for the composition:

> I used to call this girl up from the road who I was in love with, but I'd never actually met. I used to talk to her all the time on the phone, usually late at night because of the time difference. And I'd wake up in the morning feeling so good.[14]

As a typical seventies Young love song "Love In Mind" might appear somewhat out of place on *Time Fades Away*, but it does share several characteristics with some of the cuts on side one. Like "L.A." and "Time Fades Away", it is less passionate than resigned. Young appears to realize the transient nature of human relationships, even as he recognizes the symptoms of love:

> And I've seen love make a fool of a man
> He tried to make a loser win
> But I've got nothing to lose I can't get back again.

Apart from the realization that time does indeed fade away, "Love In Mind" also contains some more of Young's self-righteous opinions on institutionalized religion:

> Man made rules been holding back by love
> Can't hold it back no more
> Churches long preach sex is wrong
> Jesus where is nature goin'.

In common with "Yonder Stands The Sinner" and "Soldier", "Love In Mind" reveals Young's rejection of traditional Christianity. In criticizing the Church he utters the plea "Jesus where is nature going" ultimately making it difficult to decide whether the Saviour's name is being used profanely or sincerely. This is a typical example of Young's light ironic touch.

In spite of its diverse material the first side of *Time Fades Away* does retain a thread of unity with similar thematic and linguistic patterns emerging in different songs. However, aurally, it is the second side which is the most consistent, largely because it contains only three songs, two of which are long moralizing pieces from Young. The opening cut, "Don't Be Denied", is Young's autobiography neatly summarized in five short verses. It is one of the highlights of the album with an aggressive, confident vocal by Young. For the critics it proved that Young was far from completely washed-up and provided a warning that to dismiss him at this stage would be foolishly premature. The song says more about Young than probably every track on *Harvest* combined. In fact, the only criticism of "Don't Be Denied" is that this particular version is incomplete. In selecting the tracks for the live album, Young, for some unspecified reason, chose to include a recording from the Coliseum, Phoenix, in which he accidentally omitted the third verse. Despite losing a few points on continuity, lyrically the song is more impressive than some of the other cuts on the album. Young uses the autobiographical references to make a point about the necessity to achieve self-expression; a sentiment that is reflected in the title of the song. However, Young is not unaware of the false trappings of superstardom and in the final lines – "But I'm a pauper in a naked disguise/A millionaire through a businessman's eyes" – he stresses that commercial success may also bring with it spiritual impoverishment. In choosing to express himself through such a blatantly autobiographical composition, Young trod dangerous ground, but his artistry was effective enough to meet the challenge.

"The Bridge" was another of Neil's songs from the 1971 period. At his Royal Festival Hall performance that year he introduced the song revealing that it was a very recent composition:

> Hart Crane wrote a poem called "The Bridge" ... and I'd just been reading it. It started out like I was feeling I was Hart Crane so I started writing this song about the bridge. I wrote that here in the bustling city of London three days ago.[14]

The song is one of Young's more successful moodpieces and contains some of the most sexually explicit imagery he has ever used:

> And love came running down
> Like a river on your skin
> And you let me in
> You let me in.

Young's unorthodox live album closes with the stupendous "Last Dance" which, like "Yonder Stands The Sinner", includes some additional vocal support by David Crosby and Graham Nash. The song again shows Young's confidence in allowing the emotive performance to outweigh any technical shortcomings. The result is a great song and a powerful performance, equal to "Don't De Denied". "Last Dance" opens with a blast of feedback and Young's vocals are totally off-key even from the very first line of the opening verse. However, the vocal support of Crosby & Nash, and the insistent riff provide the song with an easily recognizable hook line which proved effective in live performances. Young's vocals are positively venomous in their sarcasm as he spits out the words – "It's time to go, time to go to work." As with several songs on this album Young's aim appears to be didactic; essentially, the sentiments of "Last Dance" are the same as those of "Don't Be Denied". Young preaches to his audience telling them that it is possible for them to live their own lives and escape the system. The image of an unbearable 9 to 5 existence that the song presents reiterates the days of subway riding "through a haze" that were described in the title track "Time Fades Away". In spite of the effectiveness of the song, it is easy to criticize the composition as naive social commentary. It seems very much Young the superstar, looking down condescendingly on the average working man and telling him that he can live his own life "laid back and laughing." However, Young seemingly gives no thought as to how this utopian bliss might be achieved. The lyrics might easily be dismissed as the most insensitive piece of social commentary since Marie Antoinette suggested that the starving French people should be given cake. However, as usual, Young is not totally unambiguous in his assertions and ultimately his vision may not be as impaired as it seems. For each time he advises us of the ease with which one can be laid back and laughing, he qualifies his statement with the words, "oh, no" effectively appearing to negate much of what has been said. One is eventually left with the consideration that the song is itself one great ironic comment. The effect is delightfully ambiguous and typical of Young at this stage of his development.

In spite of its roughness and technical imperfections, *Time Fades Away* remains a strong piece of work and reveals Young's desire to lay the ghost of *Harvest*. It also documents a period in Young's life when he appeared to be out of step with his audience, and even his backing musicians. Looking back at the album, Young maintained that it was very representative of a troubled time:

> *Time Fades Away* sounds nervous but even that says where I was at, because it's a direct ah, non-hit, a direct miss. It was like a live album of songs that no-one had ever heard before done in a totally different style from the one that came before it. But it stood for where I was at during that period. I was nervous and not quite at home in those big places.[21]

THIRTEEN

Out Of The Black

While the critics complained about *Time Fades Away*, Young took his "Tonight's The Night" show on the road and brought it to England in November 1973. The final gig of the British tour was a celebratory return to the Royal Festival Hall on 10 November. That night Young showed just how much he had changed since his last performance there in 1971. The Eagles opened the show and they were very well received by the audience. The group had yet to break internationally, but they were playing precise, well-executed country-rock and they were probably better at their craft than any other unit working in the same genre. Compared to the Eagles' set, Young's work-out seemed nothing less than a shambles. The audiences had been expecting to hear the "Best of Neil Young" and they were probably hoping for a little more than an updated version of his 1971 concert. However, Young totally disarmed them, as, without a word of explanation he opened his set with eight new numbers: "Tonight's The Night"; "Mellow My Mind"; "World On A String"; "Speaking Out"; "Albuquerque"; "New Mama"; "Roll Another Number" and "Tired Eyes". The members of the audience just looked at one another in amazement. Introducing new songs is something that every performer is wary of, and most artists usually like to give their followers a few solid well-known standards before they find the courage to attempt a new song. But here was Young, opening with a new number, and seemingly content to play unheard of songs for the rest of the evening. What was even more astonishing was the irreverent way in which Young approached each song. He gave the audience no explanation or apology for the new songs, but rattled them off as though they were a greatest hits repertoire. If that in itself was remarkable, Young's few words between songs must have made the audience wonder whether their favorite artiste was still in control of his senses. Young mumbled about how great it was to be "here in Miami Beach". At first, this seemed merely to be Young parodying those slick performers who always begin their sets by saying how marvellous it is to play in the host country. However, as the shows progressed, Young continued this monologue about Miami Beach almost as if he was convinced that the group was actually playing there. The audience was extremely polite, and attentively listened to Young's words as though they were of some import. After the show, Lofgren explained that the group was finding the audience's reaction somewhat unusual:

> ... there has been pressure here, particularly in London, but of a different kind. We hadn't anticipated the attentiveness of English audiences and their almost reverence towards Neil. 'Cos as I say, the whole thing was designed to be fun.

While Nils had been a little taken aback by the audience's response, they were even more shocked by what they were witnessing. Here was Young singing songs which were rough, to say the least, mumbling strange words to the audience, and openly drinking from a bottle of tequila. He seemed an almost certain candidate for rock 'n roll's next casualty, if he was not already undergoing some drug-induced personality change. In spite of such suspicions, the audience maintained an almost embarrassing reverence, something which is probably peculiar to English spectators. One volatile member of the audience attempted to stir things up by muttering a "Right on, Neil", but he was immediately rebuffed by another spectator who screamed, "Shut up!" Young seemed bemused by these strange reactions and exclaimed, "I don't know whether we can tolerate all this disagreement on the streets of Miami ..." Some members of the audience were clearly wondering whether they could tolerate any more from Young. After three quarters of an hour, Young was still singing songs that most of the audience had never heard before. Finally, Young broke the tension with the words, "I'm going to do an old tune for you now, one that you've heard before." The Royal Festival Hall erupted in spontaneous applause. At last it seemed that Young was going to give them what they had paid their money to hear. The introduction to the song did indeed sound familiar, but what was it? After a few seconds, Young began singing the words "Tonight's The Night". The audience reacted with a combination of laughter and open-mouthed astonishment as Young attempted something unheard of in any rock concert before or since. He had not merely sung all new numbers, but when these ran out, he sang his opening song again. Young's performance was devastating in its arrogance. He was even admonishing his audience to "Keep on singing" in the face of bewildered silence. During the instrumental breaks, Young would play the guitar with his teeth in imitation of Jimi Hendrix and it became more and more difficult to decide whether he was totally demented or indulging in some bewildering joke. However, the worst was yet to come. Following this second and very rough version of "Tonight's The Night", with much feedback issuing forth from the speakers, Young and Crazy Horse casually left the stage. That, it seemed, was the end of the show. An apparently drunken performance of less than 50 minutes duration consisting of entirely new songs played in an off-key manner seemed the only way to sum up that absurd evening. One might have expected an angry response from the audience or an unceremonious walk-out but they actually applauded. It was a remarkable scene. Suddenly Young re-emerged looking sober, and announced that he was now going to perform all the songs that the audience had expected to hear when they first entered the auditorium. He then proceeded to play "I Am A Child" as if he was opening one of his normal concerts. Although the remaining songs such as "Cinnamon Girl", "Helpless" and "Southern Man" were precisely what the audience expected Young still had a few surprises left to pull. He reached back six years for the Buffalo Springfield song "Flying On The Ground Is Wrong" and effectively reached forward six years with a premature introduction of "Human Highway", which would not appear until the *Comes A Time* album in 1979. Young continued to talk to the spectators between numbers and even borrowed a photographer's camera and took a shot of the audience for posterity. The bizarre evening concluded with yet another version of "Tonight's The Night", only on this occasion the song lasted a full fifteen minutes. It was probably the most controversial performance made by a major artist touring Britain since Dylan's volatile appearance at the Royal Albert Hall in 1966. Young explained the way in which he deliberately set out to confuse the audience:

> There was never a chance for the audiences to do anything because I never stopped talking. I would play and before they had a chance to applaud, I would become the M.C. I would just talk away to these people, tying songs together with these raps that I'd make up as I went along. It was a whole other period. I got to act. I had a part in the show instead of it being me, the pressure was off me a little bit. It didn't look like anything the people had ever seen. We did like a show – I wore this sleazy white jacket and big shades and then I'd go back and change into my funky Pendleton, jeans and my acoustic guitar.[21]

The critics were unimpressed by Young's idiosyncrasies and the concerts were universally hammered in the press. It was hardly a surprise. Even in the States, Young failed to attract many champions for his latest rock 'n roll vision.

The pressures placed upon Young at this point had become enormous. His live album had been panned, the *Journey Through The Past* film ridiculed, and now his onstage performances were being severely censured. Young had also met a cool response from his business managers who, according to Nils Lofgren, were not particularly sympathetic to the "Tonight's The Night" series of concerts. Returning to the States, Young met more resistance, this time from his record company. It was reported in the press that a "Tonight's The Night" album was scheduled for January 1974 release, but this was apparently far from the truth. Warners-Reprise rejected the concept, no doubt believing that such an album would sound the death-knell of Young's career. Young immediately reacted by beginning work on a completely new album in late November. This project involved not one group, but a variety of musicians including Ralph Molina and Billy Talbot from Crazy Horse, Ben Keith, Rusty Kershaw and Band members Rick Danko and Levon Helm. Also in attendance at some of these sessions were David Crosby and Graham Nash, which suggested the possibility of another attempted C.S.N.&Y. project. Although Young still appeared to be on a very different plane from his three former colleagues, it seemed that he was gradually being won around to the idea of making another album with them. It is difficult to pinpoint all the factors that prompted Young to arrive at this decision. Perhaps the managerial pressures upon Neil to make another C.S.N.&Y. album simply proved too great for him to withstand. It is generally accepted that Elliot Roberts was the catalyst in getting the quartet back together in 1974. His comments on their recent musical exploits and particuarly of Young's career development were curt and pointed: "you're all just pissing in the wind." Impressed by Roberts' audacity, Young apparently took these words very much to heart. It must also be assumed that following the Tonight's The Night tour, and the at this point unreleased *On The Beach*, Young had effectively exorcised the ghosts of Whitten and Berry and was looking to pastures new. After the depression of the last year, the idea of a Crosby, Stills, Nash & Young reunion must have seemed like a musical tonic. In addition, of course, Young may have felt that his uncompromising attitude towards his audience during the past year was beginning to adversely affect the development of his career. Working with C.S.N.&Y. again would provide the necessary proof that Young was still capable of functioning adequately in a variety of musical roles. The twin aesthetic and economic motives proved irresistible and following some preliminary discussion, it was agreed that Crosby, Stills, Nash & Young would embark on a summer tour and return during the winter to record their long-awaited follow-up to *4 Way Street*. Rehearsals for the summer tour were slated for June at Young's ranch, which, it was felt, would prove the ideal setting for the group to rediscover each other's respective musical directions.

A few weeks before the long and arduous preparations began, Young made a surprise appearance at New York's Bottom Line club, on 16 May, and played an acoustic set consisting of mainly new songs from the soon-to-be-released *On The Beach*. The gig provided a unique glimpse of Young during the transitional stage between Tonight's The Night and the C.S.N.&Y. summer concerts. Although Young played only eleven songs, they were carefully chosen as if to represent most accurately his feelings during this period. This was to be a quiet farewell to the world of small clubs before the monster stadium tours that would follow in the next few months. There was none of the hysteria that would characterize the C.S.N.&Y. concerts, nor any of the tension that had been produced on the Tonight's The Night tour. The audience seemed content to allow Young to play exactly what he wanted, and he did precisely that, explaining to the select gathering that he would be playing a set of new songs. His reasoning was simple and persuasive; he genuinely felt that he had performed the old classics so frequently that he could no longer do them justice. The only previously-released song that he included in the set was, significantly, "Helpless", one of the best known of his C.S.N.&Y. cuts. "Helpless" was both a glance at his past and an indication of his immediate future. There was little else that night, however, that brought to mind Neil Young the superstar.

The new songs were pensive, densely lyrical and, were it not for Young's continual flashes of humor, seemingly close to depressing. In his introduction to the opening number, Young hesitated, almost as if he had forgotten the title, before announcing, "I'd like to start with a quiet song, it's called . . . 'Citizen Kane Junior Blues'." The song was actually "Pushed It Over The End", one of the few indisputably great songs that Young would choose not to record for an album. Perhaps, in retrospect, Young felt that the song might have provided him with more trouble than it was worth, as essentially, "Pushed It Over The End" appears to be a somewhat sympathetic but critical approach to Women's Liberation. Young may possibly have been reacting against those who accused him of chauvinism following his recording of "A Man Needs A Maid". In "Pushed It Over The End", he portrays through a central character named Millie, the inhumanity that sometimes seems the inevitable result of placing a moral or political ideal before the needs of the individual. It is interesting to note that Young is rumored to have based the character of Millie on Patti Hearst. At various points in the song,

Young adopts a very cynical attitude to Women's Libbers:

> Good looking Millie's into politics now
> And things are looking much better
> She keeps ten men in her garage
> Knitting her fine sweaters.

Young's attack seems not so much directed against women, but rather the cynical attitude to men that the women's movement may sometimes unconsciously inculcate. Thus, Millie herself is described sympathetically, and her commitment and dedication are acknowledged:

> At the end of a weary day
> She looks hard and she works hard.

However, it is the plight of the man that most attracts Young's attention:

> And although no one hears a sound
> There's another poor man falling down
> > falling down, falling down ...

This consideration leads him in the remainder of the song to ask such questions as "how much love did you spend?" and more pointedly, "could those dreams of yours be true?" as he speculates upon the negative aspects of a positive movement. Young showed some daring and originality in tackling a song of this nature and it would have been interesting to read the critical response had he chosen to release it in 1974.

The remainder of Young's set was almost equally intriguing, revealing a selection of unreleased material which would eventually appear on several different albums. Young appeared to be emerging from his dark period, and even these new songs were preceded by amusing one-liners and entertaining anecdotes. His introduction to "Ambulance Blues" was characteristically self-mocking:

> It's kind of a long song, so if you'll bear with me while I tell you all about it. It's this thing that happened to me ... Sometimes I wonder about these long songs. I used to sit in coffee houses when I was younger and look at these folksingers up there and they used to come out and some of them would sing fast songs and shake around a little. And then this cat would come up and sing all these down songs. You know ... what am I doing here? I came to have a good time. So here's another bummer for you. It's my trip, man.[18]

That Young could so easily laugh at himself showed that he was already psychologically prepared for the whole C.S.N.&Y. circus. The audience at the Bottom Line had been given a unique selection of songs that night and most of them would not be heard again in concert. Young had even included a revival of the old Henry VIII classic, "Greensleeves", possibly the oldest song ever performed by a rock musician. Singing "Greensleeves" without a hint of satire, with just an acoustic-guitar backing, Young invested a meaning into the song that might not have seemed possible in a contemporary New York club setting. Although the set was relatively short, it was probably the most intimate performance that Young had given since his rise to commercial success as a soloist in 1970.

By June, the rehearsals for the C.S.N.&Y. summer tour were underway at Young's ranch in La Honda. Young had taken much trouble in ensuring that everything would go smoothly. He had even built an impressive 40 foot stage next to his studio to enable the quartet to rehearse outdoors in preparation for the concerts. The elaborate preparations ensured that the atmosphere was relaxed and conducive to work. The C.S.&N. trio remarked that Neil appeared to be a changed man, more open and hospitable than he had seemed in the past. It was generally felt that following a very troubled period, Young was at last content within himself and able to reflect a new, positive attitude to life.

FOURTEEN

A Purging Of The Spirit

The new revitalized Young that Crosby, Stills & Nash had rediscovered was yet to be revealed to the world at large. More and more critics were beginning to dismiss him as a self-pitying depressant. That view appeared to be substantiated when *On The Beach* finally appeared in July. The album received mixed reviews, and even the favorable ones, admitted that it was Young's most despairing work to date. This, however, was far from the truth. *On The Beach* represented the turning point for Young and was, in effect, a testament of his ability to override the problems that had been threatening the development of his musical career. The *Rolling Stone* review of *On The Beach* concluded that it was one of the "most despairing albums of the decade", but this is surely a severe misinterpretation in that the word "despair" implies the negation of hope; is the next stage downward following "depression", and is also a state which Young has never reached. *On The Beach* documents Young's depression, but there is nothing in the work to suggest despair. *On The Beach* is actually a therapeutic, rather than a depressing album. It is an enactment of Young's move to a more positive state of mind and presents what can best be described as a purging of the spirit.

What is most noticeable about the album is that although some tracks are lethargic in feel, there is never any question of despair, for Young never loses hope:

> I'm deep inside myself
> But I'll get out somehow
> And I'll bring a smile
> To your eyes

> ("Motion Pictures")

These are hardly the words of a man who has succumbed to despair, but clearly show a confidence about the future which is unambiguously positive. That same confidence can be observed in the opening and closing tracks of the album, "Walk On" and "Ambulance Blues", both of which serve as an artistic statement of intent as well as a reply to the criticism that Young had been receiving since the days of *Harvest*.

"Walk On" is clearly optimistic in tone with a mid-tempo beat, and none of the whining vocals that usually characterize Young's mournful songs.

With *Harvest*, Young had become, for many, the archetypal singer-songwriter and chronicler of his own emotions. For his listeners, Young's music provided a cathartic effect, enabling them to place their own little emotional traumas into a universal context. If Young could make loneliness, unrequited love and even death seem so sweet-sounding, romantic and profound, then maybe they weren't so bad after all. After *Harvest*, however, things had started to change, and Young's songs had begun to become uglier, rougher and less harmonious. The sweetness of melancholy had been replaced by bitterness, and the romanticism had been tinged with bleak visions of death and destruction. He was using all the old themes but instead of "The Old Laughing Lady" and "The Needle And The Damage Done", Young was giving his audiences rough live versions of such songs as "Time Fades Away", "Tonight's The Night" and "Tired Eyes". Loneliness and death were no longer pretty and romantic, but ugly and nauseating. Young's new darker vision was so intense that he could please neither the critics nor the fans. In effect, Young had abdicated his position as the forlorn folkie, but his followers were still clinging to the old ideals. Young had refused to compromise, however, and he was forcing his audience to accept him on his own terms. In "Walk On", Young appears to acknowledge the separation between himself and many of his audience:

> Oo baby that's so hard to change
> I can't tell them how to feel.
> > Some get stoned
> > Some get strange.
> Sooner or later it all gets real
> Walk on ...

What does the artist do when his art isolates him from his audience? This is the question that the song asks most forcibly. It is also a question that Young, his management and his record company may have posed from time to time. There is only one answer as Young sees it and that is to trust that sooner or later the artist, the art and the audience will meet again. In the meantime, each must simply "Walk On".

The one surprising feature of *On The Beach* was Young's decision to add an old composition to his series of recent speculations on the state of his life and his career. He had actually re-recorded three early compositions for this album: "Bad Fog Of Loneliness"; "Winterlong" and "See The Sky About To Rain". However, only the latter was deemed appropriate for inclusion. Presumably, the main reason for including the song was that its fatalistic philosophy fitted in well with some of the other compositions on the album. "See The Sky About To Rain" is an acceptance of the fact that life is, by necessity, indiscriminate in its distribution of wealth and happiness:

> Some are bound for happiness
> Some are bound for glory
> Some are bound to live with less
> Who can tell your story?

In "Walk On", which, of course, was written a couple of years after "See The Sky About To Rain", Young adopted the same tone:

Some get stoned
Some get strange.

However, in realising that "sooner or later it all gets real", Young had moved from the inertia of fatalism towards a belief that something positive would ultimately emerge from the chaos. By placing the tracks side by side, Young allows us to perceive the subtle difference in his state of mind during the composing of each song.

"Revolution Blues" is one of Young's more unusual songs and shows the songwriter moving towards satire. Although it is difficult to identify which group is being satirized, Young appears to be criticizing capitalism and satirizing political revolutionaries simultaneously. The opening lines show Young adopting the persona of a revolutionary:

Well we live in a trailer
At the edge of town
You never see us
Cause we don't come around
We got twenty-five rifles
Just to keep the population down.

Here, Young appears to be mocking the revolutionaries who kill indiscriminately, for no apparent valid reason ("just to keep the population down"). At the same time the idea of this invisible enemy living in a trailer at the edge of town and never actually being seen by the townspeople is a little too absurd to be convincing. Young appears to be parodying the middle-class concept of a revolutionary. The stereotyped revolutionary is obviously insane, predatory, lives outside normal society probably in a trailer like other social undesirables such as gypsies, and his one aim is to plot the destruction of civilization. Here, he captures society's irrational fear of political revolutionaries in much the same way that Dylan did in "John Birch Society Blues". Young, however, is more subtle than Dylan in this respect and in bringing to life the horrible creature that inhabits the imagination of the satirized he exposes the total absurdity and paranoia of white middle-class America in a few short lines. However, Young's satire is also dangerously double-edged at times, especially in such lines as

Yes that was me with the doves
Setting them free near the factory.

Is he laughing at the naivety of political revolutionaries, or is he laughing at the American middle-class conception of the naivety of political revolutionaries? In effect, he seems to be doing both. The clichéd notion that all political revol-utionaries are treacherous, deceitful and double-dealing because they have rejected the American way is parodied in the lines

So you be good to me
And I'll be good to you ...
I won't attack you, but I won't back you.

At the same time, however, these lines could be read as a direct riposte against the sixties revolutionaries who compromised their ideals when the going became too tough. The listener is never allowed to rest easily with either point of view. Young prefers to allow his satire to remain delightfully ambiguous. Towards the end of the song Young again appears to be presenting the exaggerated concept of the political revolutionary as a sick, insane misanthrope:

> Well I'm a barrell of laughs
> With my carbine on
> I keep them hopping
> Till my ammunition's gone

This appears to culminate in the image of the "bloody fountains" and the topical allusion to the Manson murders ("ten million dune buggies coming down the mountain") where Young's descriptions become so horrific that the song is finally reduced to the level of simple black humor. At this point, however, Young pulls his ace card by turing the satire inward. In Young's world, it seems that nobody is free from the satirical thrust of the songwriter, not even the artist himself:

> Well I hear that Laurel Canyon
> Is full of famous stars
> But I hate them worse than lepers
> And I'll kill them in their cars

Here, Young's contemporaries, "the famous stars of Laurel Canyon" and, by implication, Young himself, are also attacked. When the revolution comes, rock stars will be the first to go, and even those so-called sixties revolutionaries will not be able to escape the effects of the revolution. The ending is brilliantly satirical and, coincidentally enough, it recalls the final lines of "John Birch Society Blues", in which Dylan's Bircher persona exhausts associates to hound and so has to start investigating himself. Young similarly exhausts his satiric objects, so he also turns inward and satirizes his own position in the rock world. Once more, the difference between Dylan and Young in their approaches is that the former's satire is directed against a specific group whereas Young's is directed at everybody, including himself.

Young's new role as a satirist indicates the changes that he went through during the preparation and recording of the album. From an awareness of his depression to a confidence in overcoming such a state, Young ultimately emerges as a humorist. His realization that he was lost deep inside himself and his promise that he would eventually "get out somehow and bring a smile to your eyes" is fully vindicated in "Revolution Blues". Most of the critics of the period failed to see the satire or humor in "Revolution Blues", however, and regarded it simply as further evidence of Young's depressed state.

The factors which cause Young's depression, and his realization how to overcome them, are the subject of the next song, "For The Turnstiles". This song was also seen by contemporaneous critics as depressing, and they all pointed out that it contained images of violence, corruption and destruction. There is much truth in this, but surely it is not the images themselves, but the way in which they are used that tell us whether or not an artist's vision is negative. At a superficial glance, it is easy to locate images in the song that suggest a sense of loss and death:

> All the bush league batters

Are left to die on the diamonds
In the stands the home crowd scatters
For the turnstiles.

Equating baseball stars with rock stars, Young notes that after they have given their all, they are abandoned and forgotten. The spectators are equally uncaring and fickle and head for the turnstiles after the show is over leaving the performer to his fate. A comparable image is presented earlier in the song when the rock business is seen as all-consuming:

All the great explorers
Are now in granite laid.
Under white sheets for the great unveiling
At the big parade.

Even the great musical explorers are eventually subverted by the business and depersonalized to become merely giant statues for the spectators to admire. The idea of the rock business destroying the art of a performer by transforming him into a superstar is brilliantly conceived in Young's image of the musical "explorer" being laid in granite and covered in white sheets. These images of death are followed by the unveiling in which the artist, now a statue, is presented at the parade for the approval of the spectators. It is interesting that Young should equate the pomp of the big parade with a form of artistic death. This is, undoubtedly, the key to the song and makes it more than simply a depressing vision of destruction and death. For Young is here attempting to discover the cause of his depression and in doing so he will vanquish it. The opening lines again appear to attack the business, which at first seems unambiguously displayed as the villain of the piece:

All the sailors with their seasick mommas
Hear the sirens on the shore
Singing songs for pimps with tailors
Who charge ten dollars at the door.

The business is seen to be controlled by "pimps" with "tailors" (once a popular euphemism for a homosexual, though Young may not have been aware of this) who take the money at the door. However, Young invites us to take one step further, for if the business is represented by pimps, then it follows that the artists must be equated with prostitutes. In the second line, Young prefers to use a more oblique term, and identifies the artist as a siren. The siren, traditionally a beautiful, alluring and enticing figure sings sweet songs which are irresistible, but ultimately destructive. The function of the siren is to drive sailors (in turn equated with the audience in the first line of the song) to their deaths. If "Revolution Blues" has revealed Young satirically turning inward against himself then "For The Turnstiles" suggests a positive revulsion of both the artist and the art. Young appears to have come to the sudden realization that both he and his art were in danger of being totally destroyed by the record business. Young was, no doubt, under pressure to record another *Harvest* and abandon *Tonight's The Night*, but to meet these demands would make him a siren. In realizing this, Young shows that he has the capacity to change:

> You can really learn a lot that way
> It will change you in the middle of the day
> Though your confidence may be shattered
> It doesn't matter.

The recognition of what the business is doing to him brings about a sudden change which is enough to shatter Young's confidence, but that, as he says, does not matter. What does matter is that Young has learned and is capable of changing, and *On The Beach* demonstrates most powerfully the transformation that he has undergone.

The final track on side one, the plodding "Vampire Blues", is a reiteration of much that has gone before. As he has done in "For The Turnstiles" and "Revolution Blues", Young attacks the big industries and portrays them as bloodsuckers. He again adopts a persona, this time a blood-sucking oil magnate, but how much of a persona is Young's vampire and how much of it is an admission of his own guilt? The buinessmen may well suck oil from the earth for profit, but oil is also used in the manufacturing of records and Young has sold millions of those. When he sings "I'm a vampire babe/Sucking blood from the earth" there is just the possibility that he really is singing about himself. The song can be seen as a condemnation of the oil magnates, which, in turn, becomes an attack on the record industry and ultimately a criticism of the superstar. Throughout the album, Young continually analyzes the relationship between himself, the record industry and the audience. This is the source of his depression – a state which he makes every effort to expunge.

"On The Beach" is a further attempt by Young to rationalize the meaning of superstardom. In the song, he suddenly finds himself in a desperate situation when he realizes that he is out of step with the world around him:

> The World is turning
> I hope it don't turn away.

For some reason the fame that was once so important to him, and still is to the rest of the world, suddenly appears hollow and irrelevant:

> All my pictures are falling
> From the wall where I placed them yesterday

Nevertheless, in spite of his rejection of the importance of fame, Young finds that it is something that he cannot live without:

> I need a crowd of people
> But I can't face them day to day.

It is this paradox of both rejecting and needing fame that is causing Young's depression. Of course, speculating on something as apparently gratifying as fame should hardly produce a state of depression. Then again, the worst kind of depression is when you have no valid reason for being depressed and are therefore unable to find a remedy:

> Though my problems are meaningless
> That don't make them go away.

When the reasons for a depressed state are vague and unclear, then a remedy becomes increasingly difficult to discover. Young's worst fears are intensified in the oft-repeated image of the radio interview, in which he is left abandoned and forgotten:

> I went to the radio interview
> I ended up alone at the microphone.

The images of isolation and the breakdown of communication culminate in his irrational fear of rejection and the pressure of living the life of a star in the city force him to leave.

Again, the important fact is that from an initial state of inertia, Young has made a positive move. The line "I follow a road though I don't know where it ends" shows an attempt to come to terms with depression and reiterates the "sooner or later it all gets real" philosophy voiced in "Walk On". The final lines again indicate Young's absolute determination to survive:

> Think I'll get out of town
> Cause the world is turning
> I don't want to see it turn away.

In that final line, Young has significantly moved away from the state of listlessness observed during the opening of the song ("I hope it don't turn away") to a renewed determination to lift himself out of depression through positive action. The will to rouse himself to "get out of town" and the final shift from "I hope" to "I don't want to see it turn away" reveal that the introspection has proved fruitful. "On The Beach" is a song about depression but it is not depressing in itself since it shows the power of the human will to come to terms with the darker areas of the mind. In the final analysis, "On The Beach" shows how Young rationalizes his way out of an approaching despair.

That rationalization continues on "Motion Pictures" in which Young grows in confidence, and speaks optimistically about a brighter future. Young provides an amusing anecdote recounting the circumstances under which the song was written:

> This is a song I wrote in a motel room in Los Angeles ... and we were trying some "onion-slides". Do you know what an "onion-slide" is? That's real third-grade marijuana ... the worst you can get on the street ... That cheap grass is great! Anyway ... we were sitting round having a few "onion-slides", and they slow you down quite a bit. There's nothing to really get fast for anyway. And this song just sort of came to us. We were all sitting round just playing these chords; playing with my friends Rusty Kershaw, Ben Keith – sitting round the motel room. The T.V. was on; I hadn't been home in two months by then, trying to get my act together. ...[18]

The "onion-slides" story at least explains why the arrangement of the song is so lethargic. This does not necessarily suggest a mood of resignation, however, but rather a quiet contentment. Sitting in front of his television screen, Young is suddenly secure in the knowledge that he has found something worth striving for:But I hear some people have got their dream

I've got mine.

That dream is an idyllic life, far away from the motels and the city. While on the road, Young can now look back nostalgically at a different world:

I hear the mountains are doing fine
Mornin' glory is on the vine
And the dew is fallin'
The ducks are callin'
Yes, I've got mine.

That final line reveals a new confidence, with Young realizing that he has not lost all of his dreams on the road to fame. The song, like the remainder of the album, shows Young stripping away the trappings of stardom in order to discover what is really valid. In looking at the television screen, he sees famous stars, but he realizes that his new attitude makes him different from them:

Well all those people
They think they've got it made
But I wouldn't buy, sell, borrow or trade
Anything I have
To be like one of them
I'd rather start all over again.

Young is now capable of adopting a devil-may-care attitude towards the business and his audience, even in the face of plummeting record sales. Rather than compromising his beliefs to maintain a false standard, Young would rather start all over again from scratch. The ultimate dismissal of fame is expressed curtly in a single line – "All those headlines, they just bore me now." Here, Young is reiterating the feelings expressed in "For The Turnstiles" and "Walk On", that fame can easily become, artistically, the kiss of death. With this new realization Young can set about putting his life and career in order.

The closing track, "Ambulance Blues", is Young's final statement on his spiritual regeneration and explores all the themes that he had developed on the other seven tracks on this album. He adopts personae, uses oblique imagery, attempts some political commentary, employs some satire and, more importantly, reveals a humor and confidence which fully demonstrate his revival. In common with the other tracks on the album, Young resists using an elaborate production job to dramatize his statements. "Ambulance Blues" is a return to the old folky days with acoustic guitar and harmonica, but as the song progresses it also introduces a violin (cf. "Running Dry") and a barely audible tambourine in the background for extra effect. The stark instrumentation and production is mirrored in the musical structure of the song which accommodates Young's wandering speculations by abandoning such requisites as a middle-eight and a chorus.

The song opens on a nostalgic note, looking back to a time before Young was in the grips of the Big Business:

Back in the old folky days
The air was magic when we played.

This speculation leads Young to conjure up a memory of what appears to be a place he once played in named "Isabella":

> The riverboat was rocking in the rain
> Midnight was the time for the raid
> Oh Isabella, proud Isabella
> They tore you down
> And ploughed you under

It seems that "Isabella", the riverboat-club, was raided, closed and finally demolished. Without warning, Young immediately makes another statement, presumably about a person he had known during his period:

> You're only real with your make-up on
> How could I see you and stay too long

On the other hand, this statement follows so closely on the last that the subject still appears to be the riverboat "Isabella", which has now been personified. In this sense, the line "You're only real with your make-up on" suggests that following its closure, and no doubt the removal of all its upholstery, the riverboat-club had lost all its former sleazy charm. Depressed by this sight, Young prefers not to "stay too long" and moves on to the next section of the song which is set on the "Navaho trail". Here, Young conjures up another image from his past that seems familiar:

> Burn-outs stub their toes on garbage pails
> Waitresses are crying in the rain
> Will their boy-friends pass this way again?

In another song, "Country Girl", Young had first introduced us to these tearful waitresses in a different context:

> No pass out sign on the door set me thinking
> Are waitresses paying the price of their winking

In the succeeding lines of that song, Young had pictured faded stars who "dropped by to die", an image that might easily have fitted on to this album.

Rather than developing the waitress analogy, Young deliberately produces some oblique images to confuse the listener. Young introduces more destructive imagery taking a nursery rhyme ("Oh Mother Goose") from his childhood and perverting it, in order to express his own loss of innocence. These lines also reveal a hint of satire as Young mocks the communal ideal exemplified by the Woodstock generation exposing the idea that we can all live together in peace and unity as conceptually naive. It is regarded as nursery-rhyme idealism, and Young presents the real picture of such a society not as a peaceful utopia but as "on the skids" and politically and emotionally unstable. The tone is sardonic and in expressing the "Mother Goose and her shoe" philosophy Young even employs that awful pun, "I'm such a *heel* for making her feel so bad" in order to make his statement sound even more mocking.

As in the other songs on this album, however, Young's mockery once more turns inward, and the next section is both apologetic and self-critical in tone:

> I guess I'll call it sickness gone
> It's hard to say the meaning of this song

An ambulance can only go so fast
It's easy to get buried in the past
When you try to make a good thing last.

This is probably Young's most revealing statement on the whole album and evidence enough of his change of direction. The last two lines express Young's awareness of how easy it would be to go on regurgitating albums such as *Harvest* in order to try and make a good thing last. In doing so, however, Young would be burying himself in the past and stifling his own development. It is here that he chooses to introduce the "ambulance" motif. The ambulance comes to rescue Young's artistic life which, as we recall from "For The Turnstiles", was close to being laid in granite and covered in white sheets. As Young apologetically points out, however, "an ambulance can only go so fast", and it has taken this long to sort out his own ambiguous feelings about the state of his career. The emergency measures that Young takes consist not only of re-evaluating the relationship between himself, his audience and the business, but also taking a critical look into his own past. It is very easy to get buried in the past when you try to make the best parts of it last, and this, Young realizes, is precisely what he has been doing. Songs such as "Sugar Mountain", "I Am A Child" and "Helpless" all present the past as a golden period of idyllic bliss. Part of Young's charm had always been that in bemoaning his current state of loneliness or lost loves, he could at least look back to better days. It was always Young's last refuge, and when present emotional traumas became too great his mind would commute effortlessly into the good old days. For Young and his audience, the gap between the past and the present produced not pain, but rather a satisfying nostalgia. Sentimentality was the final layer that Young had to remove and it proved the most difficult as his technique of using the past as a yardstick for the present had become habitual.

In "Ambulance Blues" he finds himself opening with the same old lines:

Back in the old folky days
The air was magic when we played.

It looks as though Young is again escaping into nostalgia in order to avoid coming to terms with the present. But what follows is different. "The old folky days", Young reminds us, were not all glitter, glamor and magic, but had their bleaker moments. The tearing down of Isabella; the burn-outs; the crying waitresses and the distorted picture of Mother Goose, all serve to remind us that childhood, adolescence and youth are not idyllic refuges but can be as dark and terrifying as the present. "Ambulance Blues" sets out to tear down "Sugar Mountain" and expose the sentimentality of longing for the "yellow moon" and "big birds" of Young's favorite town in North Ontario. Young's self-analysis ultimately leads him to the conclusion that the future must be faced uncompromisingly. Having reached that conclusion Young can confidently exclaim: "I guess I'll call it sickness gone." This re-evaluation of the past becomes a crucial factor in Young's self-therapy.

In the next section Young once more employs some satiric thrusts:

I saw today in the entertainment section
There's room at the top for private detection

To Mom and Dad this just doesn't matter
But it's either that or pay off the kidnapper.

Some commentators have suggested that Young may be alluding to Patricia Hearst in these lines and though any such connections are somewhat tenuous in the context, that supposition seems reasonable enough. However, it is important to remember that Young's satire on this album is always double-edged and when he makes topical allusions, as he appears to do in both "Revolution Blues" and "Vampire Blues", he is never simply mocking one specified group of people nor excluding himself from satirical attack. Young's comments about there being room at the top for private detection is a case in point. This seems to be an amusing gibe directed at himself, the rock critics and the record industry. Young, it should be noted, reached the top of the entertainment industry by indulging in a form of "private detection". On his most commercially successful albums, he can be seen investigating his private feelings and revealing them to his audience. Young is satirizing the way in which the songer-songwriter exposes his own thoughts and inner feelings as a method for gaining commercial success.

These speculations on the workings of the rock music industry lead Young to question the credibility of the so-called rock critic:

So all you critics sit alone
You're no better than me for what you've shown
With your stomach pump
And your hook and ladder dreams
We could get together for some scenes

Young's wry observations are a continuation of the notion that both artists and critics are in the business of "private detection", and one is no better than the other. Young expresses his feelings more effectively by introducing the paradoxical metaphor "stomach-pump". Here, he mocks those critics who were interested only in hearing variations of *After The Goldrush* and *Harvest*, and who will be disappointed to discover *Time Fades Away* or *On The Beach*, which will show how sweetness when forcibly regurgitated tastes like the bitter saliva of cud-like vomit. However the stomach-pump, like the ambulance, is something that is used during an emergency in order to save a life. Its use is associated with the curing of indulgent excesses. This places the critic in a more positive light and reveals him as a figure whose function is necessarily to deflate the artist when he has become too overblown. For some critics then, the "stomach-pump" is an instrument used to try and force Young to regurgitate old ideas and feelings, while for others it is employed as an emergency-device to prevent Young from poisoning himself by satiating the body of his work with excessive consumptions of sweetness. Young ultimately seems to be saying that critics can be both selfish in their demands and committed to their profession. Of course, there is also the additional implication that, given their respective roles, the critic needs the excesses of the artist as much as the artist needs the stomach-pump of the critic. It is no wonder that Young makes the sarcastic suggestion that they should get together for some scenes.

The reference to "hook and ladder dreams" suggests the tendency of some critics mistakenly to assume that an artist's development is comparable to the gradual scaling of a ladder. Young appears to be suggesting here that the quality of his recorded output is likely to be erratic depending on his state of mind during the recording process. This is a plea for the right to be allowed to record albums such as *Time Fades Away, Tonight's The Night* and *On The Beach* without having to suffer accusations that he can no longer cut it adequately.

Towards the end of the song Young provides us with a revealing account, indicating one of the factors that caused him to re-evaluate his career. The scene is set in a city in the hours following a late gig by Young. He sarcastically refers to the gig as "keeping jive alive" and then provides a visual description of the streets in what appears to be the early hours of the morning:

> And out on the corner it's half past five
> But the subways are empty
> And so are the cafes
> Except for the Farmer's Market
> And I still can hear him saying,
> "You're all just pissing in the wind
> You don't know it but you are"
> And there ain't nothing like a friend
> Who can tell you you're just pissing in the wind.

Young later revealed that the friend who told him that he was "pissing in the wind" was manager, Elliot Roberts. In the song, Young uses the words as a damning comment on the recent state of his own career and as a condemnation of his depression.

In the final lines of the song, Young, no longer introspective, treats us to some more satire:

> I never knew a man could tell so many lies
> He had a different story for every set of eyes
> How can he remember who he's talking to
> 'Cause I know it ain't me and I hope it isn't you.

It is something of a critical commonplace to point out that Young is here referring to Richard Nixon, and this was even more obvious at the time of the album's release when the Watergate scandal was still a hot subject of debate. However, in every other instance on this album, Young's political commentaries and satirical thrusts have been blatantly ambivalent. In spite of the obvious connection with Watergate, Young again teases the listener's curiosity by not actually naming Nixon, as he had done in "Ohio" and "Campaigner". Here again, Young wishes to retain a degree of ambivalence by forcing us to look deeper into the words for a secondary meaning. If we apply the dictum that all Young's satirical songs on this album ultimately turn inward upon himself, then the lines gain added force by being Young's final condemnation of his former self. Following his regeneration, Young can look back at his former attitude and expose it unmercifully. He has been doing that throughout this album in songs such as 'Revolution Blues'', "Vampire Blues" and even "On The Beach" in which all his pictures had fallen from the wall where he placed them yesterday. Now Young exposes his tendency to falsify his own emotions on albums such as the sentimental *Harvest* ("I never knew a man could tell so many lies") and hopes that neither he nor his audience will accept such an artistic compromise in the future. Although this interpretation of a possible secondary meaning to these lines may seem a little extreme, it is not without some foundation. Young himself, when discussing "Out On The Weekend", admitted his tendency to disguise his true feelings and he noted that even when he was happy he made his songs appear to sound sad. On an album that so effectively strips away the illusions of both the artist and the audience, it is hardly inconceivable that Young would question his own sincerity with such venom. That he is at once placed alongside Richard Nixon makes the statement even more provocative and self-realizing. *Rolling Stone*, in common with several other rock periodicals, considered "Ambulance Blues" the highlight of Young's recording career. It remains unquestionably his greatest recorded statement, and is probably the finest song he ever wrote.

It was ironic that having exorcised his demons and produced an album that effectively documented a new positive attitude towards his art and career, Young should be criticized for, of all things, producing a despairing work. A few weeks after the release of *On The Beach*, however, one critic was intelligent enough to perceive the full implications of Young's latest work. Writing in *New Musical Express*, Ian MacDonald reviewed the album from an unusual standpoint:

> *On The Beach* is his equivalent of Lennon's *Plastic Ono Band* in terms of being a reaction to and rejection of his earlier work but, whereas Lennon's change was both gradual (starting, really, from "Help!") and included in its course pieces like "Lucy In The Sky With Diamonds" (the gap between which and something like "Remember" cannot fail to be noticed), Young has made his artistic stock-in-trade from the very beginning.
>
> Thus, that an album as bleak and miserable-sounding as *On The Beach* has been preceded by no less than six other albums almost all equally bleak and miserable-sounding, can easily obscure the fact that the record represents a departure; indeed, even if people were to credit Young with doing something vaguely new in *On The Beach*, a lot of them would be fairly justified for dismissing his "new" bleakness as a bleaker version of the one they ... er, already knew and loved. And that's the catch really.[26]

The "catch", as MacDonald perceived, was that the album seemed a conscious attempt by Young to face the truth about himself and his art.

Having determined the faults in much of Young's earlier work, MacDonald was in a strong position to realize the extent to which this new work represented a departure:

> And that could be the main reason why the majority of Neil Young fans won't get into *On The Beach*. The pill is no longer sugared – either by Sweet Melody or by garlands of posies ...
>
> Young has, quite simply, welched on the deal. Which, in turn, suggests he's Woken Up ... *On The Beach* isn't, as previously interpreted, the fag-end of Neil Young's romance with rejection, but actually a quite positive piece of work in the Merciless Realism bracket of Lennon's primal period.[26]

MacDonald's equation of *On The Beach* with Lennon's *Plastic Ono Band* album was an intriguing perception, perhaps more than even he realized. Both albums if played to the casual listener might seem bleak and despairing in tone. The reason for this is that they are each attempts at stripping down the artist's personality in order to determine what is really important. In each work, the artist views his past with a critical eye and it is only after he has examined his former feelings that he can hope to be regenerated. Lennon, like Young, can speak with bitter sarcasm about his role in the rock world: "If you want to be a hero, well just follow me." For both artists, fame is ultimately exposed as an empty, hollow dream. Generally, Lennon is even more uncompromising than Young, and on songs such as "I Found Out" says directly what Young refers to more obliquely. However, both artists have the courage to show a total disdain for their audience at times, and just as Young pleads, "I can't tell them how to feel", Lennon also dismisses the illusions of his followers – "And so dear friends, you'll just have to carry on/The dream is over." Those last four words might well serve as an alternative title for both albums. Lennon committed the ultimate heresy when he exclaimed at the end of "God" – "I don't believe in Beatles", and Neil repeated that statement by employing the famous quote about Crosby, Stills, Nash & Young – "you're all just pissing in the wind." In their respective ways, Lennon and Young had re-evaluated their own careers, and the effects were finally therapeutic rather than self-destructive. Lennon had at least discovered what really mattered in his life – "I just believe in me, Yoko and me, and that's reality", while Young had found the confidence to say "sooner or later it all gets real." Still his most misunderstood work, *On The Beach* showed Young's outstanding capacity for change and survival.

FIFTEEN

A Series Of Superstar Gigs

Crosby, Stills, Nash & Young made their spectacular return to the stage on 9 July at Seattle. It was probably the most exhausting gig they had ever suffered for they gave the audience that rarest of phenomenons, a four-hour show. As Crosby remembers, the chance to play again as C.S.N.&Y was too great a temptation to resist:

> I wanted to play. I wanted to be in that band. I love that band. Playing at those big places was something Stills and Neil wanted to do and they demanded it. That's what the managers wanted to do. That's what the agents wanted to do. That's what everybody wanted to do except me and Nash. We were the only hold-outs.

It may seem contradictory that after the *Time Fades Away* tour and Young's avowed distaste for large venues that he would be so willing to play at giant stadiums. Since the recording of *On The Beach* and the winter "Tonight's The Night" tour, Young seemed more able and willing to reconcile his contradictory attitude to stardom and the record industry. In spite of his supposed idealistic attitude in appearing at small clubs, Young was also anxious to further his own career by reaching greater numbers of people. Taking an overview of Young's career, Crosby reminds us that the "unwilling superstar" has not exactly restricted himself to playing at only small venues:

> Neil has played in enormous halls too. He is very aware of the economics of rock 'n roll. And it's not so much a question of being more so than me and Nash since we did pretty well while we were managing ourselves. With regard to the 1974 tour, I think Stills in particular liked playing the enormous places because he liked being big. And in 1974, we probably were the biggest group in the world. At that moment it was either us or the Stones. Stephen liked that. It was enormously satisfying for him to have the Beach Boys, Santana, the Band and Joni Mitchell open for us. That was quite something. I don't know how much Neil dug it. I think he dug playing and I think he dug what it would do ... I think he wanted to play the big places. It was my memory of it that he did.

According to Crosby, Young was in good spirits for most of the tour. Although his *On The Beach* album had recently been released, Young was still not actively promoting it and as the tour progressed he introduced another new batch of songs. The first gig had seen the introduction of a further two new numbers: "Love Art Blues" and "Traces". The former, a singalong acoustic number featuring Neil on piano, appeared to sum up his feelings about his career at this point. Since the purgative *On The Beach*, Young had been free to take a more sardonic look at his work, and in "Love Art Blues" he noted, "My songs are all so long and my words are all so sad." Young appeared to realize that his cloying love songs were hardly his highest form of artistic expression and wryly exclaimed:

> Why must I choose between the best things I ever had? I got the Love-
> Art blues, don't know which one to choose

"Traces" expressed a similar clash between love and art, with the former seeming to have an upper-hand at this point. Young sang about the joys of finding a new love but warned that, in artistic terms, his destination was still unnamed and therefore it was "hard to leave the traces for someone to follow." During the summer tour, two other unreleased songs were also introduced: "Hawaiian Sunrise" and "Home Fires". The former, alternatively titled "Maui Mama" was similar in theme and tone to "New Mama", which would eventually appear on *Tonight's The Night*. "Hawaiian Sunrise" boasted an unusual arrangement with Young sounding like a modern day West Coast George Formby. The melodic "Home Fires" was later described by Young as a personal song dealing with the break-up of his relationship with Carrie Snodgrass. However, the lyrics also related to the love-art dichotomy:

> I'm not the same man I was awhile ago
> I've learned some new things. I hope that it shows.

These words might equally apply to the change in musical attitude that had been revealed in *On The Beach*. Most of Young's new songs from this period contained references to either his love-life or art, but the sentiments were positive in tone with little hint of introspection. Reports of Young's performances with Crosby, Stills & Nash indicated that the songs were a fairly accurate reflection of his state of mind. Young seemed confident and content on stage and after the gigs he maintained his independence by traveling separately from the other members of the group. In this way, Young managed to avoid the tensions that might easily have resulted from the aftermath of playing before over 50,000 people at a time. As the tour reached its climax, more and more transatlantic reviews boasted of a revitalized, rejuvenated Young totally unlike the moody, melancholic character of the last two tours.

Over 72,000 British fans managed to see this new Young when C.S.N.&Y. finally reached their final date at London's Wembley Stadium on 14 September 1974. In spite of the glowing reviews Crosby still feels uneasy about his involvement in the stadium shows:

> The doom tour pissed me off. It's one of the reasons we're not playing
> together. It was a rip-off by us of the audiences. If a person can't see
> your face they can't tell how you're feeling about what you're doing.

116

And if they can't tell how you feel about what you're singing, they're not getting it. And to charge somebody 10 bucks to sit on a piece of mud, 300 yards away *literally* – it doesn't matter if you've got a P.A. system bigger than God – it's not fair.

In spite of these reservations the foursome still talked about releasing a live double album of the tour and promised to record a new C.S.N.&Y. album upon their return to the States.

Following that Wembley performance, however, the foursome went their separate ways and both projects were shelved. This at least put paid to any lasting suspicions that they had temporarily reunited simply for the money. A live double album following such a big tour would have been a guaranteed massive seller and it was assumed that they would release this material after having spent so much time and trouble recording it. But, in spite of their talents, Crosby, Stills, Nash & Young have never acted as the businessmen one might have expected them to become. Part of their charm lay in this tendency to make illogical moves and always remain ambiguous in their motives. Following the tour, Young spoke of the difficulties that he faced playing before such enormous crowds, and contrasted it to life in his early folk days:

I started playing for 25 people at a time and I was getting off. Now it's just so mammoth that you've gotta get by that all over again to get off. Money doesn't ... the biggest thing that affects it is the amount of people. That's where it is, how big the music is. Money's just a side-effect of that. It's really different, though – that part of it's really blown my mind. It's such a high to get really personal with 60,000 people.[21]

In spite of his willingness to play the stadiums and his realization of how it would benefit his career, Young had clearly experienced some psychological challenges in confronting such an enormous audience. Perhaps the sheer exhaustion of playing 30 gigs before so many people was the main factor which prevented C.S.N.&Y. from continuing their lucrative relationship after the summer tour. Some critics have felt that ego problems had probably caused a rift, but there is nothing to substantiate such a claim, and Young clearly does not remember any such clashes:

I thought there wasn't a problem at all. Last time we went out, and every time we've gone out, it's been great.

We just didn't make an album. And it's not even that it didn't happen – we just didn't *do* it. If we don't do something people put together all these trips about, you know, Stills and Young are fighting so they can't do this. That's all a bunch of bullshit.

For a month or so after the Wembley gig, Young seemed unsure precisely what he might try next. Before returning to the States, he took a vacation in Amsterdam accompanied by Graham Nash and Tim Mulligan. While there, he spoke with confidence about having come through a dark period and revealed that he was ready to record no less than 24 songs, several of which had been heard during the summer tour. Young's tendency to get excited about new projects and speak in terms of half-baked conceptual ideas was never made more evident than during this Amsterdam visit. He claimed that he had written a number of new songs dealing with water, and therefore felt it would be a good idea to record them on an island. Ibiza was deemed a suitable choice and Elliot Mazer was named as the probable producer. Young then went on to discuss six songs which he felt should be included on this "water" album: "Frozen Man"; "Star Of Bethlehem"; "Maui Mama (Hawaiian Sunrise)"; "Deep Forbidden Lake"; 'Love Art Blues" and "Vacancy". Like many of Young's projects, however, this latest idea was aborted because of what were later described as "technical problems".

Returning to the States, Young began work on a new album, *Homegrown* towards the end of the year. The sessions took place in Nashville and were produced by Mazer, with backing musicians including Tim Drummond (bass); Ben Keith (steel guitar/dobro); Karl T. Himmel (drums); Rufus Thibodeaux (violin) and Emmylou Harris on additional vocals. Early in the New Year, the album was ready for release and the cover artwork had been completed. The full track listing was selected from the following: "Homegrown"; "Vacancy"; "Homefires"; "Separate Ways"; "Deep Forbidden Lake"; "Love Is A Rose"; "White Line"; "Try"; "Star Of Bethlehem"; "Little Wing"; "The Old Homestead"; "Hawaiian Sunrise"; "Pardon My Heart"; "Love Art Blues"; "Human Highway"; "Changing Highways". Clearly, from those songs alone, the album would have been Young's most commercially successful recording since *Harvest*. Virtually all the tracks were acoustic, with strong melodies and singalong choruses. The majority of them were also easily memorable love-songs with instant mass appeal. In short, the album seemed to be guaranteed platinum. Young invited several of his friends to a playback party for the album, hoping to elicit their approval. Coincidentally, on the same reel of that tape there happened to be a resequenced version of the old *Tonight's The Night* session from 1973. After Warners had vetoed the projected album, the tapes had been left in their incomplete form with nine songs recorded. Following these sessions, manager Elliot Roberts salvaged the tapes for possible use in a Broadway show based on the life of Bruce Berry, and for which a script had been completed. Roberts and Young decided to resequence the "Tonight's The Night" songs and combine them with three earlier recordings, "Borrowed Tune", "Look Out Joe" and Danny Whitten's "Come On Baby Let's Go Downtown" in order to make a cohesive story. Unfortunately, the projected Broadway musical failed to reach fruition and the tapes were returned to Young.

It was during the playback reception that an extraordinary thing happened. As the party progressed, the tape kept rolling and those present were given the unique opportunity of hearing *Homegrown* alongside *Tonight's The Night*. As the drink flowed, many of those present found it a lot easier to relate to *Tonight's The Night*. Eventually, Rick Danko suggested to Young that *Tonight's The Night* had a lot more spirit and ought to be released in preference to the easy-listening *Homegrown*. Impressed by this enthusiastic response, Young rejected *Homegrown*, and persuaded Warners to release the resequenced *Tonight's The Night* in its place. In discussing his surprise decision, Young admitted that *Homegrown* was by far the most commercially viable record of the two:

> A lot of people would probably say that it's better. I know the first time I listened back to *Tonight's The Night* it was the most out-of-

tune thing I'd every heard. Everyone's off-key. I couldn't hack it. But by listening to those two albums back to back at the party, I started to see the weaknesses in *Homegrown*. I took *Tonight's The Night* because of its overall strength in performance and feeling. The theme may be a little depressing, but the general feeling is much more elevating than *Homegrown*. Putting this album out is almost an experiment. I fully expect some of the most determinedly worst reviews I've ever had. I mean if anybody really wanted to let go, they could do it on this one. And undoubtedly a few people will. I don't know. That record might be more what people would rather hear from me now, but it was just a very down album. It was the darker side of *Harvest*. A lot of songs had to do with me breaking up with my old lady. It was a little too personal … it scared me.

While finalizing the release of *Tonight's The Night* Young managed to find time to appear at the S.N.A.C.K. Benefit concert in the Kezer Stadium on 23 March 1975. Young's friends from the Band had persuaded him to accept an invitation from organizer Billy Graham and appear at the concert. While Neil's addition to the show helped to increase ticket sales, there was also a rumor of a special mystery guest who would be included on the bill. That man turned out to be none other than Bob Dylan, and an unusual footnote was added to rock history that day when Neil Young, Dylan and the Band appeared on stage with each other. It was certainly not the most memorable performance that any of them had given, but the sight of those three acts onstage at one time was ample reward in itself for most spectators.

SIXTEEN

At Last – Tonight's The Night

It was nearly four months later when *Tonight's The Night* finally hit the shops in July 1975. For Young, it was enormously gratifying to see the album released since it was one of the projects that had provided him the greatest artistic satisfaction. The sales of the album were not pleasing but the critical reaction was better than many might have expected. Although some critics did slam the album and few praised it without qualification, there was a notable respect for Young's artistry. Following the C.S.N.&Y. tour, it was clear that many critics had woken up to the fact that Young was not in the process of artistic decline but had been fully aware of the consequences of his musical aberrations from the outset. This realization that Young had not lost his talent and, in fact, had been capable of producing commercial albums such as *Harvest* when and as the whim took him, made the release of *Tonight's The Night* an even more daring artistic venture. Even if some critics felt unsure about the musical quality of certain parts of *Tonight's The Night* they at least had to admit a new grudging respect for an artist who had staunchly refused to compromise his musical ideals. This renewed critical interest in Young as an artist would be a crucial factor in his subsequent return to commercial success.

Young's concern that *Tonight's The Night* should be reasonably well publicized was demonstrated in his willingness to invite a select gathering to, of all things, a press conference and party. This was the first time since the premier of *Journey Through The Past* that Young had felt the need to make some kind of public statement about his artistic intentions. It was evident that Young felt a little out of place actively promoting his record in this way:

> The record business ... I don't even think I'm in it anymore. I really don't. I've never done anything like this before – interviews and the party and everything. But I never had a record you could party to and interview to before.

Young went on to reveal that another of the factors that contributed to the delay of the release of *Tonight's The Night* was his feeling that more work needed to be done on the record:

> *Tonight's The Night* didn't come out right after it was recorded

because it wasn't finished. It just wasn't in the right order, the concept wasn't right. I had to get the color right, so it was not so down that it would make people restless. I had to keep jolting every once in a while to get people to wake up so they could be lulled again. It's a very fluid album. The higher you are, the better it is. And it really lives up to that, a lot of records don't ... you should listen to it late at night.[21]

Although the album is generally regarded as bleak in tone, Young encourages us to look beyond the apparent negativity in order to perceive that the album is very much a document of something that has passed. Talbot had compared the album to an "Irish wake", and ultimately that is the mood that it evokes. A wake is a ceremony that is, paradoxically, a celebration of death and an affirmation that life must continue. In spite of its somber theme *Tonight's The Night* stresses the same philosophy and can therefore finally be seen as a positive statement. This is obviously how Young saw the album which he even went as far as to describe as a "happy record".

The story that *Tonight's The Night* is based upon is summed up in the dedication "To Bruce Berry and Danny Whitten who lived and died for rock 'n roll". Young's biography in song of the late C.S.N.&Y. roadie Bruce Berry, captures the sense of shock that Neil experienced when he learned of his friend's death. The sentiments are expressed without ostentation. The first verse captures the feeling that usually accompanies the announcement of such a tragedy. Berry's death could not have been totally unexpected; Young stresses that he was a junkie: "... A sparkle was in his eyes but his life was in his hands". In spite of the seeming inevitability when the tragic news finally reached Young it still came as a shock. Although Berry's death was unheralded in the rock press and the roadie may not have had the necessary qualities to become a famous rock star in his own right, Young still praises his talents:

> Late at night when the people were gone
> He used to pick up my guitar
> And sing a song in a shaky voice
> That was real as the day was long

Young's elegy extended beyond the lyrics and into the playing. He actively persuaded guitarist Nils Lofgren to imitate the style of Bruce Berry in order to give the song even greater emotional force.

The Berry style of playing can be heard to even greater effect on "Speakin' Out" in which Young shouts "All rights Nils" as the young player bursts into an intriguing solo. Although the song is somber in tone with its rough vocal and rolling piano work, the sentiments are essentially celebratory:

> I've been a searcher, I've been a fool
> I've been a long time coming to you.
> I'm hoping for your love to carry me through
> You're holding my baby and I'm holding you.
> And it's all right.

Taken at a faster pace and given a quality production with overdubbed vocals, a song such as this might easily have appeared on one of Young's more commercial albums. It has become a commonplace in discussing *Tonight's The Night* to describe it in Young's words as "a horror record", but on an album that is supposedly obsessed with death and the drug culture, it is worth noting that in "Speakin' Out" he spends much time singing about the contentment produced by a baby's birth.

Young's desire to restructure the album in order to place the faster cuts between the slower numbers is evident from the placing of "World On A String" in the middle of side one. It is used as a bridge between "Speakin' Out" and "Borrowed Tune" and as Young says, it livens up the listener at a crucial point. In the original sequencing, "World On A String" was placed before "Speakin' Out" and it is clear that Young has chosen to keep them side by side on the album probably because both songs, in spite of their totally different tempos, have strong thematic links. "Borrowed Tune" is the first of three songs that were added to the album in order to provide a more varied mood:

> If you take out "Lookout Joe", "Downtown" and "Borrowed Tune",
> all the others left just gather in intensity so much that you can't take
> them all. Each one I liked so much I wanted them all on there. I made
> all kinds of lists to get them in the right order so that all the songs
> would set the others up, mentally, for people.[21]

The inclusion of "Borrowed Tune" was a very appropriate choice mainly because it fitted well with both the songs relating to the drug culture and the general fatalistic tone of much of the other material on the album. In common with "Speakin' Out" and "World On A String", it is essentially contemplative in tone and included Young's familiar speculations on the apparent worthlessness of fame:

> I'm climbing this ladder my head in the clouds
> I hope that it matters, I'm having my doubts.

These speculations lead to a sense of ennui which is the predominant mood of the piece. The ennui that the song reflects is seen partly to be drug induced:

> I'm singing this borrowed tune
> I took from the Rolling Stones
> Alone in this empty room
> Too wasted to write my own.

What is most remarkable here is that Young comes out and blatantly admits his plagiarism of the Rolling Stones' "Lady Jane". These lines disorientate the listener and Young's admission that he is too wasted to write his own tune is a chilling reminder that his lifestyle may be only a few steps removed from those of Danny Whitten and Bruce Berry.

"Come On Baby Let's Go Downtown" is a further example of the care taken in choosing extraneous material for this album. The song, co-written by Whitten and taken from a Neil Young and Crazy Horse performance at a 1970 Fillmore East concert serves as the perfect tribute. It is faster and more raucous than the original version that appeared on the first Crazy Horse album and effectively captures one of Whitten's most manic live performances.

The final track on side one, "Mellow My Mind", seems to have been recorded at a point during the "Tonight's The Night" sessions when Young was noticeably wasted. His vocals are slurred and off-key but in his drunkenness he does manage to invest some intensity into the song. According to Young, "Mellow My Mind" was particularly appropriate for *Tonight's The Night* since it dealt with the problems facing the rock star in re-adapting to normal life following the madness of a hectic touring schedule:

> This is a song about wanting to stop. After a long tour you just want to be able to slow it down. Even when it's over you can't stop. You get going so fast from place to place, then when it ends you keep going for a while.[27]

On the opening cut of side two, "Roll Another Number", Young sounds as stoned as he had done on "Mellow My Mind". Although Young provides the song with a strong country 'n western flavor by allowing Ben Keith's steel to dominate, the mood is very far from that of *Harvest*. In a few short lines Young says farewell to the burgeoning hippie generation that made *Harvest* his biggest-selling album:

> I'm not going back to Woodstock for awhile
> Though I long to hear that lonesome hippie smile
> I'm a million miles away from that helicopter day
> Oh I don't believe I'll be going back that way.

These lines summed up just how much Young had changed since the superstar days of 1972.

Although the succeeding cut, "Albuquerque" presents Young "rolling another number", there is little evidence of the slurred vocals that were so evident on the previous two songs. "Albuquerque" is surprisingly ordered when contrasted to some of the other cuts on *Tonight's The Night* and its placing on the album shows Young's concern not to allow any single mood to dominate for too long.

While *Tonight's The Night* is a dark album and uses death as one of its main themes, the pervasive mood remains essentially like that of a wake. From out of the chaos comes the determination of the survivors to continue living. This feeling is emphasized in "New Mama", a song dealing not with death, but with birth. The off-key vocals are replaced by strong harmonies and the tone seems unambiguously optimistic. Significantly, this was the only song on the album that was covered by another artist, and it was a fitting tribute that the person should have been Young's former colleague, Stephen Stills.

"Look Out Joe" was the third track on the album borrowed from an earlier session. It is actually Young backed by the Stray Gators, a fact which, not surprisingly, caused Billy Talbot to object to its inclusion on the album. He maintained that the extraneous material had been added because Young was afraid that the finished album might sound too extreme. Talbot's objections to the song seem rather less than convincing. "Look Out Joe" was probably one of the most "extreme" songs on the album with its sleazy images of hip drag queens and side-walking street wheelers. Young borrows the persona of Millie from "Pushed It Over The End", but now she is presented as a heroin addict with "a hole in her arm". The title, "Look Out Joe" is an ironic warning to G.I.s returning from the war that times have changed and they may be shocked to find a world of bloodshed, drug addiction and prostitution that is not so different from the horrors of Vietnam. Young was a little critical of the track:

> "Look Out Joe" and "Borrowd Tune" were written during my *Time Fades Away* tour. I never hit "Look Out Joe" the way I wanted to. It was recorded at my ranch during the rehearsals for the *Time Fades Away* tour just after Danny Whitten O.D.d. He'd been working on the song with us and after he died we stopped for awhile. When we started playing again, that was the first thing we cut and I wrote "Don't Be Denied" that day. So "Look Out Joe" is one of the oldest songs on the album.[21]

"Tired Eyes" goes one step further than the other drug-related songs on the album by giving Young the opportunity to enact several different roles in a fictitious drama:

> It's like being an actor and writing the script for myself as opposed to a personal expression. There's obviously a lot of personal expression there, but it comes in a different form, which makes it seem much more explicit and direct. All these people they're all in there. That's why there's so much talking on the record. It's all the things that I hear people saying.

In relating the tale of a junkie who was shot in a cocaine deal Young adopts several personae, conversing with himself about the circumstances of the murder:

> Well tell me more tell me more
> I mean was he a heavy doper or was he just a loser?
> He was supposed to be a friend of yours
> He tried to do his best but he could not.

That last line becomes a refrain and it is an epitaph that might well be applied to both Danny Whitten and Bruce Berry.

The album closes with another refrain, the "Tonight's The Night" theme. It is a more intense version than the opening cut with rougher guitar breaks and an instrumental crescendo towards the end of the song. Young explains why it was necessary to include a second version of the title track:

> It's just that there was a lot of spirit flying around when we were doing it. It was like a tribute to those people, you know? Only the ones we chose no one had really heard of that much, but they meant a lot to us. That's why it gets spooky, 'cause we were spooked.

Although *Tonight's The Night* was a comparative flop sales-wise, it won back many of the critics who had consistently ignored Young since the release of *Harvest*. Many influential critics, both in the States and in England, nominated *Tonight's The Night* as one of the best albums of the year. Young agreed with the most perceptive of them and still regards the album as one of his finest.

Although the individual songs are reasonably impressive it is the overall mood of the album which gives it real power. It is probably Young's most cohesive work and even though some tracks are different in tone, none of them sound out of place. If one were to attempt a list of Young's greatest songs, the selections on *Tonight's The Night* might appear under-represented, yet the album will always remain a very strong contender for the title of Young's finest work.

SEVENTEEN

The Time Travel Concept

The belated release of *Tonight's The Night* was preceded by the reunion of Young and Crazy Horse. Talbot had invited Young to his home in Silver Lake to rehearse some new material. Young was suitably impressed with the sound and began playing along with Frank Sampedro on a Les Paul guitar that he had previously used on *Everybody Knows This Is Nowhere*. After a few days, it became clear that Neil Young and Crazy Horse were back together again and looked more powerful than ever. Young had first met Sampedro in Chicago just before the recording of the unreleased *Homegrown*. Billy Talbot maintains that it was this meeting which later inspired Young to engage the services of Crazy Horse for his next album.

Young reveals his feelings about the decision to reunite with his former backing group:

> Crazy Horse is a very soulful feeling for me. They give me a support that no one else can give me, they afford me the possibilities of doing more with my guitar and my voice and feeling than anybody else. So that's why we still play together.[9]

Following the sessions with Crazy Horse, Young decided to set to work immediately on a new album. He already had a lot of new material written and he remained extremely confident that the recording sessions would be productive and enjoyable.

It was mid-way through these recording sessions that Young decided to take time off to do some promotional work on the recently released *Tonight's The Night*. He spoke with exuberance, not only about *Tonight's The Night* and his as yet unrecorded new album, but also about a major tour that was apparently scheduled for the autumn of 1975:

> I don't know what this new tour will be like. I'll be doing a lot of the stuff that I'm recording now. A lot of long instrumental guitar things – progressive ... progresso supremo? It's about the Incas and the Aztecs. It takes on another personality. It's like being in another civilization. It's a lost sort of soul form that switches from history scene to history scene trying to find itself, man, in this maze. I've got it all written and all the songs are learned. Tomorrow we start cutting

them. We're ready to go. We're gonna just do it in the morning. Early in the morning when the sun's out. Sunny days ... just ... play.[21]

Young explained that the projected tour would probably include a series of new songs and he stressed that he had no intention of actively promoting any specific album:

> In concert what I play all depends on how I feel. I can't do songs like "Southern Man". I'd rather play the Lynyrd Skynyrd song that answered it. That'd be great. The thing is, I go on a different trip and I get a different band together, or I group with some old friends, then they don't know how to play the stuff that I did with some other group and I have to show them. That takes a lot of time and I'd rather be working on new stuff. So a lot of it is just laziness. I don't even know some of the songs with the bands, you know? I'm not going to even try to do "Tonight's The Night". If I go out in the fall I probably will take this band I'm working with now. We could get into doing these songs anytime, but I'd have something new in my head by then that I would be even more into. We'll do some of them.
>
> I'm working right now, recording. That's what I'm mainly interested in because I have a lot of new songs that I haven't finished recording.

In spite of Young's assertions the proposed concert tour with Crazy Horse did not take place until the following year. The new album also underwent several changes during the next few months. The proposed title was to be *In My Llama* though it was also rumored to be called *In My Old Neighbourhood* and *My Old Car*. Eventually, the work emerged as *Zuma* in November 1975. It was obvious that Young's original concept of an album dealing with time travel and different civilizations had altered substantially since the early recording sessions in the late spring. Songs that were relevant to the "time travel" concept such as "Ride My Llama", "Pocohontas" and "Powderfinger" were mysteriously deleted, leaving only "Cortez The Killer" and the *Zuma* title as evidence of Young's ambitious concept. Why Young decided to restructure the album has never been explained and remains a further example of his idiosyncratic tendency to make dramatic last minute alterations to his work. *Zuma* contained elements of both *Everybody Knows This Is Nowhere* and *After The Goldrush* with a selection of commercial songs revealing some stunning electric guitar work. In short, its various components were sufficient to please both the critics and the general public.

The opening cut, "Don't Cry No Tears" ably demonstrated that Young was once more interested in performing commercial ditties. It was one of his earliest songs, part of it being written during his adolescent years. The lyrics are repetitive and inconsequential, a mere backdrop to the melody with its instantly recognizable title hook. This was the type of song that would return Young to the playlists of commercial radio and must have been greeted with a mixture of enthusiasm and relief by his record company. Much the same can be said for "Lookin' For A Love" which was later released as a single.

In spite of the strong commercial appeal of "Don't Cry No Tears", and "Lookin' For A Love", *Zuma* could not be dismissed as a retrogressive album. "Danger

Bird" revealed Young's determination to recreate the intensity that characterized the work of Crazy Horse on *Everybody Knows This Is Nowhere*. One rock performer who was very impressed with Young's work on "Danger Bird" was Lou Reed. He not only stated that the guitar playing was excrutiatingly beautiful but added that it was probably the finest he had ever heard. This was undoubtedly the greatest compliment given to Young by any other rock performer.

Although *Zuma* had obviously undergone some track changes during the few months prior to its release, it was still a very carefully constructed album. Young seemed determined to reveal every facet of his musical personality, moving gradually from the simple to the intricate and frequently alternating between soft and hard rock. "Pardon My Heart" showed his mastery of the acoustic ballad and was irrefutable evidence that Young, Molina and Talbot could produce some striking harmonies.

"Lookin' For A Love" was the obvious single from *Zuma*, although it lacked the charm of either "Heart Of Gold" or "Old Man" and did not re-establish Young as a singles artist. In common with both those songs it reeked of romanticism with Young singing confidently about the possibility of discovering a perfect love. Like several of the songs on *Harvest*, however, the idealism was tinged with just enough pessimism to make it sound convincing.

By contrast, the strident "Barstool Blues" was the first of a series of songs that Young would write about getting drunk in American bars. The opening lines neatly describe the preliminary stages of drunkenness:

> If I could hold on to just one thought
> For long enough to know
> Why my mind is moving so fast
> And the conversation is slow.

According to Frank Sampedro Young's interest in investigating American bar culture was nurtured during the *Zuma* recording sessions:

> Everybody thinks Neil's so serious, so they want to talk real serious with him. But really he's just a simple guy. One night when we were doing *Zuma* he was feeling real down and he was gonna go home and feel lousy. So I said "C'mon Neil, let's go out and get drunk". We must have hit every bar in Malibu.
>
> The next day he called me up and said, "I don't know when I did it but I wrote three songs last night and I woke up sleeping on them". And a couple of those songs ended up on *Zuma*.[28]

The first side of *Zuma* had shown the lighter side of Young with a couple of tracks vaguely reminiscent of the *Harvest* and *After The Goldrush* periods. "Stupid Girl" and "Drive Back", however, were reminders of how aggressive Young could be when discussing the subject of past loves.

The undisputed key cut on *Zuma*, however, was the ambitious "Cortez The Killer". For many, this was the long awaited return to the extended guitar solos that made "Cowgirl In The Sand" and "Down By The River" such impressive pieces of work. "Cortez The Killer" provided a positive answer to the question of whether Young would ever produce an epic to rival his previous Crazy Horse collaborations. In doing so, Young had also written a song which contained some of his most intriguing lyrics. "Cortez The Killer" documented the veritable genocide of the Aztecs by the Spanish invaders led by Cortez. Young fully displayed the horror of this invasion by emphasizing the almost carefree manner in which the voyage was undertaken:

> He came dancing across the water
> With his galleons and guns.

Strangely enough, Young does not attempt to characterize Cortez, who is simply cast in the role of a "killer". Montezuma and his subjects are symbols of archetypal innocence and Young carefully glosses over their barbaric pagan rites:

> They offered life in sacrifice
> So that others could go on.

The "New World" was once it seems a utopia:

> Hate was just a legend
> And war was never known
> The people worked together ...

Cortez is the snake in Eden, the harbinger of primitive man's fall from innocence. In the final verse, however, Young complicates his narrative by placing himself and his lost love in the fictional landscape:

> And I know she's living there
> And she loves me to this day
> I still can't remember when
> Or how I lost my way.

Through this extraordinary last verse, Young equates the destroyed innocence of the Aztecs with his own loss of innocence and inability to find the imaginary perfect woman. "Cortez The Killer" was the track that reunited the critics and the general public in their appreciation of Young as one of the most important rock figures of the seventies.

The final track on *Zuma*, "Through My Sails", presents nothing less than the recorded reunion of Crosby, Stills, Nash & Young. It was fitting that having included material which reflected his various musical styles Young should end with a typically acoustic C.S.N.&Y. harmony number. The contrast is heightened by placing this track next to the electric "Cortez The Killer". Here, Young stresses that he is equally adept at recording acoustic ballads or electric guitar workouts in the style of *Everybody Knows This Is Nowhere*. However, his colleagues did not always agree with him that Crosby, Stills, Nash & Young and Crazy Horse could be equally valid. Crosby clearly preferred C.S.N.&Y.'s treatment of Young's material:

> I preferred our version of "Down By The River". I didn't like Crazy Horse. I thought they were dull. He liked it because it was a totally different sound and he wanted to be different at that point. He felt a great need to separate himself. I didn't like it.

Although *Zuma* was not a great album, it served as an effective reminder of Young's musical versatility. One of the reasons why *Zuma* was so well received was not only that it spared the general public the merciless realism of *On The Beach* and *Tonight's The Night*, but simultaneously contained enough musical adventurousness to satisfy those critics who preferred Young's less melodic work.

Following the release of *Zuma* Young found himself back in the news for other reasons. He became involved in a dispute over the staging of a rock concert. Young appeared at a meeting of the San Mateo County Planning Commission not to support the concert, but to provide a list of reasons why the projected series of performances should be banned. Officials were amazed to see the reticent superstar speaking frankly about the worst aspects of rock festivals and vividly describing drug overdoses and the dangers of overcrowding. This was no mere anti-star pose, however, for Young had personal reasons for ensuring that the projected rock concerts be suppressed. The site for the outdoor concerts was a 600 acre ranch in the mountains, fifty miles south of San Francisco, dangerously close to Young's own Broken Arrow Ranch. It was here that C.S.N.&Y. had rehearsed their 1974 reunion tour and for Young it was the closest thing to an outdoor sanctuary. The thought of his favorite refuge being defiled by autograph-seeking fans and unwelcome tourists was apparently too much for Young to take and prompted his involvement in the dispute between the locals and organizer, Monte Stern. The opposition from Young, coupled with the objections from planning authorities finally persuaded Stern to abandon the idea.

By the end of 1975, Young once more became the center of attention when rumors filtered through the press that a reunion with Stephen Stills on record was imminent. Characteristically unpredictable Young neither announced news of a projected tour with Stills nor of any extensive touring plans with Crazy Horse. Instead, he spent the whole of December playing small unannounced gigs in imitation of Dylan's celebrated Rolling Thunder Revue, and unlike Dylan's show it remained low-life and never reached stadium proportions. Young generally played without fee at bars in obscure places such as Cotati or seaside Marshall which boasted a population of fifty. The appearance at the Marshall Tavern was particularly low-key. The doors were open to all and sundry and nobody was bothering to charge for admission. Although the bar held a capacity of 100 people, it was only half-full, indicating that news of Young's appearance had been a well kept secret. The set consisted mainly of songs from the recently released *Zuma* as well as some longer numbers such as "Down By The River" and an under-rehearsed "Southern Man". Following his set, Young did not disappear to an awaiting black limousine but hung round at the bar and entertained the punters with some witty conversation. It would not last for long, but for a time Young succeeded in escaping the pressures of playing enormous halls and rediscovered the satisfaction of appearing before a small and diverse audience.

EIGHTEEN

On The Road Again

The Rolling Zuma Review continued touring throughout January 1976, but reports of Young's activities were swiftly becoming news items and it was proving increasingly difficult to play unannounced gigs. By the time the national press were reporting the story, Young was already winding up this short series of performances. Neil later admitted that it was Dylan who had inspired him to take to the road and rediscover his roots:

> Dylan has always had my total respect. He has shown so many of us, especially with that *Before The Flood* album tour with the Band, that a major performer can live with his people.[24]

With this new found confidence, Young was ready to undergo an extensive tour of Europe with Crazy Horse. An arduous series of European gigs culminated in four consecutive nights at London's Hammersmith Odeon (28 March–31 March) and a final gig at Glasgow's Apollo Theatre (2 April). The performances were carefully structured by Young to include a representative proportion of old and new songs, with both acoustic and electric sets. Unlike his previous tour with Crazy Horse during 1973, Young was now gradually introducing his audience to new material and opening with a medley of old favorites such as "Tell Me Why", "Old Man" and "After The Goldrush". By satisfying the audience's need to hear the old hits Young could more comfortably slip in a few new numbers mid-way through his set. Although some reviewers detected signs of disinterest in Neil's interpretation of his older material, Young felt satisfied with his performances:

> But I like those songs, I am now able to detach the Neil Young of today from the person who wrote them. I'm older – clearly – and if all those songs are going to help me reach people with newer stuff, that's fine by me.
>
> I've never liked it though, when they shout out for the old songs immediately after you've finished a new one. Kinda deflating. You know, you pour yourself into a song you've just written, lose yourself in your lyrics. Applause. Great! You think: "Ah, that one made it." Just as the applause dies down, someone shouts out, "SOUTHERN MAN!" And you think: "Awwwwww, they still prefer the old ones."

To HELL with the old ones.

It was not the old songs that won the day during the European tour, however, but a new number titled "Like A Hurricane". Towards the end of the electric set Young would introduce this song "about bars of America" and proceed to dazzle the audience with some incredible guitar interplay between himself and Talbot. During the song, a giant electric fan which was placed on stage would be switched on and it literally made Young appear as though he were playing in the eye of a hurricane. As the final chords were played, the audience spontaneously jumped from their seats to give Young a long standing ovation. Considering that almost nobody in the audience had heard the song before, the response was unprecedented. "Like A Hurricane" was clearly the stand-out track in Young's latest live repertoire, just as "Cortez The Killer" had been on the last album. Apart from "Like A Hurricane", Young introduced a varied selection of new songs at different stages during the tour. Perhaps not surprisingly several of these songs have yet to be recorded including "Too Far Gone"; "Stringman"; "Don't Say You Win, Don't Say You Lose"; "Country Home" and "Day And Night We Walk These Aisles". As usual, these new items were extremely diversified and showed the full range of Young's songwriting ability. "Too Far Gone" was a vivid description of an all-night drinking session with Young boasting "we had pills and we had booze, but we still had plenty to lose." Along with "Like A Hurricane", this was no doubt originally intended for a whole album dealing with the subject of American bar culture. Some of the other songs revealed that Young was also still content to tread familiar ground. The electric "Country Home" with its celebration of a pastoral retreat reiterated the "Homegrown" theme. "Day And Night We Walk These Aisles" was an interesting attempt at expressing a personal relationship through the analogy of a cinema visit. Finally, "Don't Say You Win, Don't Say You Lose" was a fatalistic ballad similar in mood to "See The Sky About To Rain". With its haunting piano-work, reminiscent of "A Man Needs A Maid", the song remains one of Young's finest unreleased songs.

The generous selection of different songs at almost every performance and the characteristically self-effacing stage persona made Young appear the perennial laid-back singer-songwriter. Certainly, Young's performances were seldom song by song rehashes and he seemed capable of far greater spontaneity than almost any other professional rock star. It might seem heretical to speak in terms of Young's "stage-act" since most of his performances were free of the posturings that characterized many of the theatrical rock acts of the seventies. It would be naive, however, to suggest that Young was unaware of the value of theatricalism. The giant fan was a mildly satirical device and displayed an interest in using props on stage which would be developed in later years. Even at this point in his career, however, Young was well aware how to manipulate an audience in the subtlest fashion. His stage garb consisted of patched jeans and jackets which since the days of *After The Goldrush* had been recognized almost as a uniform by his followers. On stage Young would wander around forgetting items, inserting his mouth-harp into his harp-holder upside down and generally making himself look as vulnerable and untogether as possible. It might seem cynical to question what many feel is spontaneity, but even Young admits that many of his actions on stage are calculated examples of audience psychology:

> Do you know why I fiddle around with the instruments during the acoustic set which begins the show? To give people something to look at. It's very important ... Helps them to focus, deviates from looking at my face all the time. Boring, just looking at an artist with guitar in hand for half an hour, no matter how good his songs are. You must interest the audience. I don't need to fiddle around so much with guitars, and I sure don't have anything to say to anyone, except the next song, but if I change instruments, change them about a bit, that helps them. Makes them think I know what I'm doing too.[24]

For Young, the constant need to re-evaluate his performances stemmed from the fear of becoming staid:

> Also the more nervous I make myself, the better I perform. I need that edgincss. Keep myself uncertain. On the precipice of disaster. It's the only way I can function.[24]

Young's reasoning explains his all too frequent moves from one group to another; from acoustic gigs at small halls to rock 'n roll venues with Crazy Horse and massive stadiums with C.S.N.&Y. As Young's career unfolds one sees that his only real security lies in change. Even a one-off European tour with Crazy Horse is in danger of becoming predictable unless the artist widens his repertoire at every opportunity. At times, Young does feel stuck on the rock 'n roll treadmill and he explains the pervading sense of unreality that life on the road can produce:

> It's been like taking in Europe through one of those viewmaster slides. All the halls are a blur. The people backstage in each hall think we're crazy – we nod and talk to them as if we saw them the previous night, whereas it was in a different country and we don't know where we are.

Looking back at the long tour, it was not Britain that most impressed Young and Crazy Horse, but the reception they received in Japan. Talbot recalls Young playing perhaps better than he had ever played before, and he concluded that in comparison to their live performances *Zuma* was a non-starter. Young had particularly fond memories of Japan and spoke warmly of the adulation that he and Crazy Horse received during their visit:

> Nobody spoke English to us there, and the response was very different from Western responses, but they understood us, I think, and gave us a great reception.
>
> My first time in Japan was those four cities, and it was amazing to see people had come to the shows and copied even the way I dress, the patterned trousers. This has always happened everywhere, but when it happens among people of a differnt culture, whose whole background is so different from the West's, it's nothing less than staggering.
>
> Apart from that, the main thing that occurred to me was the size of the people, we towered above them all in Japan! A psychological advantage which I needed.[24]

Young returned to the States during the first week of April leaving behind a wealth of glowing reviews. It was a remarkable contrast to his last series of gigs in Britain when the "Tonight's The Night" tour had been panned. The visit had not only been a commercial triumph for Neil Young the musician, but also provided him the opportunity to continue his expensive hobby as a semi-professional filmmaker. During the tour Young had been extravagant enough to hire a film crew who were busy capturing almost every moment of Neil Young's life on the road. Young had even allowed them to film the incredible sight of the star waking up in the morning and arising from his bed. Apparently, Neil was also arranging a visit to London Bridge where he intended to do some impromptu busking for the benefit of his film crew. He had even agreed to throw a party for the press at Maunkberry's in Jermyn Street. Naturally, the whole extravaganza was captured on film, including a pie-throwing contest between himself and a photographer. Observing the vast numbers of hangers-on, Young was moved to say:

> Some people think I'm the phenomenon, but it's all these people around me who're the real phenomenon.

From his comments at the time, it was clear that in spite of the setbacks of the last couple of years, Young was even more determined to succeed as a filmmaker:

> Just love getting some good film. I've got loads of footage of film back home at my ranch; my music will continue, at least on record, but eventually I'd like to make films. I have all the movie equipment you'd imagine back home, and it's more than just a hobby – it's an obsession.[24]

Following his return to the States however, neither movies nor the successful gigs with Crazy Horse were uppermost in his mind. For Neil was now channeling his energies into a Stills/Young collaboration. The duo flew out to Miami to begin work on the project before Young even had time to recover from his recently completed tour. The sessions at Criteria Studios were progressing when Young was forced to take a break and travel to Japan. While there, he decided that it would be a natural step to transform the Criteria sessions into another attempted C.S.N.&Y. reunion. The results of that decision were to have far-reaching effects and without realizing what he was about to set in motion, Young phoned Graham Nash in Los Angeles and arranged a meeting. Nash vividly remembers his reaction to Young's proposition:

> We'd just finished cutting *Whistling Down The Wire* and Neil called from Japan, and he said "Listen – Stephen and I have been making this album in Miami, and we've got great tracks and great lead vocals, but we don't have that special sound." I said, "yeah that's right. That's me and David you don't have" – and he agreed ... We left for Miami at 8.30 the next morning.[29]

The spontaneous decision to reunite C.S.N.&Y. seemed as though it was about to bear fruit. For the next two weeks, Crosby & Nash worked hard on the Stills/Young tunes providing numerous overdubs and gradually attempting to fashion the project into a C.S.N.&Y. venture. A couple of Nash tunes were recorded and it seemed that a new C.S.N.&Y. album would be a certain summer release. It was at that point that events took a strange turn. The suddenness of the reunion had interrupted the plans of both sets of duos. Neil and Stephen had prepared a three month tour as the Stills/Young Band, beginning in June, and now they would have to face the pressure of singing songs from a C.S.N.&Y. album without the support of their colleagues. In effect, this should not have been a problem as the quartet were continually rearranging their old material for performances in different groups as trios, duos or soloists. However, as the fortnight progressed Stephen Stills seemed to see this as a niggling problem which might conceivably affect his performance during the summer tour. The pressures on Crosby & Nash, however, were more imminent. They had abandoned a half-completed album in order to commit themselves to the C.S.N.&Y. project and contractual problems necessitated that they complete *Whistling Down The Wire* at the earliest opportunity. Having laid the foundations for the new C.S.N.&Y. album, they decided to return to Los Angeles, complete the work on *Whistling Down The Wire* and return to Miami as quickly as they could.

While Crosby & Nash were hurriedly completing their album, Stills began to have second thoughts about the reunion venture. Eventually, he and Neil decided to scrap the C.S.N.&Y. project, and revert to the idea of a Stills/Young album. The result of Stills' decision was that the backing vocals that Crosby & Nash had spent over two weeks overdubbing were literally wiped clean from the tape. Not surprisingly, both Crosby & Nash were shattered. Their disappointment quickly turned to anger, however, following some interviews in the music press in which both Stills and his manager had implied that the reunion was not fruitful because Crosby & Nash were "not hungry enough".

Nash's anger was so great that at one point he insisted that he would never work with Stills and Young again. The fiasco in Miami that had come so close to reuniting C.S.N.&Y. was now threatening to destroy permanently any possible future projects as a quartet. Nash's final comments on the situation appeared to leave little hope for any reconciliation and seemed to show how far the quartet had drifted from each other:

> They're not in it for the right reasons. They're in it for the bucks, the manipulation and career moves and I'm in it for great music. It sounds corny, but that's the way I feel. C.S.N.&Y. is, to me, an incredibly special thing that we should not fuck around with. We have no right as individuals ... I see Stephen's career going downhill and I see Neil's career going downhill ... They're desperate and I was saying don't be desperate. We can have it all. Me and David can have albums, and you and Stephen can have albums and C.S.N.&Y. can have albums.[29]

The many words of reproach, however, did ultimately have a positive effect by clearing the air and allowing the foursome to see precisely where the Miami reunion had gone wrong. All the rushing to and fro and the sudden decision to record an album had led to a lack of communication. Ironically, it was Neil's original notion to re-form single-handedly Crosby, Stills, Nash & Young that had caused all the problems. Stills later confirmed that no matter how strained their relationship might seem to be, it was always a likelihood that another joint album would appear at some point in the distant future. This confidence in their spirit of cameraderie would finally be proven the following year when Crosby, Stills & Nash would reunite and release a studio album. For Neil, however, even though the plan to reunite the foursome in Miami had backfired, the results were not ultimately disastrous.

After completing the album at Criteria, Stills and Young immediately set out on tour with Stephen's backing group (George "Chocolate" Perry on bass; Jerry Aiello on organ and piano; Joe Lala on congas; and Joe Vitale on drums and flute). Both artists had cancelled their respective summer tours in order to ensure that this latest project could be promoted on the road. The scheduled three month tour of the States was the same one originally planned for Young and Crazy Horse, which meant that there were no administrative problems in organizing dates. The tour turned out to be one of the most erratic affairs in the turbulent history of either performer. The reviews were not only mixed but often contradictory. The critics who attended more than one of the dates were often confused to discover that the group could abruptly switch from a promising to an abysmal performance for no apparent reason. Stills was severely criticized for his singing which was continually off-key, especially on ambitious songs such as "Suite: Judy Blue Eyes" which could not be competently performed without the harmonies of Crosby & Nash. Predictably, Young was treated with greater kindness by the critics, though the quality of his performance was equally erratic. The gigs at Springfield, Washington, Hartford and Los Angeles showed that Young's guitar-playing was less impressive than on the recent Crazy Horse tour. By the time the duo reached Cleveland, however, there was a noticeable improvement. It finally seemed as though the duo was about to fulfil its promise and the next four gigs at Cincinnati, Pittsburgh, Greensboro and Charlotte were reasonably received. Ironically, it was at this point that Young chose to disappear, leaving Stills to play Atlanta alone, following which the tour abruptly terminated.

The reason for Young's sudden departure has never been adequately explained. Official reports from the period reveal that he was suffering from a throat illness and had been told to rest by his doctors. Certainly, following his departure, Young had returned to his Northern California ranch and refused to discuss the incident. The abrupt nature of his departure, however, has led to persistent rumors of a disagreement between the two musicians. Stills agreed that there may have been some unforeseen pressures that were gradually building up as the tour progressed:

> He got to oversinging a little bit and maybe there was too much pressure. It was all so sudden that I don't know, but whatever happened was cool. Neil stopped the tour very suddenly, just cold like that, but up until then it had been going great.

Young was considerate enough to send Stills a sarcastic telegram with the words "Dear Stephen, funny how some things that start spontaneously end that way. Eat a peach, Neil." The throat infection notwithstanding, one cannot escape the feeling that Young simply lost interest.

David Crosby provides an intriguing insight into Young's decision-making:

> Neil's a very smart man ... very, very intelligent. He's quite charming

when he wants to be and very friendly and seemingly very upfront and nice. But he's also got another side to him where he thinks very carefully on his own behalf and that decides a lot of his actions. And he does that when he's not around you.

Following the anticlimactic departure of Young, the public were left to consider the merits of the duo's much publicized album *Long May You Run*. The album confirmed the critical opinion that this latest Stills/Young coupling was nothing more than a non-event. Neither artist appeared to have any exciting material to contribute and the work was marred by a pervasive listlessness. Stills' cuts were little more than average and far below the standard of even his better solo material. "Make Love To You" and "Black Coral" were probably his best moments and it must be said that Young's involvement here is strictly negligible. Young might have offered any number of interesting songs from his past, but only "Long May You Run" seemed to be regarded as significant enough for inclusion.

The remainder of the album consisted of compositions written within the last few months, some of which had been heard on the European tour with Crazy Horse. Songs such as "Midnight On The Bay", "Ocean Girl' and "Let It Shine" were pleasant enough, but extremely lightweight when compared to the material on *Zuma*. Stills conceded that the songs may have represented a departure from Young's more arresting work, but argued that the album was a valid product:

> For Neil it was a departure from some of his darker moments, mainly because we had a great time and looked forward so much to going in the studio. I think it was very educational for me and him both because we picked up on what was right about the way we each recorded and also corrected some of the things we had been doing wrong.

The final irony came when the sales returns revealed that Crosby & Nash's *Whistling Down The Wire* had outsold *Long May You Run*. The coupling of Stills and Young had produced neither aesthetic fulfilment nor commercial success.

NINETEEN

Life Through Hazy Bars

Following the abortive Stills-Young collaboration Neil decided to prepare another album and buried himself in studio work. He re-emerged in November 1976 in order to complete a brief series of gigs with Crazy Horse. Suddenly, Young had even more new songs and it was clear that selecting material for the next album would present him with some problems. His concerts were equally varied, even on the same night. At the Boston Music Hall he played two contrasting sets, dropping half a dozen songs and replacing them with five others as the evening progressed. One of the highlights of the show was an orchestrated version of "A Man Needs A Maid" in which the strings were employed sparingly, but effectively. Such restraint ensured that the fragility of the song was not sacrified as it had been to the pomp and circumstance of the L.S.O. version. The first set had opened with, of all things, "The Old Laughing Lady", but Young completely transformed the song. The haunting ballad had changed into a fast strumming number which made the sentiments sound positive rather than death-laden. This manipulation of his own material was worthy of Dylan.

If Young's concerts were becoming more ambitious, his recording plans seemed even more elaborate. A three record compilation, appropriately titled *Decade* was set for imminent release. It had been specially complied by Young and was rumored to include several previously unreleased tracks. In addition, Young was also completing work on another album, which had been tentatively titled *Chrome Dreams*. At the end of 1976, however, Young revised his schedule and postponed the release of *Decade* for one year, feeling that the timing was somehow not quite right. He also revised *Chrome Dreams* and in the process changed the title of the album to *American Stars 'n Bars*. Young explained that this would enable him to use songs about American bar culture on one side and compositions dealing with American folk heroes on the other.

By the time *American Stars 'n Bars* was released in June 1977, it had altered considerably. The side dealing with "American stars", on which Young had intended to include such songs as "Pocahontas" and "Ride My Llama" was eventually scrubbed as Neil explained:

> Well, originally the concept was to have two sides on the album. One was going to be American history and the other was going to be

American social comment, the bar culture kind of thing where I was at at the time — you know, drunk on my ass in bars. So I couldn't remember the American history part so we left that out. So that's where that one came from.[9]

The revised version of *American Stars 'n Bars* showed Young's willingness to make dramatic last minute changes when a new idea captured his imagination. Perhaps influenced by the music he had heard while exploring American bars, Young quickly recorded a selection of recently composed country 'n western tunes. Incredibly, the entire first side of his new album consisted of material which had been cut less than two months before. During the hasty proceedings which had precipitated the recording of these new songs, Young unwittingly brought attention to a singer named Nicolette Larson:

Linda Ronstadt introduced me to her. I called Linda up one day as I was doing *American Stars 'n Bars* and I said, "Do you know any girls who can sing really good? I want them to come down to my ranch and sing a couple of tunes. It won't take very long." So she said, "Yeah, I know, there's Nicolette — and I'll come too." And I didn't expect her to come and I really felt great that she came. So they came up for a couple of days and we ran through the tunes and I was recording in the other room and once I got a good recording I just sent them back and that was it. They thought we were rehearsing and going in the studio but we were finished before that ... They're nice girls. We called ourselves The Crazy Horse And The Saddle Bags.

The addition of Ronstadt and Larson ensured that these country 'n western songs sounded totally different from any other material in the Young canon. The experiment was partly successful, although it must be conceded that the material was not of a consistently high standard. Most of the songs on the first side are superficial re-creations of what are generally characterized as Nashville obsessions — marriage, alcohol and adultery. Young adopts the persona of a Nashville stereotype in many of the songs which occasionally makes the performance sound like a country 'n western parody. In "The Old Country Waltz" Young becomes the predictable melancholic alcoholic; "Saddle Up The Palomino" presents the witty adulterer; "Hold Back The Tears" shows a love-sick optimist who finally re-emerges as a crazed suitor in the raucous "Bite The Bullet". For the most part the melodies were pleasant but predictable, and songs such as "Hey Babe" unfortunately displayed some of Young's most atrocious rhymes. Although it is easy to fault these hastily conceived country 'n western outtakes, it would be wrong to dismiss them without some positive qualifying comments. Amid the embarrassing rhymes, Young occasionally manages to produce some witty lines and genuinely original images. The equation of unrealized love with a cold bowl of chilli in "Saddle Up The Palomino" shows that Young can be a true humorist:

I want to lick the platter
The gravy doesn't matter.
It's a cold bowl of chilli when love lets you down
But it's the neighbor's wife I'm after.

In "Bite The Bullet", the impassioned performance is so overwhelming that the lyrical content seems hardly relevant. However, it is worth noting that Young blasphemes his self-confessed romanticism here by promoting an unusually brutal sexuality:

> Carolina Queen
> She's a walking love machine
> I like to make her scream
> When I bite the bullet.

It is the odd sparkle of humor and originality among the predictable which saves the first side from unqualified critical castigation.

What is most puzzling about *American Stars 'n Bars* is Young's decision to bypass so much of the material that he had introduced to his audiences during the 1976 tour. While the first side consisted entirely of songs written only months before, side two delves into the Young archives to plunder material from as far back as November 1974. The oldest song, "Star Of Bethlehem" was taken from a 1974 session at which Emmylou Harris guested. It is difficult to decide why Young chose to resurrect this light, acoustic number for inclusion on the album. Perhaps he found the darker elements in the song suddenly less depressing than they had once seemed. The song is most memorable for the final verse which, in its blasphemy, becomes a metaphor for his own disillusionment in love:

> Yet still a light is shining
> From that lamp on down the hall.
> Maybe the Star of Bethlehem
> Wasn't a star at all.

"The Will To Love", although the most recent song on this side of the album was actually recorded as early as May 1976. Young sang the song into a two-track Sony cassette recorder while sitting at his fireplace on the ranch. It serves well as a mood piece, and part of the song's charm comes from the unusual imagery. Young uses the extended simile of an ocean fish and its fight for survival, in order to express the mystery of romanticism:

> It has often been my dream
> To live with one who wasn't there.
> Like an ocean fish who swam upstream
> Through nets, big hooks, and hungry bears.
> When the water grew less deep
> My fins were aching from the strain.

After six verses in this vein, Young concludes that just as the fish is required by nature to survive the perils of the deep, so man will never lose the will to love. The song remains an interesting albeit unusual approach to one of Young's favorite themes.

For most of Young's followers "Like A Hurricane" was the real meat on *American Stars 'n Bars*. Yet, it is difficult not to be a little disappointed with this version of the song. Written about a bar in Redwood City, California, "Like A Hurricane" was obviously part of the original American bar album concept.

Throughout the 1976 tour, the song was a showstopper and received standing ovations wherever it was played. The studio version, however, fails to capture the excitement that the song generated during those concerts and one is left with the conclusion that Young would have been better employed to have included a live take of the number. In discussing the song, Young reminds us that though many critics have applauded his lead-guitar work-out, the playing is hardly like that of a heavy-metal speed-freak:

> If you listen to that, I never play anything fast. And all it is is four notes on the bass, just keeps going down. Billy plays a few extra notes now and then, and the drum beat's the same all through. It's like a trance we get into. Sometimes, it does sound as if we're really playing fast, but we're not. Everything starts swimming around in circles, and everything starts elevating and it transcends the point of playing fast or slow or anything like that – lucky for us because we can't play fast ...

The closing cut on the album, "Homegrown" seems to have little relevance to American stars or bars but serves as an effective paean to both farmers and those members of Young's audience who like to cultivate their own type of weed. Like "Cripple Creek Ferry", "Homegrown" reveals Young's tendency to end certain albums on a light note. Perhaps lightweight is the best adjective to describe one of Young's most patchy albums. Having abandoned most of the projected bar songs, Young seems to have lost sight of his original idea and hastily put together a hotch potch of new and old songs almost at random. The country songs on the first side are erratic in quality, while the second side appears to lack any sense of continuity. *American Stars 'n Bars* ultimately emerges as one of Young's strangest and most perplexing recordings.

Almost immediately after the release of *American Stars 'n Bars*, Young became involved in another bizarre musical venture. Rumors began to filter through from Santa Cruz that he was appearing at bars in the area backed by an unknown group. These apparently wild speculations were dismissed by most people in the record business who felt certain that Young would not be wasting time playing around bars when he and Crazy Horse could be promoting his new album all over the country. Neil has never been an artist to attempt the expected, however, and it was typical of the man to confound the music world for the umpteenth time. His latest aberration had been correctly reported, and Young was now an honorary member of a group known as the Ducks. The collaboration had occurred while Young was visiting Jeff Blackburn, a musician he had known from the Buffalo Springfield days. Jeff, once part of the San Franciscan duo Blackburn and Snow, had formed a group with former Moby Grape bassist Bob Mosely and drummer Johnny C. Craviotto. They were searching for a lead guitarist when Young conveniently appeared in the area. In true fairy-tale fashion, Young agreed to join the group for a series of summer gigs at bars in the Santa Cruz area.

The situation was very similar to the Rolling Zuma Review at the beginning of the year but Young was hoping that the Ducks might be able to remain incognito for a longer period. This was not Neil Young and Crazy Horse and most of the songs that the Ducks performed were written by Blackburn. Although they occasionally opened with the Buffalo Springfield's "Mr. Soul", the majority of Young's songs consisted of new material. It is a pity that the Ducks could not have been heard by more people because their sound was totally different from any group that Young had previously played with. They were a classic club group and to hear Young's material in this new context was nothing short of revelationary. Neil performed some fast, rock 'n roll songs such as "Crying Eyes", which included strong and very soulful backing vocals from Blackburn and Company. The sound bore no relation to that of either Crazy Horse or the Stray Gators and on some nights Young must have been sorely tempted to take this project even further. The highlight of their set was a scorching new song titled "Windward Passage". It was classic Young in the tradition of "Cortez The Killer" and "Like A Hurricane", but different from both in its rawness and spontaneity. Yet, there was no mistaking Young's familiar lead-guitar work, gradually building in its intensity as this 7 minute epic reached its climax. The audience was kept on the edge, awaiting the inevitable chorus, but it never came. Young kept on playing and brought this unique instrumental to a thundering close. Whether this was simply an instrumental work-out or a new song for which the lyrics were yet to be written remains debatable. Whatever it may have been, "Windward Passage" has never since been played at any Neil Young show; the fate of the song sums up the transience of the "tour". Young had spoken to one person too many in the bar after a gig and his words had been reported in the local press. Within days, Santa Cruz was invaded by over-zealous fans, sensation-seeking pressmen and even record company officials. As soon as Young received word of the invasion, his days as a Duck ended.

In spite of his abrupt departure from the Ducks, Young had not lost his love of surprise appearances and in August he again astonished his followers this time by appearing onstage at the Civic Auditorium with David Crosby and Graham Nash. Crosby was performing solo and brought on Nash half-way through his concert, but the best was yet to come. Crosby teasingly introduced a local picker whom he wished to give a break. Apparently, this unknown played in a local band, but they hadn't yet found the confidence to try and hit the big time. At that moment former Duck Neil Young casually walked onstage to a rapturous welcome. The trio then involved themselves in a long argument about which songs to play. They began, appropriately enough, with "Human Highway" from the album that Crosby, Stills, Nash & Young had almost recorded together. Young was allowed three more songs and chose "New Mama" and "Only Love Can Break Your Heart" in order to highlight the three-part harmonies. The concert ended with a surprising version of "Sugar Mountain", a song Young normally sang alone. The harmonies sounded impressive and added a new dimension to a well-worn number. Even Young was moved to comment: "These guys sure sing good, don't they Santa Cruz?" It was a perfect ending to an eventful summer.

Having fulfilled his recent musical ambitions, Young decided to spend more time with his son. His long-standing relationship with actress Carrie Snodgrass had ended. Carrie apparently had no regrets about the separation which seems to have been amicable:

Neil and I had six good years together. We never bothered with a marriage license. I wanted him to think of me as somebody *different*, not a wife. When we had problems we had to *talk* to each other about them, not to a court. And no judge tells Neil that he can visit his son on weekends only. Oddly enough, everything worked out just as we had planned from the beginning. We always said that when one of us wanted to end it, we would end it. We never had bad times, and we still see one another.[30]

Neil shared custody of their only son, Zeke, whom he took on a long bus tour of the States during the autumn. Zeke had been crippled since birth with cerebral palsy and Young clearly felt an additional need to contribute to his son's childhood years.

In October, the long-awaited *Decade* triple set was finally released. It showed that Young's taste for his own material was not as suspect as might have been supposed. The songs he had chosen from every stage of his career were undeniably representative of his finest work. In compiling the album set, Neil chose to include several previously unreleased songs plus two compositions that had originally been issued on singles. It seems hard to believe that this was the first occasion on which the oft-released b-side "Sugar Mountain" had appeared in album form since the song remains one of the oldest in the Young repertoire. According to Neil, he wrote it on either his nineteenth or twentieth birthday (he has frequently given conflicting accounts of the precise year!). Like "I Am A Child", "Sugar Mountain" can sound remarkably insipid on occasions, but at certain performances Young has fully expressed its potential naive charm. In concert he has often used the song as a form of light relief and taken much comfort in explaining his embarrassment about singing one of his most banal verses:

> When I wrote this song, I wrote 126 verses to it. Now, you can imagine I had a lot of trouble deciding which four verses to use. I was "underneath the stairs" at the time. Anyway, there was this verse that I wrote and it was the worst verse of the 126 that I wrote. So I decided to put it in the song just to give everybody a frame of reference as to what can happen. What I'm trying to say is ... I think it's one of the lamest verses I ever wrote and it takes a lot of nerve for me to get up and sing it in front of you people.[15]

It was that kind of onstage patter which made "Sugar Mountain" such a favorite with the less discriminating members of Young's audience.

The previously unreleased material on *Decade*, although of interest, was generally erratic in quality. Young had included two unquestionably excellent cuts: the Buffalo Springfield's "Down To The Wire" and the recently completed "Campaigner". The latter, originally titled "Requiem For A President" had been written on Neil's bus during the 1976 Stills/Young Band tour. After seeing a television broadcast announcing Pat Nixon's stroke, Young was struck by the sight of a pathetic, dejected Richard Nixon visiting his wife in hospital. Young was sufficiently moved to write a song in which he openly sympathized with the fallen premier. The chorus reminded us that even the man whom Young had pointed the finger at in "Ohio" did indeed have soul. As David Crosby noted: "Neil has got a lot of compassion."

The remaining three unreleased songs on *Decade* were pleasant though unspectacular. "Winterlong", written as early as 1969, was taken from a much later session around the time of the *On The Beach* recordings. "Love Is A Rose" was little more than a blatant re-working of "Dance Dance Dance" and probably less impressive. Young had written the song while traveling in a car to Maui and it had been recorded at his California ranch during rehearsals for the 1974 Crosby, Stills, Nash & Young tour. The final "new" cut, "Deep Forbidden Lake" was another outtake from the unreleased *Homegrown*. Young argued that its placing on *Decade* was significant:

> It hopefully signified the end of a long dark period which started with *Time Fades Away*.[8]

In a rock world weary and suspicious of triple album sets, *Decade* was generally accepted as a valid artistic statement and a tribute to Young's development as a creative artist.

While *Decade* was selling in the record stores, Young made another of his impromptu guest appearances at the star-studded "Last Waltz" extravaganza. This Thanksgiving Day celebration was a final tribute to the Band who were about to end their 15-year association. The concert attracted an enormous number of established stars who were determined to pay tribute to one of the world's most respected groups. Young found himself in the company of such artistes as Bob Dylan, Joni Mitchell, Van Morrison, Neil Diamond, Muddy Waters, Ronnie Hawkins and Dr. John. Young contributed a competent version of "Helpless", which was later included as part of the three album movie soundtrack.

Continuing his bus tour across America, Young arrived in Nashville where he decided to cut a new album. He gathered together a host of players, many of them local country session musicians. He then contacted Nicolette Larson who flew out to Nashville at short notice in order to provide additional vocal support. Their duets were very impressive and Nicolette learned the songs with extraordinary rapidity. Young kept the twenty-two musicians, who were dubbed the Gone With The Wind Orchestra, until the recordings were completed. During a break in the sessions, the ensemble agreed to play a one-off charity performance for children's hospitals in the Miami Beach area. Following the initial recording sessions the outfit flew out to Florida, well rehearsed and ready to give a unique performance. It was 12 November 1977 and the concert served as a memorable birthday celebration for Neil. Having introduced many of the songs on the forthcoming album, Young closed the show with a stirring version of Lynyrd Skynyrd's "Sweet Home Alabama", (a cynical rejoiner to his own "Alabama") which was a fine tribute to the musicians who had died so tragically in a plane crash that year.

By December, the new album tentatively titled *Gone To The Wind* had been completed. However, due to a series of indecisions and revisions the work would not be issued until the autumn. As the months passed Young began to turn his thoughts to completing another film in the near future. His decision was no doubt partly prompted by the attention given to the Bob Dylan movie *Renaldo And Clara* which was due for release in the summer. By the late Spring, filming had begun on a documentary-style western which was to be titled *Human Highway*. Young recruited his old friend Dean Stockwell to share directing and writing credits and a list of co-stars was announced including Dennis Hopper, Sally Kirkland and Devo.

144

Apparently, the film was an attempt to combine concert footage with scenes from Young's life on the road. A number of sequences had already been discussed including a dramatic attack by robbers on Young's tour bus. Young also hoped to add further footage shot at his ranch and in Taos, New Mexico. Learning of the diverse material that Young was intending to include in his latest cinematic venture, many critics feared that this new work would merely be a re-make of *Journey Through The Past*.

The determination to complete the *Human Highway* movie had the positive effect of encouraging Young to play a short series of eight concerts at New York's Bottom Line club towards the end of May 1978. The concerts were filmed and Young, who sang without a back-up group, was wired up with a hidden wireless microphone which enabled him to roam freely around the stage. The filming continued at a private gig, the punk venue Mabuhay Gardens, where Young flew in Devo to join the show. It transpired, however, that Young's intention was not to perform with Devo but to use them as a dramatic counterpoint in the movie. According to Mark Devo, director Dean Stockwell had taken Neil to see the group and he was extremely impressed by their bizarre act. Young then decided that the juxtaposition of Devo alongside himself would be a spectacle not to be missed. So it was that Devo appeared as support at the Mabuhay Gardens, miming their own songs and singing a hilarious parody of "After The Goldrush" with lines such as "I was sitting in a burning basement when a pinhead knocked on the door ... evolution is on the run in 1984." Young did manage to stumble across the stage before Devo completed their set, but the much-vaunted collaboration failed to occur.

Almost all the songs that Young played during this short series of gigs were unfamiliar to his audience. Several would appear on the as yet unreleased *Comes A Time* while several others including the famous "My My Hey Hey (Out Of The Blue)" would be held over for a future project. As usual, a couple of the new songs were destined to remain in the vaults until such time as Young felt ready to release them. The haunting "Shots" with its images of children in the sand attempting to re-build their fathers' crumbled castles was one of Young's more complex songs of the period. Yet, the closing lines seemed bathetic: "I promise to you whatever we do, I will always be true." Here, the complexities submit finally to a single, commonplace message. This is typical of Young's writing and reminds us how difficult it is in discussing his work to draw a line between what are commonplace truths and profound observations on human nature. Much the same might be said of "The Ways Of Love" which, lyrically, is no more impressive than the love songs Young had been writing during the Springfield days. This kind of accusation has often been levelled against Young during his career but it is based on a false assumption – "the hook and ladder dream". Young's entire recorded output is erratic, and his writing is sometimes seemingly retrogressive, especially when he tackles a love song. Yet, this is the nature of the artist. He is continually re-evaluating old ideas, both through simple direct statement and complex imagery. For Young, there can be no progression without retrogression. Indeed, Young questions the nature of artistic progression in both aesthetic and commercial terms. By the summer of 1978, it was clear from both his new recordings and his choice of venue that Young was still questioning the meaning of success in the rock business.

TWENTY

The End Of A Decade

The long delay in the release of *Comes A Time* was further elongated when Young insisted that Warners/Reprise re-press the album and in order to ensure that his wishes were obeyed he cunningly revised the track listing. The album finally reached the shops in September 1978 amidst universal critical acclaim. For once, public and critical opinion concurred and *Comes A Time* was to provide Young with his most commercially successful recording since *Harvest*. Several critics compared the two albums arguing that they were both examples of Young in lighter mood and should be seen as temporary diversions from his more complex material. While this seems reasonable enough, the difference in quality between *Harvest* and *Comes A Time* is a crucial factor. The latter reveals Young totally in control of the proceedings and in spite of the fact that he employs a cast of hundreds the musical vision is never sacrificed to over-indulgent arrangements.

This is evident from the opening track, "Goin' Back", one of Young's best crafted songs. Neil's playing and signing are carefully studied, as they are in the succeeding title track. One is immediately impressed how professional and polished this album is when placed alongside *American Stars 'n Bars*. Lyrically, the songs are necessarily uncomplex but they are never sloppy or embarrassing like their predecessors on the last album. Even the simplistic philosophy of "Comes A Time" uses a singalong chorus with surprisingly apocalyptic undertones:

> Oh this old world keeps spinning round
> It's a wonder tall trees ain't layin' down
> There comes a time.

Even the urbane mood of "Goin' Back" entertains similar apocalyptic visions:

> When fire fills the sky, I'll still remember that day
> These rocks I'm climbing down
> Have already left the ground
> Careening through space.

In general, however, it is not the lyrics but the arrangements which one finds most impressive. "Look Out For My Love" shows Young's ability to add different musical textures in order to increase the listener's attention. Some fine acoustic playing is gradually supplemented by the subtle introduction of a fiddle half-way through the song. The juxtaposition of some choppy guitar work by Crazy Horse towards the end of the number gives the song an additional bite and shows Young's ability to interweave acoustic and electric instruments to maximum effect.

Another strong feature of the album is the powerful harmony work of Nicolette Larson particularly on "Peace Of Mind" and "Lotta Love". According to Nicolette, Neil had originally intended to include "Lotta Love" on *American Stars 'n Bars* but in a fit of generosity he allowed her to use it on her solo album. Its enormous success as a Stateside hit ensured that much attention was focussed on the duo. For many people the powerful duets were a welcome reminder of Neil's earlier more melodic work in the early 70s. David Crosby obviously saw *Comes A Time* as representing the Neil Young music that he most admired. As a craftsman, Crosby was less than impressed with Young's less commercial material:

> He lets the art happen and the inspiration but then he refuses to apply the craft. On *Comes A Time* he did apply some craft because he had Nicolette there to do it. He was making albums – and he was doing it on purpose and I understand the stance he wanted to take. But I disagreed with it because I think he's one of the best songwriters ever and I wish he'd polished his stuff the way that we did. I think his best material was the stuff that either we did with him or that he did after in the same mould. I like Neil's stuff when the songs are developed. I don't like the idea of leaving them in their bare, stark form.

Though the critics would be appalled by Crosby's words, his opinions are probably a true reflection of those of the general record buying public.

The appearance of "Human Highway" on the album must have pleased those punters who had despaired of ever hearing the track on record. It had long been an audience favorite at Young's concerts and Neil was not adverse to re-writing some of the lyrics at times. "I went looking for the D.J.'s daughter" was often altered to "I married" or even "I buried the D.J.'s daughter", depending upon Young's playfulness.

More serious in tone is the plaintive "Already One", a song written about the first birthday of Neil's son, Zeke. Its speculations on the transience of love are made even more poignant by the evident autobiographical references to Young's recent divorce:

> I can't forget how love let me down
> And when we meet, it still gets in my way
> But we're already one, already one
> Now only time has come between us
> 'Cause we're already one
> Out little son won't let us forget.

Listening to this song, one can see why Young once suppressed an album such as *Homegrown* because of its intensely personal revelations.

Young's return to a form approaching open confessional might have caused some suspicion among critics wary of 70s singer-songwriters. As if realizing this, Young included the amusingly self-castigating "Field Of Opportunity":

I've been wrong before and I'll be there again
I don't have any answers my friend
Just this pile of old questions ...

In reviewing the album almost every critic quoted the key line "In the field of opportunity it's plowing time again" as a perceptive comment on the album as a whole. It was typical of Young to remind us that this new batch of love songs guaranteed commercial success. What is most amusing is that in using the "plowing time" analogy he wryly compares this album to a "harvest". "Field Of Opportunity" demonstrated that unlike many of his contemporaries Young could never take his emotional traumas too seriously. What other singer-songwriter would be self-effacing enough to exclaim: "Let me bore you with this story: 'How my lover let me down'"? Although these tracks may be thematically similar to those on *Harvest*, it is clear that the artist's perspective is totally different.

In order to deflate any further romanticism Young almost heretically included the wailing "Motorcycle Mama". For many listeners, "Motorcycle Mama" with its screeching, high pitched vocals from Nicolette Larson, is justifiably regarded as an unfortunate abberation which spoils the mood of the album although it clearly serves a purpose by reminding us not to take Young's introspective work too much to heart. Indeed the decision to place "Motorcycle Mama" amongst a series of well-crafted love songs is further evidence of Young's unorthodox, even perverse attitude when faced with the problem of collating material for an album.

The final track, Ian Tyson's "Four Strong Winds", was an equally surprising move on Young's part, especially when we consider the number of his own songs that are still unrecorded. Tyson's old chestnut is something of an M.O.R. standard in Canada and can be heard everywhere from the folk club circuit to the cabaret halls. That Young should attempt such a sentimental song may seem unusual, but it highlights his problem in effectively covering other people's material. "Four Strong Winds" was probably the most commercial song on *Comes A Time* and received extensive airplay which no doubt contributed enormously to the sales of the album. The song reveals how easily Young could be accepted as an M.O.R. artist if he ever chose to limit his musical vision. For Young, however, the enormous popularity of *Comes A Time* seemed of little relevance:

> I like it when people enjoy what I'm doing but if they don't I also like it. I sometimes really like aggravating people with what I do. I think it's good for them. It may sound pretentious to say something like that but I like to read about somebody who saw "Tonight's The Night" or heard *Tonight's The Night* who's just so mad that I would put out a distorted record and have no respect for the craft I'm in. They don't know what they're talking about. As far as I'm concerned they don't because if I put out the same thing over and over again and made a perfect kind of record as I could, like a *Harvest* or *Comes A Time*, well, two's enough. Maybe in five years I'll try another one like that, just to convince myself that I can still do it.[9]

By the time he received the reviews of *Comes A Time*, Young had already begun his next project, an extensive one month tour of America taking in 23 dates. It was to be the most bizarre and controversial tour that Neil and Crazy Horse had played since the "Tonight's The Night" series of concerts in 1973. Young had specially designed a set which included a huge bandstand rigged with oversized amps, an enormous microphone and ostentatiously oversized instruments. Young remembers how the idea of using props was originally conceived:

> I think it all started when I looked at the pile of amplifiers I had when I was rehearsing. It was just such a gross pile of junk. I thought that onstage it would just look like we had this huge pile of stuff, so I thought maybe we could cover it with something ... and then I thought we could make a model of a little tiny Fender amp, but that's huge ... It just started and it didn't stop until it got to be what it is. There was no concept. It all just fell together.

The concerts invariably began with Jimi Hendrix's "Star Spangled Banner" (as performed at Woodstock) and The Beatles' "A Day In The Life" being blasted over the sound system. Following this the roadies, or "road-eyes" as Young called them, would dart across the stage dressed in the long brown robes and flashy red eyes of the Jawas of *Star Wars*. They would then accidentally uncover Neil from atop one of the giant speakers and he would "awaken" and look around in childish wonderment before picking up an acoustic guitar to sing a series of songs spanning his entire career from "I Am A Child" to "Comes A Time". He would then return to his "sleep" while preparations were being made for the emergence of Crazy Horse. During the break between sets, the audience were "entertained" with stage announcements borrowed from the soundtrack of the *Woodstock* film. It was this use of theatricalism that bothered some of the critics. Generally, the reviews were reasonable and Young found himself being compared favorably with Bob Dylan who was also touring at the time. Young's performance did not please everybody, however, and some critics argued that rather than enhancing the music, Young's use of theatricalism distracted from it. In reviewing Young's concert at the Madison Square Garden on 28 September 1978, John Rockwell felt that the theatrics belittled Young and almost cheapened his artistic integrity. Young remained unrepentent, however, and argued that this latest venture was an expression of his audience's need to idolize a star:

> At first people told me I was belittling my music by having all these props and everything around ... Actually, one reviewer did use the term "belittle" because everything was so big. I don't know if he knew that was a play on words or not. I like it like this to be able to do it and not be too serious about it ... I mean people want a star to be flashy and they want something that they don't have to relate to as being human. Things that are human, you have your moment then you go away, but stars are supposed to represent something else I guess; a super quality of, it's great – and once it isn't great people don't want to hear about it because that doesn't satisfy their illusion.

The mixed reviews that these concerts received were indicative of a period of fluctuating fortunes. Recently married, Neil was probably happier than he had been for some years, but life was not without its problems. The birth of his second son, Ben, in November, was accompanied by the news that the child was a victim of cerebral palsy. It was a tragic coincidence. Young contacted various doctors but, as far as he could ascertain, the susceptibility to the condition was non-hereditary. More bad news was to follow. The night before his tour ended, Young learned that his Zuma beach house had been burned to the ground. Four major fires had swept through Southern California that day but the fiercest was the Agoura/Malibu blaze which devastated Young's home. The police confirmed that the fire was started by an arsonist in Agoura and the blaze was propeled into a storm by sixty-mile-per-hour winds which razed over 28,000 acres of land and caused a reported sixty injuries and one death. For Young, the house, once owned by F. Scott Fitzgerald, had been a perfect refuge and vacation spot. In spite of the depressing news, Young quickly recovered his spirits and continued work on a variety of projects destined for release in 1979.

It was hoped that the *Human Highway* movie might be completed and ready for release by the spring but Young for some reason abandoned the project in favor of a later film shot during his recent tour. The film, *Rust Never Sleeps* opened in July and it was a surprise to those people who had been expecting another *Journey Through The Past*. Contrary to his statement following the premier of *Journey Through The Past* this new film was primarily about Young and his music. *Rust Never Sleeps* was not a documentary of life on the road but simply a film of his concert at the Cow Palace, San Francisco on 22 October 1978. There were no revealing backstage shots and no off stage dialogue from Young or anybody else. Neil's intention seems to have been to capture his performance onstage as seen from the audience's point of view. Though less ambitious than his previous cinematic ventures *Rust Never Sleeps* modestly achieved its limited aims. The worst one could say of the film is that it is a poor substitute for seeing Young in performance. Surprisingly Young disagrees with this viewpoint:

> This is better than the concert, especially for all my friends who could never handle a concert scene anyway, and I know that most of the people who listen to my music don't want to go to the Forum. Some of them will – the Forum is great, we had a good show and everything – but they don't want to go through all that. In a film you can see it up close if you want to see it. If you're into my music you'll enjoy it, probably.

In spite of Young's arguments one cannot help feeling that *Rust Never Sleeps* would have been a more interesting film if it had been presented in the form of a documentary. There are no insights into Young's feelings about his performance and there are no clues as to how the artist prepares for his concerts or unwinds after the curtain has fallen. Even taking the film on its own terms as a cinematic version of a live concert, it is still not without its failings. The acoustic half of the concert sounds hackneyed and unconvincing – a performer going through the motions and unsuccessfully attempting to invest new energy into old tunes. In concert, Young's physical presence on the stage was probably sufficient to suspend his audience's disbelief but seeing the artist on screen in the impersonal surroundings of a cinema one fully realizes the inadequacies of his performance. The success of Young's acoustic set partly depends upon his ability to mesmerize

150

his audience, and it is this quality which fails him on the big screen. The gap between audience and performer is too great and the acoustic songs are devoid of even nostalgic charm. Fortunately the film is saved by the excitement generated by a series of electric songs such as "Cinnamon Girl", "Like A Hurricane" and "My My Hey Hey (Into The Black)" all of which transcend the problems inherent in transforming a live show into an exciting movie. In this respect, the film is only partly successful and hardly recommends Young as a filmmaker to be reckoned with. *Rust Never Sleeps* is certainly no *The Last Waltz* and the final impression one gets from the film is that Young is a very private person who appears to value his own mystique. Perhaps another reason why Young chose to present such an objective representation of his art is that he finds the perfunctory function of film making laborious. The possibility of Young ever penning a worthwhile script is hardly likely, as he is more than willing to admit:

> I could never write something down. I can never write more than half a page at a time. I guess I've read 50 to 100 scripts – but not really because I only read the first couple of pages and then I just put it down because I just can't relate to it. Some people write great scripts and they sit on executive desks and they decide that it's fantastic and they spend millions of dollars on it and I'll read the same script and say it's a piece of crap. I don't understand what it is, and then you'll see the movie and it'll be great, but the script … I don't know.

While Young's film had been greeted with less than unanimous enthusiasm by some critics there were no such reservations concerning the album *Rust Never Sleeps*. This time Young had collected together the best of his acoustic and electric material in order to produce one of his finest works. The title of the album and several key cuts, most notably "My My Hey Hey (Out Of The Blue)" and its electric counterpart "My My Hey Hey (Into The Black)" explained the central theme of the work – the transience of rock stardom. The idea for the album and its subsequent title *Rust Never Sleeps* were partly fostered by the group Devo whom Young had been rehearsing with during this period.

"My My Hey Hey (Out Of The Blue)" was generally acclaimed in the press as one of Young's finest songs to date but some of the more conservative critics took exception to several of the lines. The main contentions were that Young appeared to be glorifying rock 'n roll suicides and at the same time immortalizing the memory of Johnny Rotten. Of course one might justifiably reply to these critics that Young has every right to state these views but this is not even necessary. It seems clear from the song that Young's main aim is not so much to glamorize the idea of sudden death but to stress the fact that "rock 'n roll can never die". Young recognizes the fleeting nature of rock stardom and realizes that the worst thing that can happen to a performer is to watch his career gradually hit the skids. Having realized this, however, Young draws strength from the fact that although the artist wilts, the musical form continues. There is, ultimately, it seems, constancy in change. The choice of Johnny Rotten to exemplify Young's ideal has bothered those who feel that Lydon's contribution to rock 'n roll is somewhat less than his illustrious predecessors. In one line Young appears to describe Rotten in the highest possible terms:

"The king is gone but he's not forgotten"

The *Rolling Stone* critic who reviewed the album was so shocked by this "blasphemy" that he persuaded himself that Young was referring to Elvis Presley in this line. It's a nice delusion but Young states unambiguously in the very next line – "This is the story of a Johnny Rotten". The song is not about Johnny Rotten but "a Johnny Rotten" – a type of that character rather than the man himself. Young has not set out to apotheosize Johnny Rotten or the Sex Pistols but to pay tribute to all those artists who have gone and can never come back. The Johnny Rotten phenomenon ended not in death but in a name change and a refusal to falsely maintain one image for an entire career as many performers have done. It is this determination to avoid a staid image or as Young would say to resist "the rust" which is the true theme of the song.

The concern with the transience of stardom in relation to the permanence of rock is again presented in the succeeding track, "Thrasher". The most complex song on the album, "Thrasher" ably displays Young's recent tendency to use an elaborate metaphor to elucidate his main point. In "Cortez The Killer" he had used the ravaging of the Incas to express a personal loss and the same technique could be observed in "The Star Of Bethlehem" in which the religious allusion was employed to describe his own disillusionment in love. "Thrasher" ostensibly describes the effects of mechanization on the lives of a farming community. The "rolling thrashers" are seen as aimless blades of science flailing the idyllic pastoral life of a rural community. The narrator ultimately loses his friends as a result of the advancing "thrashers":

> I searched out my companions, they were lost in crystal canyons
> When the aimless blade of science slashed the pearly gates ...
> How I lost my friends I still don't understand.

What is interesting here is the way that this "thrasher" image is gradually applied to Young's own situation in the rock world. Just as the members of a rural community are alienated from each other through change so the increasingly affluent rock star is gradually forced into an inevitable process which isolates him from his fellows. With "nothing left to find" artists lose themselves in "rock formations" (a phrase that cleverly puns on superstar get togethers).

In the final lines Young reveals his determination to avoid the excesses of superstardom by recognizing his own mortality as an artiste and by demonstrating a willingness to accept the blade of the thrasher when it comes to end his career:

> But me I'm not stopping there, got my own row left to hoe
> Just another line in the field of time
> When the thrashers come and I'm stuck in the sun
> like dinosaurs in shrines
> Then I'll know the time has come to give what's mine.

When Young gets stuck like a dinosaur in the ever-advancing world of rock he assures us that he will accept his enforced retirement with grace. The extended metaphor of the "thrasher" is one of Young's most effective and sophisticated methods of expressing his vision of the rock world.

"Ride My Llama" is one of Young's most amusing songs and was written around the time of *Zuma* when Young was discussing the possibility of writing an album consisting of compositions about time travel. The idea of meeting a man from Mars allows Young to speculate on the Alamo or even llama riding from Peru to Texarkana. The time travel motif continues in "Pocahontas" in which Young vividly describes a massacre:

> They killed us in our tepee
> And they cut out women down
> They might have left some babies
> Cryin' on the ground.

His bitterness is reinforced by the description of himself as a twentieth century Indian suppressed by city life:

> The taxis run across my feet
> And my eyes have turned to blanks
> In my little box at the top of the stairs
> With my Indian rug and a pipe to share

In the final verse the bleak images are replaced by wish-fulfilment as Young imagines sleeping with Pocahontas and sharing a camp fire with Marlon Brando, who had recently proved himself a champion of the Red Indian cause.

The closing track "Sail Away" combines all these images in an attempt to express the notion that stardom does not necessarily mean greatness. Young recognizes that he might easily have been poor or rich, successful or unsuccessful:

> I could live inside a tepee
> I could die in Penthouse thirty-five

His final observation is that greatness and success are not necessarily even incidental:

> See the losers in the best bars
> Meet the winers in the dives.

In all these songs Young continually seems to question the relevance of his own success.

The electric "Powderfinger" becomes in the context of the album a reiteration of the "Thrasher" motif. With the same destructive force of a Cortez the white boat's guns mercilessly blast out the life of a young man unable to defend himself in the face of devastating odds. In common with "Cortez The Killer" and "Thrasher", "Powderfinger" expresses Young's fear that man's perennial desire for advancement can all too frequently cause pain and suffering and even death. "Powderfinger" is the first of four songs on side two that gradually build in intensity as Young fully displays his ability as an electric guitarist.

"Welfare Mothers", Young's comment on the lovemaking prowess of divorcees, includes some of his most aggressive guitar breaks and confirms his standing as a first division rock 'n roller. Much the same can be said of "Sedan Delivery" with its alternating slow and fast guitar work. Here Young's writing is reminiscent of early Dylan, complete with stream of consciousness lyrics. The sudden shift from a description of a pool hall game to the delivery of a shipment of drugs and the brief description of a mad scientist enhance the speed-freak paranoia that the song dramatizes.

The album reaches its most powerful moment with the closing electric refrain of "Hey Hey My My (Into The Black)". Slightly phased guitars chop back and forth as Young reiterates his faith in the permanance of rock 'n roll. He even plays around with the lyrics and deliberately teases those listeners who felt that the song was simply a tribute to the Sex Pistols by asking: "Is this the story of Johnny Rotten?" Young's question is a reminder that he knows what he is doing and a warning that "there's more to the picture than meets the eye". With *Rust Never Sleeps* Young showed the world that his best work was not necessarily in his past. The album is undoubtedly one of his most consistent, and displays a new level of sophistication and maturity already suspected but previously unheard. For Young, *Rust Never Sleeps* remains a significant musical statement:

> I can relate to *Rust Never Sleeps*. It relates to my career you know; the longer I keep on going, the more I have to fight this corrosion. And now that's gotten to be like the World Series for me. The competition's there, whether I will corrode and eventually not be able to move anymore and just repeat myself until further notice or whether I will be able to expand and keep the corrosion down a little. So that's it.

The release of *Rust Never Sleeps* encouraged Young to promote his film by talking to specially selected members of the press and radio. He waxed eloquently on the merits of the film, even making strong claims for what he called "Rust-O-Vision":

> It enables certain people in the audience to see the rust falling off ... Mind you, not everyone can see it. You have to be in the right frame of mind to see it. It's a very high tech thing. Few people understand it actually, but you put on these glasses and at certain points, especially in the older songs, you can see it and you can tell where the band starts to falter.

At least one cannot deny the potential power of Young as a soft salesman. He cleverly plays upon the audience's vanity by stating that only certain people will be able to see the rust through these wondrous glasses. Of course, it's such a "highly technical" concept that even he cannot begin to explain it. This is classic Young at his most humorous and the Rust-O-Vision spoof had audiences adjusting their glasses and constantly removing them in an attempt to see this technological miracle. In reality, the glasses seemed to have little function beyond intensifying the color brown and distracting the audience from the film's shortcomings.

Undeterred by good or bad reviews, Young is clearly set on continuing as a filmmaker and his belief in his talent seems unquenchable:

> I'd like to do more films and I probably will. I'm set up to do it. I have a studio for editing films and doing soundtracks. It's something I planned on for a long time and I knew I was going to get into. But this is my second film – probably the first film most people would notice – and in the future I'd like to do more.

154

Having just released one of the finest albums of his career Young should have been content with his standing in the rock world as the decade drew to a close. One project remained to be fulfilled, however. Young was determined to release a soundtrack of the movie *Rust Never Sleeps* in order to give even greater promotion to the film. This was to prove his greatest artistic blunder since the disastrous *Journey Through The Past*. It is very strange but whenever Young becomes involved with a film he appears to lose all sense of artistic perspective in promoting his music. The *Live Rust* double album which was duly released in the winter of 1979 smacked of the same unhealthy opportunism which had marred Young's reputation following the release of his last soundtrack album. It contained not one new track and indeed, over half the album consisted of inferior live recordings of songs that had just been released a few months before. To make matters worse, Young was even planning to call the album *Rust Never Sleeps* until his record company persuaded him that he would simply confuse the record buying public. The release of *Live Rust* calls into question Young's much vaunted integrity and makes him appear a calculating cynic, ready and willing to take advantage of his audience's willingness to buy any product with his name on the cover. In discussing his motives, however, Young seems blissfully unaware of such considerations and even has the audacity to suggest that *Live Rust* is evidence of his altruism:

> The first album that came out was all new songs, which was to give people an even break if they didn't want to buy the soundtrack album, which is going to have maybe 10 old songs on it. I don't like to repeat that over and over and say that if you want to buy these new songs you've got to buy these old songs. If they don't want to hear the old songs again they don't have to buy it (*Live Rust*) to hear the new ones. That's why I did that ...

What is most amusing here is that Young apparently fails to see the absurdity of his reasoning. He claims that he doesn't want to repeat himself over and over and wishes to protect his public from having to buy material that they already have in another form. Yet his solution is to record two separate albums called *Rust Never Sleeps* which, of course, means that he *is* repeating himself "over and over" while simultaneously encouraging his devoted folowers to purchase an entire double album of old material. In critical terms, Young paid dearly for his error and the album was rightly panned in the majority of music papers.

155

TWENTY ONE

Is He Ready For The 80s?

After such a busy year as 1979, it was inevitable that Young would decide to take a break from recording. For most of 1980 Young sailed off on his schooner and continued work on a yet to be announced movie. For long it seemed that Neil's only appearance on vinyl in 1980 would be the soundtrack of *Where The Buffalo Roams* in which he attempted a less than amusing version of "Home On The Range". Suddenly towards the end of the year a new work appeared, *Hawks and Doves*. It was given a fair though unexceptional welcome by the critics, largely because it was an acoustic album and seemed to lack the power of much of Young's greatest work. In many respects, the album was a return to the kind of material Young had been recording during the early Seventies. "Little Wing" and "Lost In Space", for example, were evidence of Neil at his acoustic best. It is easy to complain of trite rhymes, clichéd imagery and self indulgent romanticism when discussing these songs. In fact, one might point out that "Lost In Space" with its account of a broken relationship would have fitted well into the framework of *Harvest*. But there is a crucial difference here. This may be standard Young, but it lacks the extreme self-consciousness of the *Harvest* material and the songwriter avoids explicit self revelation, preferring to express his feelings more obliquely.

One of the most perplexing features of the album was the inclusion of "The Old Homestead", a song Young had written as early as 1974. It is a song which almost begs an allegorical explication, though so far no critic has felt confident enough to attempt one. David Crosby once told me that his "Cowboy Movie" was an allegory of the history of C.S.N.&Y., complete with Rita Coolidge in the role of an Indian girl. I cannot help feeling, though there is no evidence to support such a contention, that "The Old Homestead" might be some sort of a reply. Certainly, Young allocates distinctive voices for the different verses in the song: The Shadow, The Rider and the three Birds. One might speculate that The Shadow who holds "the reins" is Elliot Roberts, who had once told Young that he was "pissing in the wind". In attempting to reunite Crosby, Stills, Nash & Young, Roberts would have been just the man to demand of The Rider (Neil):

"Why do you ride that Crazy Horse?"
Enquires the Shadow with little remorse.

156

The three Birds (Crosby, Stills & Nash) eventually "ditch this rider, shadow and all" leaving Young alone on his ranch still feeling the pull of stardom, a moon which is no longer quite full. Such a purely speculative interpretation leaves many lines to unravel and, ultimately, one has to conclude that the song is a very private statement requiring a specific key to unlock the hidden allegory. Why Young chose to include it on vinyl in 1980 remains unclear, but, suffice to say, it is probably the strongest cut on the album.

"Captain Kennedy" is the second high point of the album. Melodically, it sounds very similar to Stills' "Know You Got To Run", but it is a much stronger composition. Thematically, it is not dissimilar to "Powerfinger" on *Rust Never Sleeps* and, indeed, it was on the short list for inclusion on that album at one point. "Captain Kennedy" reveals Young's latest tendency to create a fictional drama rather than relying purely upon the love songs of yore. It is typical of his almost unconscious handling of American mythology that the central figure in the song should be named Kennedy. As a young mariner sets out to war he recalls the life of his father, "Captain Kennedy", who had lost his wooden schooner fighting the Germans. The mariner relates how Kennedy spent his later days desperately saving up to buy another schooner and how he hoped to sail away in peace. It is a simple tale relating, microcosmically, the story of human struggle in the face of adversity. Just as the assassination of Kennedy reinforced rather than destroyed his family's resolve, so the young mariner sets out like his father before him. The strength of a dynasty lies always in the ability of the siblings to take up the banner from their illustrious predecessors.

The entire second side of *Hawks And Doves* consists of country 'n western material recorded in 1980. In common with his efforts on *American Stars 'n Bars* one feels that the excursion into country has not proved as fruitful as expected. For Young, however, these provide an opportunity to express an important feature of his musical personality and history. On *Hawks And Doves* the country material is at least not as predictable as it might have been. Instead of tributes to American bars or love lost melancholia, Young turns his attention to a variety of emotional and political feelings. "Staying' Power" and "Coastline" are celebrations of love in which Young fully expresses the strength and longevity of a wholesome relationship in disarmingly simplistic lines:

We don't back down from no trouble
We do get up in the morning.

"Union Man", by contrast, heralds the return of Young the satirist. Here he parodies the meetings of the Musicians Union where the main conclusions appear to be that "live music is better" and "bumper stickers should be issued". The song is one long romp with Rufus Thibodeaux excelling himslf on fiddle, while Young screams out the lyrics.

Towards the end of the album Young turns his attention to politics. In "Comin' Apart At Every Nail", which highlights the harmony work of Ann Hillary O'Brien, Young observes the plight of the working man. As in "Last Dance", however, Young's sentiments hardly sound convincing. His basic feelings about America are an unusual mixture of patriotism and uncertainty:

Oh this country sure looks good to me
But these fences are comin' apart at every nail.

This ambivalent attitude is reiterated in "Union Man" in which he appears to satirize the patriotic expressions that he voiced in the previous number:

Ready to go, willing to stay and pay
U.S.A., U.S.A.

The lines indicate his realization that happiness and money are inextricably bound in the American ethos. Young is also at pains to point out that American history has painted some "grim pictures" and he warns that "we might feel that way again". In the final verse, Young turns inward in an oblique comment on his own career in the rock world – an arena in which he appears to be both loved and attacked:

Hawks and doves are circlin' in the rain
Got rock and roll, got country music playin'.

And for those "hook and ladder" critics, like myself, who may argue that his excursions into country music are less than satisfactory, Young provides a final scathing line:

If you hate us, you just don't know what you're saying.

An amusing end to yet another unusual album in the Young canon.

The worst thing one could say of *Hawks And Doves* is that its best songs date back to the mid-seventies. Young has deliberately attempted to resist any monistic classification by splitting the album into two separate sides in order to demonstrate the breadth of his musical vision. Structurally, *Hawks And Doves* is not dissimilar to *Rust Never Sleeps* though the material is considerably less impressive. Although *Hawks And Doves* hangs together reasonably well and sounds less diffused than *American Stars 'n' Bars*, it is far from a consistent piece of work. The musical quality varies enormously and it is difficult to avoid the conclusion that the stylistic juxtaposition is detrimental rather than complementary. One wonders how much longer Young will continue to raid his own vaults in order to construct albums with often diametrically opposed musical styles. Ultimately, one is forced to ask whether such a precise and calculating way of producing albums is of benefit to the artist. It seems clear that Young is consciously writing his own myth, carefully ordering album releases to include different aspects of his own personality, often borrowed from different eras. It is an intriguing artistic ploy that has already produced some great work, yet one wonders whether it is all becoming rather predictable. Even the country tunes which are designed to break the vault searching are little more than vain attempts at a spurious spontaneity. Perhaps Young needs to capture on vinyl some of the immediate intensity of a *Tonight's The Night* before successive album releases become little more than authorially disguised Neil Young samplers. His challenge in the 80s will be to continue one step ahead of a world that is becoming increasingly averse to the old and predictable. And no rock artist realizes that fact of life more than Neil Young.

Young has no regrets about either *Hawks And Doves* or *Rust Never Sleeps* and does not feel that their success or failure will affect his future development:

> How could it? It really doesn't affect anything. It's just the last thing I did. I don't know what I'm going to do next. I know I'm not just going to go out and make another album because I'm supposed to. I have to wait until something happens to make me want to do it.

What Young will attempt next is anybody's guess. Even a reunion album with his old colleagues Crosby, Stills & Nash is not impossible though Young feels it to be unlikely:

> Who cares? It's better for them to remember it the way it was. That's why Muhammed Ali isn't fighting anymore.[9]

Those words are a little ironic now that Ali has partly destroyed his own myth by sacrificing himself to Larry Holmes, in a vain attempt to reclaim a surrendered crown. Is it any less likely that Young would worry about spoiling the C.S.N.&Y. myth? One person who does not support Neil's contention that C.S.N.&Y. should remain buried is former colleague David Crosby:

> I disagree. We're all different cats. It would be a different band. It's a different chemistry every time we see each other. I think it'd be fantastic. I think we'd be better than we were then. We're all older and smarter and we could stay out of each other's way a hell of a lot more. For instance, Stills and I don't butt heads anymore. We still argue in the studio, but it's friendly. I think our work now is better than it was then.

Few people would agree with Crosby's optimistic appraisal of the situation and most critics believe that musically Young has grown away from his former colleagues. One also suspects from his words that Young's attitude to the music scene has altered drastically during recent years:

> I think I don't take it so seriously anymore. When you look back at the old bands they're just not that funny. People want to be funny now; people want to have a good time. That's why this punk thing is so good and healthy because the people aren't taking themselves seriously. They're saying, "you take yourselves too seriously". The whole rock establishment, they're so carried away with themselves, and now they're there and everything – it doesn't really mean anything anymore. People make fun of the established rock scene, like Devo and the newer groups that are out now and several other groups like The Ramones and everything. They are much more vital, to my ears, than what's been happening in the last four or five years ... Mostly the old rock 'n roll groups are just taking themselves too seriously. It's just like they know they're human and they're going to die pretty soon and they're all falling apart. It's not funny.[9]

Young's speculations on death are hardly surprising when we consider the number of people that he has seen destroyed by drugs. One might expect him to be morbid and fatalistic but as his albums have shown Young has already managed to maintain a tragi-comic perspective on life. It is typical of the man that he can even compose his own epitaph with a sardonic smile:

> This man, the longest living rock 'n roll star, died searching for a Heart Of Gold. He never found it, but he turned a few people on.[24]

NOTES

In addition to my own interviews and correspondances I would like to credit the following:

1. *Rolling Stone* 8/2/79 Int. Cameron Crowe
2. *Rolling Stone* 14/3/71 Int. Allan Mc. Dougall
3. *Zig Zag 27* Int. Michael Wale
4. *Trouser Press 35* Int. David Koepp
5. *Fusion 31* Int. Gary Kenton
6. *Melody Maker* 1971. Int. Michael Watts
7. Extracted from a letter to Rassy Young dated April 1966.
8. *Decade* liner notes
9. Mary Turner Interview
10. *Rolling Stone* 14/8/75 Int. Cameron Crowe
11. *Hit Parader* 1966 Int. Don Paulsen
12. *Rolling Stone* 30/4/70 Int. Elliot Blinder
13. Neil Young speaking at his La Honda Ranch
14. Neil Young live onstage 27/2/71 Royal Festival Hall
15. Neil Young live onstage 1/2/71 L.A. Music Center
16. Neil Young live onstage 10/2/70 Cincinatti Music Hall
17. *Zig Zag 37* Int. Chris Briggs
18. Neil Young live onstage 16/5/74 Bottom Line, New York
19. Neil Young live onstage 5/12/70 Carnegie Hall, New York
20. Neil Young live onstage 30/12/70 Boston Music Gardens
21. *New Musical Express* 28/6/75 Int. Bud Scoppa
22. *Dallas Times Herald* Reviewer Bob Porter
23. Neil Young live onstage 23/3/73 L.A. Forum
24. *Melody Maker* 25/8/73 Int. Ray Coleman
25. Neil Young 23/2/71 B.B.C. T.V. In Concert
26. *New Musical Express* 17/8/74 Reviewer Ian MacDonald
27. Neil Young live onstage 24/3/76 Ahoy-hal Rotterdam
28. *Trouser Press 35* Jon Young/David Koepp
29. *Sounds* 18/9/76 Int. Ted Joseph
30. *New York Times* 19/8/77

DISCOGRAPHY

BUFFALO SPRINGFIELD

Singles:

	U.S.A.	U.K.
Nowadays Clancy Can't Even Sing/Go And Say Goodbye	6428	—
Everybody's Wrong/Burned	6452	—
For What It's Worth/Do I Have To Come Right Out And Say It	6459	584077
Bluebird/Mr. Soul*	6499	—
Rock 'n' Roll Woman/A Child's Claim To Fame	6519	584145
Expecting To Fly/Everydays	6545	584165
Uno Mundo†/Merry Go Round	6572	584189
Kind Woman††/Special Care††	6602	—
On The Way Home/Four Days Gone	6615	—
Pretty Girl Why/Questions	—	226006

*Two separate versions of "Mr. Soul" were released in the States.
The alternate take has a 1.59 minute version of "Bluebird" on the flip-side.
†The U.S. version of "Uno Mundo" is a different mix.
††Edited versions

E.P.:

Buffalo Springfield	—	K10237
Bluebird; Mr Soul; Rock 'n Roll Woman; Expecting to Fly		

Albums:

	U.S.A.	U.K.
*Buffalo Springfield**	33-200	—
Buffalo Springfield	33-200A	587070
Again	33-226	K40014
Last Time Around	33-256	K40077
Retrospective	33-283	K30037
Expecting To Fly	—	2363012
The Beginning	—	K30028
*Buffalo Springfield***	SD2-806	K70001

*The original *Buffalo Springfield* includes the subsequently deleted "Baby Don't Scold Me".
**This compilaton includes the elongated version of "Bluebird".

Neil Young

Singles:

	U.S.A.	U.K.	Notes
The Loner/Sugar Mountain	0785	RS 23405	

Title			
Everybody Knows This Is Nowhere/			
The Emperor Of Wyoming	0819	—	A
Down By The River/The Losing End	0836	—	B
Down By The River/Cinnamon Girl	—	RS 23462	B/C
Oh Lonesome Me/Sugar Mountain	0861	RS 20861	D
Oh Lonesome Me/			
I've Been Waiting For You	0898	—	D/E
Cinnamon Girl/Sugar Mountain	0911	—	C
Cinnamon Girl/			
Only Love Can Break Your Heart	0746	—	C
Only Love Can Break Your Heart/Birds	0958	RS 20958	F
After The Goldrush/			
When You Dance I Can Really Love	—	RS 23488	
When You Dance I Can Really Love/			
Sugar Mountain	0992	—	
Heart Of Gold/Sugar Mountain	1065	K 14140	
Old Man/			
The Needle And The Damage Done	1084	K 14167	
War Song/			
The Needle And The Damage Done	1099	—	G
Heart Of Gold/Old Man	1152	—	
Time Fades Away/Last Trip To Tulsa	1184	—	H
Walk On/For The Turnstiles	1209	K 14360	
Looking For A Love/Sugar Mountain	1344	K 14416	
Drive Back/Stupid Girl	1350	—	
Don't Cry No Tears/Stupid Girl	—	K 14431	
Long May You Run/12-8 Blues	1365	K 14446	I
Midnight On The Bay/Black Coral	1378	—	I/J
Hey Babe/Homegrown	1390	—	
Like A Hurricane/Hold Back The Tears	1391	K 14482	K
Sugar Mountain/			
The Needle And The Damage Done	1393	—	
Comes A Time/Motorcycle Mama	1395	—	
Comes A Time/Lotta Love	—	K 14492	
Four Strong Winds/Human Highway	1396	—	
Four Strong Winds/Motorcycle Mama	—	K 14493	
Hey Hey, My My (Into The Black)/			
My My, Hey Hey (Out Of The Blue)	49031	K 14498	
Cinnamon Girl/The Loner	49189	—	L
Hawks And Doves/Union Man	49555	—	
Staying Power/Captain Kennedy	49641	—	
Southern Pacific/Motor City	49870	—	

A. Some promo pressings feature an earlier take of "Everybody Knows This Is Nowhere" from the first album sessions without Crazy Horse. This astonishing version would have fitted well into the context of the first album. An unusual feature of the backing is the extended use of what sounds like a recorder!

B. Edited version of "Down By The River".

C. Different vocal mix on "Cinnamon Girl".

D. Elongated version of "Oh Lonesome Me".

E. Different vocal mix on "I've Been Waiting For You".
F. U.S., Canadian and some European pressings have an alternate take of "Birds".
G. "War Song" recorded by Young with Graham Nash.
H. "Last Trip To Tulsa" is a live version from the "Time Fades Away" tour.
I. Recorded as the Stills/Young Band.
J. Edited version of "Midnight On The Bay".
K. Edited version of "Like A Hurricane".
L. Taken from *Live Rust*.

N.B. According to Neil, he released a song titled "Image in Blue" in Canada in 1962 but I
     have been unable to trace its existence.

Albums:

1.69 *Neil Young*	RS 6317	K 44059	
69 *Neil Young*	RS 6317	—	A
7.69 *Everybody Knows This Is Nowhere*	MSK 2282	K 44073	
9.70 *After The Goldrush*	MSK 2283	K 44088	
3.72 *Harvest*	MSK 2277	K 54005	
12.72 *Journey Through The Past*	2XS 6480	K 64015	
9.73 *Time Fades Away*	MS 2151	K 54010	
7.74 *On The Beach*	R 2180	K 54014	
6.75 *Tonight's The Night*	MS 2221	K 54040	
11.75 *Zuma*	MS 2242	K 54057	
8.76 *Long May You Run*	MS 2253	K 54081	
6.77 *American Stars 'n Bars*	MSK 2261	K 54088	
11.77 *Decade*	3RS 2257	K 64037	B
12.78 *Comes A Time*	MSK 2266	K 5499	
6.79 *Rust Never Sleeps*	HS 2295	K 54105	
11.79 *Live Rust*	2RX 2296	K 64041	
11.80 *Hawks And Doves*	RS 2297	K 54109	
11.81 *Re-ac-tor*	HS 2304	K 54116	

A. U.S. remix – matrix RE.
B. In addition to the unreleased material discussed in the main text, *Decade* also features
    an alternate take of "Long May You Run". The initial test pressings of the disc included
    an elongated version of "Campaigner" complete with an extra verse. The original
    artwork reveals that three other tracks were once intended for inclusion: "Pushed It
    Over The End" (C.S.N.&Y. Chicago 1974), "Don't Cry No Tears" (Japan 1976) and
    "The Old Laughing Lady".

Crosby, Stills, Nash & Young

Singles:

Teach Your Children/Country Girl	2091 002	2735
Woodstock/Helpless	2091 010	2723
Ohio/Find The Cost Of Freedom	2091 023	2740
Our House/Deja Vu	2091 039	2760

Albums:

Deja Vu	SD 7200	K 50001
Four Way Street	SD 2-902	K 60003
So Far	SD 18100	K 50023

164

Woodstock	SD 3-500	K 60001
Woodstock II	SD 2-400	K 60002

Guest Appearances

Ladies Of The Canyon – Joni Mitchell
If I Could Only Remember My Name – David Crosby
She Used To Wanna Be A Ballerina – Buffy Saint-Marie
Grin
Hejira – Joni Mitchell
Last Waltz
Crazy Moon – Crazy Horse
Light of The Stable – Emmylou Harris
Where The Buffalo Roam

Cover Versions

(A selection of Young songs recorded by other artistes)

Elkie Brooks:	"Only Love Can Break Your Heart".
Byrds:	"Cowgirl In The Sand"; "See The Sky About To Rain".
Cascades:	"Flying On The Ground Is Wrong"; "Out Of My Mind".
Merry Clayton:	"The Loner"; "Southern Man".
Rita Coolidge:	"I Believe In You"; "Journey Through The Past".
Crazy Horse:	"Dance Dance Dance"
Dave Clark Five:	"Southern Man"
Nicolette Larson:	"Lotta Love".
Kathy McDonald:	"Down To The Wire".
Buffy Saint-Marie:	"Helpless".
Buddy Miles:	"Down By The River".
Prelude:	"After The Goldrush".
Linda Ronstadt:	"Love Is A Rose"; "Birds"; "I Believe In You"; "Look Out For My Love".
Stephen Stills:	"The Loner"; "New Mama".
Ken Viola:	"High School Graduation"
Yellow Hand:	"Sell Out"; "Down To The Wire".

UNRELEASED SONGS

There Goes My Babe	Demo. (1967)
One More Sign	Demo. (1967)
Kahiera Sunset	Demo. (1967)
Extra Extra	Demo. (1967)
The Rent Is Always Due	Demo. (1967)

Sell Out	Demo. (1967)
High School Graduation	Demo. (1967)
Baby Go	Demo. (1967)
I'll Wait Forever	Demo. (1967)
Wondering	Music Hall, Cincinatti. 10/2/70
It Might Have Been	Music Hall, Cincinatti. 10/2/70
Everybody's Alone	1970 Tour
Big Waves	1970 Tour
I Need Your Love To Get By	1970 Tour
Bad Fog Of Loneliness	Carnegie Hall, N.Y. 5/12/70
Dance Dance Dance	B.B.C. T.V. London. 23/2/71
Lonely Weekend	Milwaukee. Wis. 5/1/73
Sweet Joni	Bakersfield, Ca. 1973
Vacancy	*Homegrown* sessions 1974
Separate Ways	*Homegrown* sessions 1974
White Line	*Homegrown* sessions 1974
Try	*Homegrown* sessions 1974
Home Fires	*Homegrown* sessions 1974
Frozen Man	Demo. 1974
Home Fires	Milwaukee, Wis. 5/1/73
Traces	Wembley Stadium, London. 14/9/74
Hawaiian Sunrise	Wembley Stadium, London. 14/9/74
Love Art Blues	Wembley Stadium, London. 14/9/74
Pushed It Over The End	Wembley Stadium, London. 14/9/74
Too Far Gone	Osaka, Japan. 6/3/76
Country Home	Osaka, Japan. 6/3/76
Don't Say You Win, Don't Say You Lose	Falkonerteatret, Copenhagen. 16/3/76
Day And Night We Walk These Aisles	Eppelheim, Germany. 18/3/76
Stringman	Hammersmith Odeon, London. 31/3/76
Give Me Strength	Boston Gardens, Massachusetts. 26/6/76
Just Like Tom Thumb's Blues	Santa Monica Civic Center. 28/8/76
Like A Rolling Stone	Santa Monica Civic Center. 28/8/76
Open Road/Changing Highways	Fort Worth, Texas. 20/10/76
Lady Wingshot	Demo. 1976
Crying Eyes	Catalyst, Santa Cruz. 28/8/77
Windward Passage	Catalyst, Santa Cruz. 28/8/77
Sweet Home Alabama	Miami Beach, Florida. 12/11/77
Spud Blues	Demo. 1978
Four Walls	Demo. 1978
Shots	Boarding House, San Francisco. 24/5/78
The Ways Of Love	Boarding House, San Francisco. 24/5/78
Winter Winds	Greek Theater, Berkeley. 3/10/80

Needless to say the above is merely a selection of what lies buried in Neil Young's vaults!

BOOTLEGS

BUFFALO SPRINGFIELD

Springfield Roots
Down By The River; Hard Luck; My Kind Of Love; Bluebird Revisited; And So Begins The Task; Bluebird; Baby Don't Scold Me.
Bluebird Roots
Bluebird; Baby Don't Scold Me; Hard Luck; My Kind Of Love; 49 Bye Byes; And So Begins The Task; Bluebird Revisited; Down By The River.
Stampede
Neighbor Don't You Worry; We'll See; Down To The Wire (1); Down To The Wire (2); Do I Have To Come Right Out And Say It; Raga One; Raga Two; My Kind Of Love; Come On; Baby Don't Scold Me (1); Baby Don't Scold Me (2); Pay the Price; Nobody's Fool/ Nowadays Clancy Can't Even Sing; Rock 'n Roll Woman.
Buffalo Springfield can also be heard on two bootleg compilations: *Gulp!* (live version of "Bluebird") and *Rock 'n Roll Circus* (We'll See; Down To The Wire; Come On Lover).

CROSBY, STILLS, NASH & YOUNG

Wooden Nickel (a.k.a. *Bluebird Live*)
Guinevere; Birds; 4 & 20; You Don't Have To Cry; Suite: Judy Blue Eyes; Bluebird Revisited; Sea of Madness; Down By The River.
Ohio Wooden Nickel
As above with the addition of the single "Ohio"/"Find The Cost Of Freedom".
Live At the L.A. Forum
Suite: Judy Blue Eyes; On The Way Home; Teach Your Children; Tell Me Why; Guinevere; Don't Let It Bring You Down; Carry On; 49 Bye Byes/For What It's Worth; Love The One You're With; Pre-Road Downs; Long Time Gone; Helplessly Hoping; Southern Man; Ohio; Woodstock; Find The Cost Of Freedom.
Reunion Concert 25 July 1974
Sugar Mountain; Ambulance Blues; Change Partners; Word Game; Suite: Judy Blue Eyes; Deja Vu; Long Time Gone; Revolution Blues; Pushed It Over The End; Military Madness; Only Love Can Break Your Heart; Don't Be Denied; Bongo Beat; Ohio.
Nice To See You; The 1974 Excursion
Love The One You're With; Wooden Ships; Immigration Man; Down By The River; Grave Concern; Johnny's Garden; Almost Cut My Hair; Teach Your Children; Only Love Can Break Your Heart; Love Art Blues; On The Beach; Carry Me; Pre-Road Downs; Walk On; Suite: Judy Blue Eyes; Blackbird; Long Time Gone; Ohio; Carry On.
We Waited Three Years For This (a.k.a. *Traces*)
Suite: Judy Blue Eyes; Wooden Ships; Immigration Man; Traces; Grave Concern; Black Queen; Ohio; Blackbird; Human Highway; Carry Me; For Free; Prison Song; It's Alright; Our House; Long May You Run; Only Love Can Break Your Heart; Ambulance Blues; On The Beach; You Can't Catch Me; Long Time Gone; Revolution Blues; Pushed It Over The End.

CROSBY & NASH (WITH YOUNG)

Water Brothers
Wooden Ships; Harvest; Only Love Can Break Your Heart; Southbound Train; Almost Cut My Hair; Page 43; And So It Goes; Immigration Man; Heart Of Gold; Needle And The Damage Done.

STILLS/YOUNG BAND

For What It's Worth
Love The One You're With; For What It's Worth; Helpless; Southern Man; Cowgirl In The Sand; The Loner; Suite: Judy Blue Eyes.

NEIL YOUNG

Collector's Item (a.k.a. *Neil Young & Crazy Horse*; *Broken Arrow*)
Sugar Mountain; Don't Let it Bring You Down; The Old Laughing Lady; The Loner; Everybody Knows This Is Nowhere; Winterlong; Downtown; Wondering; It Might Have Been; Down By The River; Broken Arrow; I Am A Child; Helpless; On The Way Home; Dance Dance Dance.
Rocky Mountain Review
Ohio; See The Sky About To Rain; Don't Let It Bring You Down; Dance Dance Dance; Sugar Mountain; Old Man; Journey Through The Past; Heart Of Gold; A Man Needs A Maid; Needle And The Damage Done.
Young Man's Fancy (a.k.a. *Neil Live*; *Neil Young Live At The L.A. Music Center*; *Live On Sugar Mountain*; *I'm Glad You All Came Down*).
On The Way Home; Tell Me Why; Old Man; Journey Through The Past; Cowgirl In The Sand; Heart Of Gold; A Man Needs A Maid; Needle And The Damage Done; Ohio; See The Sky About To Rain; I Am A Child; Dance Dance Dance; Sugar Mountain; Don't Let It Bring You Down; Love In Mind.
B.B.C. Broadcast
Out On The Weekend; Old Man; Journey Through The Past; Heart Of Gold; Don't Let It Bring You Down; A Man Needs A Maid; Love In Mind; Dance Dance Dance.
Coming Home
On The Way Home; Here We Are In The Years; Harvest; After The Goldrush; Out On The Weekend; Old Man; Heart Of Gold; Time Fades Away; Look Out Joe.
A Bit More
As above with the addition of: Southern Man; Alabama; Don't Be Denied; Cinnamon Girl; Are You Ready For The Country; New Mama.
The Last Album
Sugar Mountain; Sweet Joni; Look Out Joe; Time Fades Away; Don't Be Denied; New Mama; Last Dance; Southern Man.
Madison Square Garden Volume I and II (a.k.a. *Neil Young January 1973*)
On The Way Home; Here We Are In The Years; L.A.: Soldier; Out On The Weekend; Harvest; Old Man; The Loner; New Mama; Alabama; Don't Be Denied; Cinnamon Girl; Time Fades Away; Southern Man; Look Out Joe; Are You Ready For The Country.
Neil Young Live At The Roman Colosseum

Old Man; A Man Needs A Maid; Once I Was In Love; Too Far Gone; Needle And The Damage Done; After The Goldrush; The Losing End; Last Trip To Tulsa; Don't Cry No Tears; Lotta Love; Hurricane.

Neil Young And Old

A two record set featuring *The Last Album* and *Neil Young & Crazy Horse*.

Old Man's Fancy

Campaigner; Human Highway; After The Goldrush; Pocahontas; Too Far Gone; Old Man; A Man Needs A Maid; Sugar Mountain; Country Home; Don't Cry No Tears; Down By The River; Lotta Love; Hurricane; Cinnamon Girl; Cortez The Killer; Just Like Tom Thumb's Blues (with Firefall); Like A Rolling Stone (with Spirit).

Rust Never Sleeps

Sugar Mountain; I Am A Child; Comes A Time; Already One; After The Goldrush; My My Hey Hey (Out Of The Blue); When You Dance I Can Really Love; The Loner; Welfare Mothers; Downtown; Needle And The Damage Done; Lotta Love; Sedan Delivery; Powerfinger; Cortez The Killer; Cinnamon Girl; Hurricane; Tonight's The Night; Hey Hey, My My (Into The Black).

Young is also featured on the bootleg album S.N.A.C.K. performing "Are You Ready For The Country"; "Lookin' For A Love"; "Helpless"; "Knockin' At The Dragon's Door" (with Bob Dylan).

In addition to the above there are over 90 tapes of Neil Young live material currently in circulation! A complete list of this material would be approximately eight times the length of this discography and has therefore been omitted. Sadly, it is extremely unlikely that Young's unreleased works and concert recordings will ever be granted the same scholarly approach as those of Bob Dylan. Nevertheless, the contents of this edited discography and the remaining 1,400 songs that space precludes listing, would provide the basis for a voluminous analysis and revealing appraisal of Young's more obscure recordings and public performances.

EPILOGUE

As 1981 closes, Young has at last re-emerged with a new album – *Re-ac-tor*. Those hoping for a return to the lyrical sophistication and musical diversity of *Rust Never Sleeps* will no doubt be bitterly disappointed by this new work. Young has taken another avenue, this time exploring rhythm 'n blues in the same uncompromising way that he approached country 'n western. Like the country 'n western outing it reveals another facet of Young's musical personality and demonstrates his continued determination to investigate different genres. The starkness of *Re-ac-tor* recalls earlier works such as *Tonight's The Night* and *Time Fades Away*, though it lacks the power and intensity of either of those albums. Tracks such as "Motor City" and "Get Back On It" seem insubstantial and "T. Bone", in spite of some occasionally interesting guitar work, meanders on for too long and ultimately emerges as rather tedious. Yet, track by track criticisms of this kind must be qualified by the fact that Young is deliberately working in the context of a musical format that demands repetition and simplicity. It is a deliberate attempt to recapture the minimalism of early rock 'n roll by stripping down songs to their core and refusing to modify the raw live sound. Reviewing *Re-ac-tor* presents the same problem as discussing Dylan's *Saved*. One is impressed by each artist's determination to explore a new form so thoroughly – yet the results are far from aesthetically pleasing. Young's excursion into r 'n b territory is interesting but on this particular album he seems almost as ill-suited to the genre as Dylan is to gospel music. Ultimately, *Re-ac-tor* seems intriguing as another chapter in Neil Young's musical journey – but it is hardly classic r 'n b material. In short, there are too many people out there in the rock world who could do the same job a lot better.

What is pleasing about *Re-ac-tor*, however, is Young's refusal to conform to anyone's standards, even his own. In reviving "Shots", for example, Young totally transforms the song from a soft acoustic number into an aggressive electric effort. It's an uneasy, though startling transition, and on first hearing I could hardly believe it was the same song. In discussing the original version, I mentioned Young's tendency to fall into bathos, as demonstrated in the lines:

> And so if you give your heart away
> I promise to you, whatever we do
> I will always be true.

There can be no room for such sentiment in an electric version and it's pleasing to note that the 1981 adaptation omits those lines entirely. Although the revamping of "Shots" from acoustic to electric is somewhat unsatisfactory, especially when we consider supremely successful mutations such as "Cowgirl In The Sand" and "My My Hey Hey", it does at least testify to Young's innovatory spirit. Ever restless, often perverse, but always interesting, Young shows no sign of surrendering that stubborn and obsessive individuality that has made him one of the world's few truly intriguing rock stars.